Creation as Sacrament

"In this timely book, John Chryssavgis offers a sacramental account of the natural world as a creation that finds its true identity in Christ as the body of Christ. It is rare to find a book that is attentive to the sciences, theologically rich, and able to speak practically to some of the major challenges that we are currently facing in this world. *Creation as Sacrament* succeeds on all these fronts and should have pride of place on the bookshelf of anyone interested in the doctrine of creation. There is no question in my mind that this is one of the best books available on theology and ecology."

Andrew Torrance, University of St. Andrews, UK; coeditor of *Knowing Creation: Perspectives from Theology, Philosophy and Science*

"It is difficult in a few lines to do justice to this beautifully written and inspirational book. The author weaves together a rich tapestry of ideas on the theme of creation as sacrament drawn from Orthodox traditions and practices in a way that can inspire real hope in the transfiguration of the shattered image of the world around us. The reader is taken into a profound recognition of different aspects of the mystery of divine revelation that is both revealed and concealed at the same time. The frank acknowledgment of human sin sits alongside a call to asceticism and gratitude. This is not just about promoting a change in attitude to ecological responsibility in the light of scientific knowledge, but a vision of the church that is both ancient and fresh in its relevance for our world today. This is theological writing at its best: profound, informed, inspiring, and relevant, not just for those in the Orthodox Church, but for many others as well."

Celia Deane-Drummond, University of Notre Dame, USA; author of *A Primer in Ecotheology: Theology for a Fragile Earth*

"Long before the current ecological crisis, the theology of Eastern Christianity had developed a sophisticated and harmonious picture of the interweaving of spiritual and material reality in a universe animated at every point by the radiant, creative agency of God. For human beings to flourish as God intends, they need to learn how to see and attend to this mystery; the contemplation of the divine can grow in us only as we learn to recognize this uncreated act as reflected in all we encounter. John Chryssavgis has played a major role in articulating the resources of Orthodox theology in tackling our environmental catastrophe, and this excellent book could not be more timely as we seek for a spirituality that will genuinely transform our sinful and mindless ravaging of God's world."

Dr. Rowan Williams, former Archbishop of
Canterbury and currently Master of Magdalene College,
University of Cambridge, UK; author of *Christ,
The Heart of Creation*

"John Chyrssavgis's capacious, reflective book is a wonderful, rigorous, and accessible meditation on ecological theology as intrinsic to Orthodox Christian thought and practice over the centuries. His theological finesse is unique and unparalleled in mediating Orthodox thought between the currents of contemporary environmentalism and theological shoals of the past. Readers of all levels will benefit from his reflections on how transfiguration, sacrament, and spirituality in Orthodox theology resist any blithe, firm distinctions between humans and nature. Eminently readable and assignable, this text is also guaranteed to become a staple in courses on Christian ecotheology."

Christiana Zenner, Fordham University, USA;
author of *Just Water: Theology, Ethics,
and the Global Water Crisis*

Creation as Sacrament

Reflections on Ecology and Spirituality

John Chryssavgis

t&tclark

LONDON · NEW YORK · OXFORD · NEW DELHI · SYDNEY

T&T CLARK
Bloomsbury Publishing Plc
50 Bedford Square, London, WC1B 3DP, UK
1385 Broadway, New York, NY 10018, USA

BLOOMSBURY, T&T CLARK and the T&T Clark logo are trademarks of
Bloomsbury Publishing Plc

First published in Great Britain 2019

Cover design: Terry Woodley
Cover image © The Holy Monastery of Roussanou at Meteora, Thessaly,
Greece. Photo by Dimitrios Tilis/Getty

A catalogue record for this book is available from the British Library.

Library of Congress Cataloging-in-Publication Data
Names: Chryssavgis, John, author.
Title: Creation as sacrament : reflections on ecology and spirituality /
John Chryssavgis.
Description: 1 [edition]. | New York : T&T Clark, 2019. |
Includes bibliographical references and index.
Identifiers: LCCN 2019007759 | ISBN 9780567680709 (pbk.) |
ISBN 80567680716 (hardback) | ISBN 9780567680723 (epub) |
ISBN 9780567680730 (epdf)
Subjects: LCSH: Creation. | Ecology–Religious aspects–Christianity. |
Wisdom (Biblical personification)
Classification: LCC BT695.5 .C4975 2019 | DDC 231.7/65–dc23
LC record available at https://lccn.loc.gov/2019007759

ISBN: HB: 978-0-5676-8071-6
PB: 978-0-5676-8070-9
ePDF: 978-0-5676-8073-0
ePUB: 978-0-5676-8072-3

Typeset by Newgen KnowledgeWorks Pvt. Ltd., Chennai, India

To find out more about our authors and books visit www.bloomsbury.com
and sign up for our newsletters.

CONTENTS

ACKNOWLEDGMENTS

I am grateful to "a great cloud of witnesses" (Heb. 12:1), who helped shape this book. Among them, especially:

His All-Holiness Ecumenical Patriarch Bartholomew: Thank you for your persistent advocacy of caring for God's creation. Your decisive leadership and humble ministry have taught me that Orthodox Christianity can actually make a difference in our world.

His Eminence Metropolitan John of Pergamon: Thank you for your bold approach and eloquent theological voice on creation care, as well as for the gracious Foreword to this publication.

My son Alexander: Thank you for motivating me to live more simply, subsist with less, and tread lightly on our planet.

My son Julian: Thank you for opening my eyes to the intimate and intricate connections between economy and ecology, as well as property and poverty for a fairer world and just society.

My editor Marilyn Rouvelas: I have literally run out of words to express my gratitude sufficiently or efficiently. Thank you for your affectionate ownership, generous championship, and faithful stewardship of this book.

FOREWORD

For a very long time, it was assumed—by religion and science alike—that theology has very little to do with ecology; the environmental crisis and climate change were matters handled only by specialists and technocrats, by politicians and activists. In reality, however, the relationship between theology and ecology is profound and pronounced, even while the reasons for any misunderstanding are positive and negative.

From a positive perspective, Scripture and tradition underline the sanctity and dignity of all creation, including the animals and the natural and material environment, which humans must respect and treat as a gift of the divine Creator. Christ came to save the whole creation—and not just humankind—through the Incarnation; this is why, according to St. Paul, "the whole creation groans in travail and is suffering" (Rom. 8:23) as it awaits its salvation through humanity.

From a negative perspective, it is unfortunately true that the ecological crisis, at least as we experience it today, to a large extent derives its roots in certain ideas that historically prevailed in the West from earlier centuries through to our own time. Christian theology has contributed decisively to the emergence of the ecological problem by—knowingly or unknowingly—promoting the view that the soul is in some way more significant than the body, that humanity is somehow superior to the rest of creation, and that human beings have a mandate from above to "be fruitful and subdue the earth" (Gen. 1:28), a biblical verse particularly misinterpreted and conveniently exploited by Protestant thought in the eighteenth and nineteenth centuries.

The Orthodox Church—and especially the Ecumenical Patriarchate—has always been sensitive and open to the problems of humanity, recognizing that the current ecological crisis constitutes a serious threat to God's creation, including human beings. Thus, in 1989, the late Ecumenical Patriarch Demetrios issued an encyclical addressed to Orthodox faithful, all Christians, and all people of goodwill, raising awareness about the seriousness of the ecological crisis and urging them to act responsibly for the protection of God's creation. Following this initiative, the present Ecumenical Patriarch Bartholomew placed the ecological crisis at the very center of his global concern, appealing to faith leaders, political authorities, and renowned scientists to consider collaborative ways of resolving our ecological problems. Moreover, Patriarch Bartholomew promoted ecological sensitivity and learning among clergy and communities, as well as parishioners and young people, in order that creation care may become part of religious education and pastoral ministry.

As this remarkable book by John Chryssavgis makes abundantly clear, the interest of the Orthodox Church in the ecological problem stems from two fundamental principles: First, there is the Eucharistic or sacramental principle. In the Eucharist, the material creation is transformed and sanctified, becoming the body of Christ. In the Eucharist, creation is solemnly declared as God's gift, and human beings act as priests of creation, rather than its proprietors.

Second, there is the ascetic or spiritual principle. The spirit of restraint and renunciation places essential and fundamental limits on human greed or selfishness, which accounts for the misuse and abuse—the exploitation and devastation—of the earth's resources. An ascetic ethos springs from a loving heart and the conviction that between the natural world and ourselves there is an organic unity and fundamental interdependence that makes us share a common fate just as we have the same Creator.

Over many years, John Chryssavgis has reminded us about our responsibility to care for God's creation and researched the classics of the Christian tradition on the sacredness of creation. He has eloquently articulated his intuition and conviction about the relationship between the way we *regard* and the way we *respect* creation. He has proved persistently critical of dismissing climate change as political or superficial but also passionately sensitive to the need for radical change in our attitudes and lifestyles. He has tirelessly advised the ecumenical patriarch in ecological initiatives and activities, humbly guided church leaders in establishing environmental institutions and producing pastoral statements, while authoritatively contributing to global, national, and local efforts raising awareness on the vital and urgent nature of creation care. This book bears testimony to the maturity of his thought and clarity of his conviction.

Metropolitan John [Zizioulas] of Pergamon

Introduction

Restoring the Shattered Image of the World

Cosmic Fragmentation

Almost every day, we witness activists, lobbyists, and theorists—each from their own perspective, occasionally with their own agenda—grappling with the ecological crisis. Climate change and global warming, flora and fauna extinction, soil erosion and forest clearance, marine and agricultural contamination, noise and air pollution receive increasing attention on a daily basis and striking prominence on an international level. Indeed, these concerns have assumed a progressive sense of urgency, even though the intensity with which they are frequently handled and resolved is far less impressive or persuasive. With the emphasis in the twentieth and twenty-first centuries on the individual and individual rights, who would have predicted that the exploitation and violation of nature would become more important than, and even equivalent to, concern and consternation for the very survival of the human race?

No matter how carefully modern man has sought to foster material prosperity and self-sufficiency, it is now clear that grave "fissures" and "faults" have appeared on the face of earth. As a result, despite past actions that sought to contain or constrain the world's forces and resources, today we face a global challenge that directly affects everyone, regardless of ecological awareness, geographical location, or social class. Nature, we know, paces like an enraged animal in a cage, and it is only a matter of time before it exacts retribution. We are already feeling the reverberations; ecological "justice" always follows suit, sooner or later, with mathematical precision. The image of God in creation has been shattered; the face of God on the world has been distorted; the integrity of natural life has been fragmented.[1] Yet, it is precisely in this shattered world that we are called to discern the caring nature of the Creator and discover the sacramental nature of creation.

This book examines the restoration of that shattered image of the world through the sacramental lenses of cosmic transfiguration, cosmic interconnection, and cosmic reconciliation. The aim is to induce personal and societal transformation in making choices that respect creation as sacrament. Such transformation is only possible through divine grace, the energy of the Holy Spirit, the creative and motivating force for everyone and everything. As Symeon the New Theologian (949–1022) asserted, "The Holy Spirit has no other name. It derives its name from the matter on which it rests."[2] The same grace communicates a vision of how creation relates to its Creator, inspiring an ethos that enables us to live on earth while having our citizenship in heaven.

Cosmic Transfiguration

One distinct focus of the book lies in the emphasis on cosmic transfiguration, as this is articulated through the centuries to this day in Orthodox theology, liturgy, and spirituality. The hymns for the Feast of Theophany, the celebration of Christ's baptism commemorated each year on the sixth of January, declare, "The nature of the waters is sanctified ... the earth itself is blessed ... and the heavens are enlightened." And the Great Blessing of Waters recited on the same day provides the reason behind the blessedness of the earth: "So that by the elements of creation, and by the angels,

---

[1]While the present book draws on material from my *Beyond the Shattered Image: Insights into an Orthodox Christian ecological worldview* (Minneapolis, MN: Light & Life, 1999 [Out of print]), it denotes an evolution and expansion of reflections on ecology and spirituality in the context of a fresh exploration of early Patristic theology, modern Orthodox spirituality, and contemporary environmental thought.

[2]*Hymn* 22, in George Maloney, *Hymns of Divine Love* (Hong Kong: Dimension Books, 1976), 111. Centuries earlier, Basil of Caesarea claimed that "recounting the Spirit's wonders" is evidence of its divinity and creativity. St. Basil the Great, *On the Holy Spirit*, chs. 23–24 (Crestwood, NY: St. Vladimir's Seminary Press, 1980), 85–9.

and by human beings, by things visible and invisible, God's most holy name may be glorified."

The theology of the Orthodox Christian tradition retains a sacramental, balanced view of nature and the environment, proclaiming a world imbued by God and a God involved in the whole world. I say retains because the essence and creed of the Orthodox Church offer the basis for its unparalleled and unfailing care for the created cosmos. It would be a mistaken identity and ideology that perceives the interest and involvement in the protection and preservation of the natural environment on the part of Orthodox theologians and leaders—most notably among them, Ecumenical Patriarch Bartholomew[3]—merely as a reaction to the contemporary ecological crisis.

Climate change provides the occasion and opportunity, but it does not prompt the cause or conviction for an Orthodox Christian sacramental worldview. Orthodox liturgy and spirituality offer compelling and concrete answers to the ultimate questions about redemption from corruptibility and liberation from death, teaching that "original sin" lies in turning away from God, manifested in a refusal to view life—and all life in the world—as a sacrament of communion. In the seventh century, Maximus the Confessor describes the Incarnation of the Word as a complete and comprehensive re-creation of the world, wherein "God is emptied and descends without change to the last extremities of nature."[4]

Inasmuch as everyone and everything bear the imprint and likeness of the divine, there can never be a sharp line of demarcation between humankind and nature. This vision surely lies at the heart of the doctrine and intention of creation; this conviction also lies at the heart of the doctrine and purpose of the Incarnation. It is why Paul can describe the eager expectation and deeper yearning that unites all people with all creation:

> From the beginning until now, the entire creation has been groaning in one great act of giving birth, and not only creation, but all of us who possess the first fruits of the Spirit, we also groan inwardly, as we wait for our bodies to be set free. (Rom. 8:22-23)

---

[3]See Chapter 10: "The Green Patriarch—A Contemporary Worldview and Witness."
[4]Maximus, *Ambiguum* 253 in PG 91.1385.

Above and beyond any conception or definition as a rational, social, or political being, the human person is primarily and essentially a liturgical celebrant of this sacramental reality of the world. The dimension of liturgy—of joyful praise and cosmic mystery in the human heart and in the natural environment—is God's gift to the world and transcends any environmental erudition or endeavor. Augustine of Hippo long ago acknowledged this truth: "Through the mouth of the good, all the lands make a joyful noise to the Lord ... No words are needed to make this joy heard ... overflowing with joy ... above the level of discourse."[5]

Cosmic Interconnection

"A human being," says Gregory the Theologian in the fourth century, "is like another universe,"[6] standing at the center of creation, midway between strength and frailty, greatness and lowliness. Humanity is the meeting point of all the created order. The idea of the human person as a bridge of union or point of contact is developed in the seventh century by Maximus the Confessor: "The whole world, made up of visible and invisible things, is a man; and conversely ... man, made up of body and soul, is a world."[7] As an image of the world, the human person constitutes a microcosm—a universe in miniature. And at the same time, the human person is a mediator, a bond of sorts[8]—integrating and reconciling the fragmentations within oneself and the divisions within the world. As another monastic writer, Nilus of Ancyra, put it in the fifth century: "You are a world within a world ... Look within yourself and there you will see the entire world."[9]

---

[5]Augustine, *On Psalm 99* in PL 37.1271.
[6]Gregory the Theologian, *Homily XXXVIII*, 11 *On The Theophany* PG 36.321–4.
[7]Maximus the Confessor, *Mystagogia* 7 PG 91.684 [and 672], in George Berthold, trans., *Maximus Confessor: Selected Writings* (New York: Paulist Press, 1985), 196. See also Maximus, *De Ambiguis* 91. Lars Thunberg, *Microcosm and Mediator: The Theological Anthropology of Maximus the Confessor*, 2nd ed. (Chicago, IL and La Salle, IL: Open Court, 1995).
[8]Maximus the Confessor speaks of "a natural bond" in *Ambiguum* 41 PG 91.1305.
[9]Nilus of Ancyra, *Epistles*, Book II, *Letter* 119 PG 79.252. See also Origen, *Homily on Leviticus* V, 2 PG 12.448–50; and John of Damascus, *On the Orthodox Faith* II.12, 4. Cf. also the study by D. S. Wallace-Hadrill, *The Greek Patristic View of Nature* (Manchester, UK: Manchester University Press, 1968), especially 66–79.

The same mystical interdependence between our lives and our planet is eloquently articulated by American farmer and cultural critic Wendell Berry, who touches in poetic and prophetic manner on the deeper implications of the global ecological crisis:

> The earth is what we all have in common, that is what we are made of and what we live from, and we therefore cannot damage it without damaging those with whom we share it. But I believe it goes further and deeper than that. There is an uncanny resemblance between our behavior toward each other and our behavior toward the earth. Between our relation to our own sexuality and our relation to the re-productivity of the earth, for instance, the resemblance is plain and strong and apparently inescapable. By some connection that we do not recognize, the willingness to exploit one becomes the willingness to exploit the other. The conditions and the means of exploitation are likewise similar.[10]

Not only, then, are we members one of another (cf. Eph. 4:25); but to press Berry's image still further and provide an identity for this interdependence, we might also suggest an uncanny resemblance between the body and the earth. If the earth is our very flesh, then it is inseparable from our story, our destiny, and our God. After all, as Paul writes in his Letter to the Ephesians, no one ever hates one's own flesh (5:29), a notion subsequently echoed in the philosophical thought of Origen of Alexandria (c. 185–254): "The world is like our bodies. It, too, is formed of many limbs and directed by a single soul. Yes, the world is an immense being directed by the power and the word of God, who is, so to say, its soul."[11] Indeed, for Origen, the parallel between nature and scripture is so complete that the person exploring nature and the person examining scripture should inevitably and invariably arrive at the very same conclusion and creed.[12]

---

[10]Wendell Berry, *Standing on Earth: Selected Essays* (Ipswich, UK: Golgonooza Press, 1991), 48–9.

[11]*On First Principles* II, i, 2–3 in PG 11.183.

[12]In Charles Upton, *Who Is the Earth: How to See God in the Natural World* (San Rafael, CA: Sophia Perennis, 1997), 59. Similarly, for Maximus the Confessor, creation resembles scripture, while the bible parallels the cosmos. See his *Ambiguum* 10 PG 91.1128–9.

Cosmic Reconciliation

While acknowledging the importance of the cosmic interconnection of all living things, one must also keep all things in perspective: their relationship to each other and the Creator, who is above all. Cosmic reconciliation includes reconciling *in humility* our relationship to God and others.

In this perspective, we gain access to other dimensions of life and are empowered to transcend ourselves and our own in order to see others and the world more transparently. After all, we constitute a part of creation and can never be considered apart from it; much less so should we dare to set ourselves up over and against the rest of creation. Surely it is inappropriate to contrast or compare ourselves with other creatures in order somehow to establish disparity or distinctiveness. Perhaps it would be more accurate to say that we *actually are* creation, that we are *truly are* the cosmos. Human beings—or at least the saints, as those who recall and realize what it means to be truly human—are "the hypostases of cosmic nature."[13] As Fr. Dumitru Stăniloae (1903–1993) expresses this,

> It is not that man is a part of the cosmos, but that all parts of the cosmos are parts of man. Man is not a microcosm sided by a macrocosm, nor is he framed within a macrocosm, but he is the actual cosmos, as he gives complete unity and complete meaning to all the parts of creation.[14]

The vision and boundaries of the world are always far broader than the limited space and narrow stake of any individual human being. The kaleidoscope of creation consistently reveals a variegated splendor of the holy and a rich diversity of beauty. As Gregory Nazianzus (also known as Gregory the Theologian, 329–391) intimates, this depth and breadth provide a glimpse into the very grandeur of God: "Study the enormous number of different kinds of birds, the variety of their

---

[13]Paul Evdokimov, "Nature," *Scottish Journal of Theology* 18 (March, 1965): 1–22 [Here at 3].
[14]Dumitru Stăniloae cited in Dragos Bahrim, "The Anthropic Cosmology of St. Maximus the Confessor," *Journal for Interdisciplinary Research on Religion and Science* 3 (2008): 28.

shapes and colors ... It gives me joy to speak of these things because they unfold to us the greatness of God."[15]

This implies that we can never exhaust the essence of even the smallest flower. When we look at a flower, we do not so much perceive its intrinsic nature as a reflection in this flower of the intrinsic nature of our own consciousness in relation to the flower. Similarly, a bee can only perceive the nectar of a flower; a snake will perceive the same flower as an infrared object; a bat perceives the flower as an echo of ultrasound. At the same time, however, the essential reality of the flower and the bee, the snake and the bat, always remains unknown and unobjectifiable, beyond our narrow interest or individual indulgence. This is why, centuries ago, the Cappadocian theologians were well aware that the essence of the slightest blade of grass and microscopic proboscis of mosquitoes evade human comprehension: "We cannot understand the nature of these things. Much less are we likely to be able to understand the nature of the first being, the unique being, who is the fullness of everything."[16]

In order, therefore, to acknowledge how the world and humanity are inseparably intertwined, and by extension intimately interconnected with God, we need to appreciate how our individual destiny is profoundly identified with the sacred purpose of creation, just as we are all inextricably susceptible to each other's influence. This is arguably the fundamental difference between a self-centered and a God-centered worldview:

> The person with a secular mentality feels himself to be the center of the universe. Yet he is likely to suffer from a sense of meaninglessness and insignificance because he knows he's but one human among five billion others—all feeling themselves to be the center of things—scratching out an existence on the surface of a medium-sized planet circling a small star among countless galaxies.
>
> The person with a sacred mentality, on the other hand, does not feel herself to be the center of the universe. She considers the center to be elsewhere and other. Yet she is unlikely to feel lost or insignificant precisely because she draws her significance and

---

[15]Gregory Nazianzus, *Oration* 28, 23–5 in PG 36.57–60.
[16]Ibid., 25 in PG 36.60.

meaning from relationship, her connection, with that center, that other.[17]

Love for the whole of creation smashes the noxious, if not obnoxious image of a self-centered, secular worldview and suggests a sense of enlarged, balanced existence, as echoed in Dostoevsky's *The Brothers Karamazov*, where the exhortation of Fr. Zossima is to

> love God's creation, love every atom of it separately, and love it also as a whole; love every green leaf, every ray of God's light; love the animals and the plants and love every inanimate object. If you come to love all things you will perceive God's mystery inherent in all things.[18]

For Paul, the difference between a secular worldview and a sacred vision lies fundamentally in the face of Christ as the center of the universe, where the ultimate cosmic transfiguration, interconnection, and reconciliation resides:

> [Christ] is the image of the invisible God, the first-born of all creation; for in him all things were created, in heaven and on earth, visible and invisible, whether thrones or dominions or principalities or authorities—all things were created through him and for him. He is before all things, and in him all things hold together. He is the head of the body, the church; he is the beginning, the first-born from the dead, that in everything he might be pre-eminent. For in him all the fullness of God was pleased to dwell, and through him to reconcile to himself all things, whether on earth or in heaven, making peace by the blood of his cross. (Col. 1:15-20)

Reimagining a Transformed Creation

By perceiving the world through the lenses of cosmic transfiguration, cosmic interconnection, and cosmic reconciliation, individuals and

---

[17]M. Scott Peck, *A World Waiting to Be Born* (New York: Bantam Books, 1993), 46.
[18]Fyodor Dostoevsky, *The Brothers Karamazov*, trans. Andrew R. MacAndrew (New York: Bantam Classics, 1970), 427.

society—with the grace of the Holy Spirit—can embark on the transformation necessary to restore the shattered image of creation. This involves a journey that acknowledges responsibility for the sin of degrading creation instead of recognizing the divine presence in all things—for moving from autonomy to dependence on God, from self-centeredness to communion with the sacred, and from anthropocentrism to theocentrism.

Heaven and earth are full of God's glory (Isa. 6:3); the world is a burning bush of divine energy, soaked in divine grace and presence. Such is the way we received creation from the Creator as a gift; and such is the way that creation was perceived by mystics as an image of God, albeit fractured. It remains simply for us to recognize this gift and restore its image. Indeed, long before any human interest or anxiety about climate change, creation itself understood the human vocation and obligation to remember and revive this reality: "From the beginning till now the entire creation, as we know, has been groaning in pain" (Rom. 8:22).[19]

The mystic grasps the same essential truth, the same sacramental vision of the world, that everything is a source of gratitude and a cause for glory. A recently acclaimed saint of the Orthodox Church, Porphyrios of Athens writes,

> Nature is the mystical gospel. It requires of us an inner grace ... Otherwise, it does not induce us to heaven. The spiritual person, who possesses the divine spirit, becomes all eyes, all scent. All of the senses come alive with the Spirit of God. The spiritual person hears and sees things differently: the birds, the rocks, and the butterflies ... Grace renders the spiritual person attentive, yearning to be one with all things.[20]

Societal transformation is of course imperative in cultures and institutions around the world. While the approach and emphasis

---

[19]See the interpretation by Cyril of Alexandria, *Commentary on Romans* PG 74.821–4.

[20]Porphyrios, *Life and Teachings of St. Porphyrios* (Chania, Crete: Chrysopiyi Monastery, 2003), 462–3 [In Greek: My translation]. Also cited in Chrysostomos Stamoulis, *Sacred Beauty: An Introduction to Orthodox Aesthetics* (Athens: Akritas Editions, 2004), 313–14. See also the English translation of *Wounded by Love: The Life and the Wisdom of Elder Porphyrios*, trans. John Raffan (Limni, Evia: Denise Harvey Publisher, 2005), 218–19.

in this book reflect the Greek Patristic worldview and Orthodox Christian way, it must be remembered that the shattered image of creation is by no means a problem solely of Western Christianity or Western civilization. No single era, faith, or culture can be held responsible or accountable for the contemporary environmental pollution and deterioration of our planet. It would be naive to suppose that classical theology and Orthodox spirituality somehow automatically or perhaps magically hold the key to answers where others have failed. If that were the case, then Athens and Istanbul, just as Moscow and Kiev, would surely present as pictures of ecological integrity and paradigm. Moreover, it would be presumptuous, if not audacious, to assume that the Orthodox worldview undeniably presents the quintessence of Christianity— that would once have been labeled as the mortal sin of pride. The truth is that every era, faith, and culture is responsible and accountable for the way it has ignored the sacramental dimension of creation.

Clearly, Western civilization represents a particular ecological worldview and environmental bias, but it would be arrogant and inaccurate—if not dishonest and unethical—to explain or blame the ecological crisis as an aberration of Western philosophy and theology, or of its scientific and technological ramifications.[21] So much fine literature has described the contemporary problems as resulting from a process that emerged in the late Middle Ages, matured in the Reformation and Counter-Reformation, and produced the more recent Enlightenment and modern civilization. Instead, everyone—of Western or Eastern background and context alike—should respond to the godless anthropocentrism that saturates and subverts our perception of creation and the world.

While science and technology may inspire humanity with a dangerous inclination toward autonomy and a perilous temptation toward self-adoration or even paradoxically toward self-destruction, one must never forget that the supreme goal of all human endeavor and advance is to achieve perpetual progress and spiritual growth in the sight of the Creator as well as in the context of a continually renewed covenant with creation. Today's immense technical and technological development in the

---

[21]I will return to this argument in Chapter 6: "On Earth as in Heaven—Cardinal Symbols and Values."

end renders humanity more responsible, accountable, and liable. And the church's principal role and responsibility in the world is to exercise clear and candid prophetic criticism within rapidly changing times and cultures.[22]

There can never be any sanctioned formula; there will never be a straightforward solution. Nevertheless, defensive or apologetic attitudes should certainly be abandoned. Instead, we must engage in responsible dialogue with and criticism of civilization as well as of the fundamental presuppositions of economy as we know and practice them. Orthodox Christianity, too, must rethink its vocation and contribution to current challenges in our world. And with regard to the ecological crisis, Orthodox theology has preserved an unequaled dynamism and unqualified optimism in its unprecedented affirmation of every person and particle in creation. Still, it must learn to recuperate these gifts from its remote, historical past and abstract, theological present in order to translate them into tangible virtues and applicable disciplines for a contemporary ecological worldview and lifestyle.

It is a fact that Orthodox theology and liturgy were in the past often distinguished—even dismissed—as a mystical, metaphysical system inasmuch presenting an otherworldly, unworldly spirituality. Paradoxically, however, in its most powerful criticism of the destruction wrought upon God's wonderful creation and the shattered image of our sublime world, Orthodox Christianity emphasizes the significance of all creation as the incarnation of God in the widest and deepest sense:

> The fact is that God is at work in the world, the same God who infuses into creation the power needed for it to continue stable throughout all time ... Through the things that are seen let us be led toward the things that are not seen. To do this there is no need to travel far. Only faith is required, because only through faith can we behold him.[23]

---

[22]See Jim Antal, *Climate Church, Climate World: How People of Faith Must Work for Change* (Lanham, MD: Rowman and Littlefield, 2018), especially ch. 2, 31ff.
[23]Theodoret of Cyrus, *The Cure of Pagan Diseases* IV, 60 in Pierre Canivet, ed., *Sources Chrétiennes* 57 (Paris: Cerf, 1958), 221. For an English translation, see Thomas Halton, trans., *Theodoret of Cyrus: A Cure of Pagan Maladies* (Mahwah, NJ: Ancient Christian Writers, 2013).

A popular Russian priest and renowned spiritual director at the turn of the twentieth century, St. John of Kronstadt described the same paradox in the early nineteenth century, when he claimed that we have arrived at the original, primeval state where "we see flesh and matter in everything; and yet nowhere, nor at any time, is God before our eyes."[24] The truth is that we do not need to travel far in order to discern the divine image in creation. Christ's countenance is perceived through the eyes of the soul; and it is perceived in every corner and fragment of creation. This is the essence and extent of the sacramental worldview. The words from the Psalms are more pertinent today than ever: "I discern before me [the face of] my Lord in everything" (Ps. 16.8). "For, all things look to [his] face ... which renews the face of the earth" (Ps. 104:27).

---

[24]John of Kronstadt in E. E. Goulaeff, trans., *My Life in Christ: The Spiritual Journey of St. John of Kronstadt* (repr. Jordanville, NY: Holy Trinity Publications, 1977), 143.

SECTION I

Theory and Theology

1

The Lens of Grace

Reintegrating the Sacred and the Profane

Laying the Conceptual Groundwork

Religious thought and political practice—in earlier eras, as in cultures that remain frozen in some distant past—were influenced by a sharp division between the sacred and the profane, between that which represented the divine or uncreated and that which was relegated to the material or created. In medieval times and traditions, people did not readily discern or easily overcome any such dichotomy between things divine and things temporal. However, this manner of thinking prevails to this day and has been expanded to many other aspects of society—including politics, economics, science, and technology. As a result, the church in the world often seems to languish with increasing irrelevance or else is resigned to filling the gaps between the sacred altar and the public square with pious statements and religious slogans.

There is, therefore, an ever-growing need today for a restored theological vision—one that is far less separatist and isolationist from or self-sufficient and self-righteous toward the world. And while this is certainly taking place on some levels, theology and the church must relearn how to affirm, inform, and transform the world, based on the foundational claim in Christian scripture that the divine Word assumed flesh and made its home in our world (Jn 1:14). There is a need once again to uphold and advance the catholic and cosmic breadth of the church's teaching, reintegrating the sacred and the profane.

Notions of World

In order to define this vision and ethos, it will be helpful to consider some of the key terms that recur throughout this book—including the fundamental concepts of world, church, and grace.

There is of course a great diversity in the way people perceive the term "world." It may be regarded as including everything outside or beyond the religious sphere or the church: nature's trees, oceans and mountains, but also worldly matters such as education, governance, and housing. Alternatively, world or nature may designate the enormous possibilities promised and promoted by technology and progress. Both views imply and involve transcending or transforming nature by reason and culture through material things or mechanical technology.[1]

However, such attitudes are insufficient and inaccurate since the church is nothing less than the entire world transfigured, the universe ordered, created nature rendered into "cosmos"—a Greek term that literally signifies "beauty." Cosmos is in fact the only Greek term for "world."[2] Moreover, any naive optimism that human intellect, ideology, or invention can somehow alone control and convert nature loses sight of the formative and transformative significance of Gethsemane and Golgotha—of the power of despair, the land of tears, and the reality of death. The recognition and assumption of the cross is a realistic confrontation and assimilation of the world in all its deficiency and possibility, all its pain and suffering, warts and all.

The fundamental scriptural and patristic principle behind this worldview is that "God so loved the world that he gave his only Son" (Jn 3:16). This love-to-the-point-of-death (Phil. 2:8), which constitutes a characteristic feature of a theological insight into

---

[1]For an interdisciplinary approach to the transformation of nature in shifting philosophical paradigms throughout the centuries and technological advances in recent times, see David Albertson and Cabell King, eds., *Without Nature? A New Condition for Theology* (New York: Fordham University Press, 2010).

[2]Other terms have more specific definitions, signifying "creation" (dēmiourgia or ktisis), "earth" (gaia or planētēs), or "people" (anthrōpoi or koinōnia).

and spiritual perspective of creation, seems to be at the opposite end of much contemporary thought. It is no surprise that early writers emphasize cosmic transfiguration, rather than dwelling on the ramifications of individual predestination.[3] Whereas medieval Christian thought under the influence of Augustine tended to distort salvation by confining it to a narrow elite, Eastern patristic thought preferred to discern the divine light pervading the whole world, affirming that everyone and everything is filled with the love of the God (1 Jn 4:8).

Even so, any discussion about the relationship between church and world should be wary of embracing an easy pantheism, where the secular is simplistically and superficially—older theological manuals were preoccupied with and prejudiced toward the term "supernaturally"—integrated into or identified with the sacred. To remain truly balanced, a Christian understanding of the world must retain a foundational biblical and theological duality, simultaneously maintaining both the continuity and the discontinuity between Creator and creation. The line of demarcation between God and world is clearly, though not always crisply, articulated in Hebrew Scripture. Thus, while a Judeo-Christian perspective accepts the creation of the world by God "out of nothing" (ex nihilo), it is simultaneously quick to affirm the creation of humanity "in the image and likeness of God." (Gen. 1:26).[4] This is why the Greek term for "church" (ekklesia) essentially implies separation or "con-vocation" (ek-kaleo) from the world in order to fulfill the true vocation of the world— namely, the realization of a dynamic relationship with God, an interpretation of the horizontal and historical in light of the vertical and eternal.

---

[3]This "cosmic" dimension of theology, anthropology, and cosmology is a prominent, if not distinctive feature of Eastern patristic and Greek Orthodox thought. See Andrew Louth, *Maximus Confessor* (New York: Routledge, 1996), 63. Hans Urs von Balthasar underlined this dimension in the writings of Maximus, emphasizing the central place of the world in the act of creation and the plan of salvation. See his *Cosmic Liturgy: The Universe According to Maximus the Confessor* (San Francisco, CA: Ignatius Press, 2003).

[4]The doctrine of creation *ex nihilo* is often gleaned through scriptural passages such as 2 Macc. 7:28, Rom. 4:17, and Heb. 11:3. For a theological, if conventional analysis of this doctrine, see John Zizioulas, *The Eucharistic Communion and the World* (Edinburgh: T&T Clark, 2011), especially ch. 8, 143–75.

Notions of Church

When defining the term "church," no one can ignore the powerful organization and institution of the Roman Catholic Church through the centuries or overlook the social and economic impact of the diverse Protestant congregations throughout the world. However, there is a rigorous distinction, if not a radical difference in the way that Orthodox Christianity perceives the church.[5]

From as early as the third century, but especially from the Constantinian era of the early fourth century, the church is gradually conceived and increasingly considered in juridical terms. This was the case particularly in the West, perhaps due to the powerful impact of the sense of law, in which Rome surely excelled. The result over centuries was a reduction of the church either to an institutional and monarchical system or else to a social and political program. The accent in both instances appeared to be more on the external, visible organization as well as on an immediate, imperial authority that combined—at times confused—the power of this world with the sovereignty of the next. While not altogether losing sight of the inspirational and sacramental aspect, the church in the West emphasized its institutional or secular dimension as an establishment and enterprise in the political or public domain.

This attitude was undoubtedly also the result, among other things, of a just and justifiable historical evolution. However, the consequence of such a development was that the church imposed its way on society and family, as if from above, with pronouncements and decrees in ethical and moral matters, at times correct and courageous but at other times inappropriate and audacious. The Orthodox Church—where, admittedly, the more outward missionary or social, and even liturgical or theological developments have frequently proved deficient through the ages— might contend that the desirable harmony or symphony between divine and human was forfeited in the West for an emphasis on human realism and worldly activism. When the church is no longer

---

[5]I would risk a cursory clarification here—again within the context of establishing a Christian worldview, for both theological and ecumenical purposes—to underscore the fact that relations and conversations among the various churches have in recent decades encouraged and developed a study of ecclesiology in order precisely to shed light upon the numerous divisions in the Christian world and to discern a methodology for their rapprochement and reconciliation.

called to transform humanity and the whole creation, but instead concedes to conforming to a worldly reality or fantasy, then it also ceases to be a promise and is reduced to mere compromise.

Therefore, any temptation to secularize the church must be avoided as another severance of the vital relationship between heaven and earth. The Greek word for devil (diabolos) implies rupture or separation. And the diabolical temptation at all times in the church is to succumb either to a form of angelism or else a form of secularism that finds its grounding either in the other-worldly or the very mundane. The result is a destruction of the equilibrium of the church in the world and of the integrity of the world in the church, both of which are ultimately a distortion of the solidarity between heaven and earth.

At the same time, the church cannot ignore the material world; it cannot properly exercise its mission unless it cares for every human person and every living creature. Nineteenth-century philosopher Ludwig Feuerbach proposed that one is what one eats. In this sense, the breadth of the church's vision lies in the bread and wine of the Eucharist, in the consumption of sacramental communion. It is ultimately with the living body and blood of Jesus Christ as the central plate of life's banquet that one can garner a glimpse of the reality of matter and of what really matters in the world.[6]

Notions of Grace

While the church is in the world and exists for the world (cf. Jn 6:51), its origin and goal—its alpha and omega—lie beyond the world in the divine initiative for creation and the divine image in humankind. As the instrument of grace, the church's earthly and institutional side reveals the energy of the Holy Spirit, which constitutes the creative and motivating force of everything and everyone. This Spirit is the giver of life and of all forms of life: personal, interpersonal, communal, ecclesial, and hierarchical.

[6]See Alexander Schmemann, *For the Life of the World* (Crestwood, NY: St. Vladimir's Press, 1973), esp. ch. 1. I am generally indebted to Fr. Schmemann as a principal inspiration in my own ministry and writing. I regard this book as radical, constituting the root of Schmemann's theology and the foundation of Orthodox spirituality.

That the church is in the world also implies that God penetrates and permeates the whole world. Neither church nor world can be conceived or comprehended independently of one another. The phrase "in the world" signifies in total solidarity and communion with the world, implying an organic relationship and not simply a moral association or social correlation. The communion between church and world is never contingent on the actions of its leaders or systems of its theology, but rather is conferred through the loving act of creation and confirmed in the loving act of re-creation through the Incarnation.

In this sense, the church *is* the world, which it is intended to transform. And the world *is* the church, which it is called to become. Of course, the danger of overemphasizing the church as the world transfigured or as new creation (Rev. 21:1) lies in the temptation to acknowledge only the divine or "other-worldly" aspect of the church. Yet, the world is fully present in the church. Similarly, the church needs always to embrace the world, always to remain down to earth. Christians are called to be faithful stewards and trustworthy caretakers of the sacramental dimension of creation (cf. 1 Cor. 4:1-2). It is by remaining faithful to the earth that the church can become new heaven (Rev. 21:1), where the heavenly pierces and pervades, without in any way oppressing or suppressing the earthly. It is a fundamental Christian premise that the earthly aspect of the church and the world is never crushed but always consecrated, never rejected but only respected. This is what safeguards the church in the world from any abuse of authority and any assertion of triumphalism.

It may be argued that Orthodox theology and spirituality ultimately propose no theoretical solution with regard to the problems of the world. What they offer instead is a compelling invitation to salvation, healing, and transfiguration; what they provide is the potential or capacity to perceive the same world in a different light. This does not imply subjectivism, for the "different light" is ultimately the grace of the Holy Spirit that renews, restores, and transforms all things. There is nothing in the world that is not a gift of the Spirit. And the goal of every human being is simply to acquire the gifts of the Spirit wherever and everywhere that they may be found.

Thus, any balanced view of church should not overlook the person and power of the Spirit in the formation and sustainability of the world. Only from this perspective can creation be understood as the work of a loving God, who acts out of love and is in love with creation—a God who is confessed as Trinity and conceived as communion, a God who passionately desires to share divine compassion and shower divine benevolence in the world (cf. Lk. 22:15). In the early fourth century, Basil of Caesarea (also known as Basil the Great, 330–379), underlined this Trinitarian aspect of creation:

When you consider creation, I advise you to think first of Him who is the first cause of everything that exists; namely, the Father, and then of the Son, who is the Creator, and then the Holy Spirit, the perfector ... The Originator of all things is the One: He creates through the Son and perfects through the Holy Spirit ... Perceive these three: the Lord who commands, the Word who creates, and the Spirit who strengthens.[7]

A passage in "The Conversation of St. Seraphim of Sarov," written toward the beginning of the nineteenth century and describing the provenance and purpose of the Christian life, illustrates the vital role of the Holy Spirit in creation. In the course of an exchange that occurred deep inside a forest on a winter morning, Nicholas Motovilov, the renowned disciple of St. Seraphim and author of these revelations, asks his elder about the peace and warmth conveyed by divine grace:

I don't understand how one can be certain of being in the Spirit of God. How should I be able to recognize for certain this manifestation in myself?

"I've already told you," said Father Seraphim, "that it's very simple. I've talked at length about the state of those who are in the Spirit of God. I've also explained to you how we can recognize this presence in ourselves ... What more is necessary, my friend?"

"I must understand better everything that you have said to me."

---

[7] Basil the Great, *On the Holy Spirit*, XVI, 38 PG 32.136. See the translation by David Anderson (Crestwood, NY: St. Vladimir's Seminary Press, 1980), 62–3. Also see Irenaeus of Lyons (writing before Basil), *Against Heresies* IV, 20. 1 PG 7.1032; and John of Damascus (writing after Basil), *On the Orthodox Faith* II, 2 PG 94.864.

"My friend, we are both at this moment in the Spirit of God. Why won't you look at me?"

"I can't look at you, Father," I replied. "Your eyes shine like lightning, your face has become more dazzling than the sun, and it hurts my eyes to look at you."

"Don't be afraid," said he. "At this very moment you've become as bright as I have. You are also at present in the fullness of the Spirit of God; otherwise, you wouldn't be able to see me as you do see me." And leaning towards me, he whispered in my ear: "Thank the Lord God for His infinite goodness towards us ... How thankful we ought to be to God for this unspeakable gift which He has granted to us both ... The grace of God, like a mother full of loving kindness towards her children, has deigned to comfort your afflicted heart, at the intercession of the Mother of God herself ... Why then, my friend, do you not look me straight in the face? Look freely and without fear; the Lord is with us."

Encouraged by these words, I looked and was seized by holy fear. Imagine in the middle of the sun, dazzling in the brilliance of its noontide rays, the face of the man who is speaking to you. You can see the movements of his lips, the changing expression of his eyes, you can hear his voice, you can feel his hands holding you by the shoulders, but you can see neither his hands nor his body—nothing except the blaze of light which shines around, lighting up with its brilliance the snow-covered meadow, and the snowflakes which continue to fall unceasingly.

"What do you feel?" asked Father Seraphim." An immeasurable well-being," I replied. "Infinite joy in heart."

Father Seraphim continued: "When the Spirit of God descends on a man, and envelopes him in the fullness of His presence, the soul overflows with unspeakable joy, for the Holy Spirit fills everything He touches with joy ... If the first-fruits of future joy have already filled your soul with such sweetness, with such happiness, what shall we say of the joy in the Kingdom of Heaven, which awaits all those who weep here on earth ... For the present we must work, and make continued efforts to gain more and more strength to attain the perfect measure of the stature of Christ ... But then this transitory and partial joy which we now feel will be revealed in all its fullness, overwhelming our being with ineffable delights which no one will be able to take from us."[8]

Toward Reintegration

Any discussion of the relationship between the church and the world, or about the establishment of heaven on earth, must therefore include an emphasis on the role of divine grace as the integral and transformative force of restoration and renewal in Christ. When as Christians we learn to die to the world and rise in the light of a world revived in Christ, then we are also able to acquire a new vision of creation. This means that, before there can be any social or ecological ethic, there must first be a personal and spiritual ethos. It is that simple, though it remains far more seductive to become embroiled in abstract programs and general plans, while neglecting the formation of the church and transformation of the world.

What is implied here by personal transformation is not the individualism that is so pervasive in our society but rather the relational aspect of all creation. By personal transformation, I imagine the human person in a network of connections, a process of communion, and an attitude of abiding reference to God and the rest of creation (including other human beings at once created in the image of God and from the soil of the earth). A person baptized and clothed in Christ (cf. Gal. 3:27) is essentially no different from any other person in the world (cf. Col. 3:11). What ultimately distinguishes a Christian is the vocation and aspiration to become and be like Christ. An early document describes the life of believers:

> They are in the world, but their piety is unseen. They inhabit both Greek and barbarian cities, as the case may be, and follow the local customs in dress, diet, and life in general ... They obey the particular laws, and transcend these very laws with their own life ... They live on earth, but their citizenship is in heaven.[9]

---

[8]Cited in V. Lossky, *The Mystical Theology of the Eastern Church* (Crestwood, NY: St. Vladimir's Seminary Press, 1976), 227–9. See also Isaac of Nineveh, *Homily* 38, where Isaac rejects any "difference" between "securing immortal life" after death and "sensing everything in God" from this life.

[9]*Letter to Diognetus* 5–6 PG 2.1173–7; cf. also *Macarian Homilies* 5, 4 in *Classics of Western Spirituality*, trans. George Maloney (New York: Paulist Press, 1982).

Christians differ existentially from others inasmuch as they have accepted and adopted a new nature, a life renewed after the image of its Creator (Col. 3:10) and through Christ as all in all (Col. 3:11). However, it is one thing to acknowledge and affirm the presence of Christ everywhere, and quite another to recognize and reflect Christ in all persons and places:

> From now on, then, therefore, we know no one from a human (literally, a fleshly) point of view; even though we once knew Christ from a human point of view, we no longer know him thus. Therefore, if any are in Christ, they are a new creation; the old has passed away, behold the new has come. All this is from God, who through Christ reconciled us to himself and gave us the ministry of reconciliation; that is, in Christ, God was reconciling the world to himself. (2 Cor. 5:16-19)

To be in Christ is an act of faith, a personal event; but the call to restoration and reconciliation shapes this act into a relationship, into an event of community and an exchange of communion. And it is precisely as an image of what the world is supposed to be that the community of the church becomes a cosmic and universal event.

This new becoming—or becoming anew—also explains the emphasis in Orthodoxy spirituality on the ascetic and ecclesial dimensions explored in the chapters that follow. It assists in making sense of the radical, albeit fundamental Orthodox concepts of reconciliation (metanoia) and divinization (theosis) discussed in this book. The early Christian tradition and entire Orthodox worldview affirm that the Word of God assumed flesh (Jn 1:14) in order that the world might be reconciled and deified, that the whole of creation might share in divine grace. Ultimately, God became human and assumed the created world in order that creation might become what it was originally intended to be—namely, divinely-transfigured and grace-filled—but also that the sacred and the profane might be restored, reconciled, and reintegrated.

FIGURE 1 *Creation of Adam: Detail from Byzantine mosaic of the Old Testament, God creates Adam, Tower of Babel, Cappella Palatina, Palatine Chapel of the Palace of the Normans or Royal Palace of Palermo, Palermo, Sicily, Italy © imageBROKER/Alamy Stock Photo.* **See p. 101**

2

Transcendence and Immanence

Ancient Concepts for a Modern Crisis

While the reconciliation of the sacred and the profane was accomplished once and for all when the Word of God assumed flesh, the question of the relationship between heaven and earth—or grace and nature—remained central to the journey of intellectual mysticism and to the process of ascetical spirituality. When we approach a conceptual awareness of God as sacred, and of divine action in the world as sacramental, we also become aware of a parallel dichotomy that affirms the dialectical, almost paradoxical character of God's presence in creation. On the one hand, there is a profound sense of divine immanence, whereby God is markedly recognizable in the beauty and sanctity of the world; and on the other hand, there is a keen sense of divine transcendence, whereby God is perceived to be above and beyond anything in the world.

This intimate realization of the immediate accessibility and inaccessible remoteness of God—the ultimate dialogue and communication between Creator and creation—has always been at the heart of religious search and spirituality. At its finest and most refined, theology becomes an exercise of balance, maintaining mutual interaction while at the same time avoiding dualistic isolation between God and world.

This chapter examines select theologians and paradoxes from the early Christian and Late Middle Ages in order to explore how they perceived creation in association with the Creator. The purpose of such a foray into the history of Christian thought is to foster an historical appreciation regarding fundamental inherited concepts, Eastern and Western alike, as well as to appreciate the source and influence of their positive and negative worldviews.

In this survey, I will consider familiar philosophers and fundamental precepts of creation that were nonetheless greatly influential and instrumental in the development of Christian attitudes and practices related to the world: Clement of Alexandria and his emphasis on cosmic hierarchy, Origen of Alexandria's Christian mysticism, Plotinus and his Neoplatonist synthesis, the dipolar theology of Dionysius the Areopagite, John Scotus Eriugena and his notion of cosmic verity, as well as the cosmic synthesis of Nicholas of Cusa. Their thinking provides the historical backdrop for an Eastern theological approach to reconciling the paradox of God's presence in creation: namely, knowing God through the beauty of creation (divine immanence), while not-knowing God perceived as above and beyond anything worldly (divine transcendence). Finally, the scriptural notion of creation *ex nihilo* and the essence-energy model of Gregory Palamas will be submitted as indispensable methods for relating the immutable divine essence to the uncreated energies of God that simultaneously reveal and conceal the mystery of God as Creator and the source of cosmic transfiguration.

Clement of Alexandria (*c.* 150–215): Christian Humanism

In the second and third centuries, the world's intellectual and cultural center, Alexandria, also came to be recognized as the capital of Hellenism. It was here that Jewish and Christian traditions came into contact with the Greek world. The Church in Alexandria did not boast excessively of any apostolic origin, although its sources are indeed very early; the peculiarity of Alexandria lay primarily in its Catechetical School. In contrast to the institutional succession and authority of bishops reminiscent of other cities such as Rome or Constantinople, Alexandria presented a more philosophical, almost charismatic progression or tradition. Thus, the Christian Platonists of Alexandria hold an undisputed place in the history and thought of Christianity as the first scholars to undertake the enterprise of constructing a Christian institution of instruction.[1]

While the founder and first master of the Alexandrian School was Pantainos, it is his successor, Clement of Alexandria, who is arguably its most renowned and influential representative. Clement gladly accepted the best gifts of non-Christian philosophy as providing pointers toward Christ as the truth *par excellence*. This unprecedented thinker, always so optimistic about the capacities and possibilities of the human mind, was nonetheless uncompromising in his teaching about God's otherness or transcendence: "Though heaven be called his throne, yet God is not contained, even while resting delighted in his creation."[2] The image of such a cosmic hierarchy comprises a vast living chain, wherein every link draws those below in response to an overpowering attraction and appeal from the divine beauty.[3]

Clement's humanism is proof of his positive attitude toward creation. This is especially evident in his reference to divine beauty and in the importance that he attaches to the proper use of worldly pleasures. Yet, Clement's Gnostic (as he likes to describe the person who reaches perfection) always enjoys worldly pleasures in a spirit of detachment, precisely because these are ultimately irrelevant to salvation. Similarly, Clement's Gnostic conveniently uses but does not actively transform the material world. The Gnostic may in many ways appear to be an admirable figure, but what is ultimately absent is any sign of struggle or stress for the transfiguration of the world. In this respect, Clement is far less a humanist than the more rigorist or ascetic Christian writers. For him, truth always remains

---

[1] Cf. E. Osborn, *The Philosophy of Clement of Alexandria* (Cambridge, UK: Cambridge University Press, 1957) and S. R. C. Lilla, *Clement of Alexandria* (Oxford: Oxford University Press, 1971). A more recent survey of early (mainly Western) Christian writers and their "ecologically harmful" or else "ecologically responsible" doctrines may be found in D. Kinsley, *Ecology and Religion: Ecological Spirituality in Cross-Cultural Perspective* (Englewood Cliffs, NJ: Prentice-Hall, 1995), especially 103–24. For further on the early scholarship, particularly the Eastern patristic tradition in relation to God's presence and perception in the world, see Paulos Gregorios, *The Human Presence: An Orthodox View of Nature* (Geneva: World Council of Churches, 1978), especially chs. 5 and 6, 54–81.

[2] Clement, *Stromateis* II, cf. the edition of O. Stählin (Berlin, 1960), 2.

[3] Clement, *Stromateis* VII, cf. the edition of O. Stählin (Berlin, 1960), 10.

a homeless stranger in the historical order and social context.[4] In
the final analysis, Clement's worldview fails to assimilate the basic
principle of Christianity that the truth assumed flesh and dwelt
among us (Jn 1:14), finding an abiding home in the simplicity of
Bethlehem, the insignificance of Nazareth, and the ignominy of
Golgotha.

Origen of Alexandria (c. 185–254): Christian Mysticism

With Origen, Clement's successor as head of the Catechetical School,
we enter the domain of specifically Christian mysticism, beyond
any mere philosophical Gnosticism.[5] Unlike Clement (before him),
Origen was not a convert from philosophy; and unlike Plotinus
(after him), Origen was not a philosopher. Origen was primarily,
if not exclusively concerned with interpreting Scripture, which he
saw as the repository of all truth. It is Scripture, then, that lies at
the heart of his mystical theology and his spiritual life. However,
Origen is always two-sided; he is never unilateral or monolithic.
There is of course the traditional, deeply ecclesiastical side of this
theological luminary; but there is also the Platonist, more speculative
side of this exceptional thinker. As an extraordinary representative
of Alexandrian Christianity, Origen reveals a far more subtle and
differentiated scheme than Clement, though one that essentially
undergoes similar challenges.

From both Greek philosophy and Christian Scripture, Origen
inherits the conviction that God is fundamentally unknowable;
yet, Origen is at the same time reluctant to entertain the notion
that God is radically unknowable. His is a mysticism of light,
never of darkness; in Origen's theological system, the summit of
mystical experience is always the illumination of knowledge. To
contemplate the light of Christ is our highest privilege as fleshly
beings. However, we are not merely flesh, and so Christian maturity

---

[4]Rowan Williams, *The Wound of Knowledge: Christian Spirituality from the New Testament*, 2nd rev. ed. (Cambridge, MA: Cowley Publications, 2003), 37.
[5]See Henri Crouzel, *Origen* (Edinburgh: T&T Clark, 1989). See also Jean Daniélou, Origen (London: Sheed and Ward, 1955), and Henry Chadwick, *Christianity and the Classical Tradition* (Oxford, UK: Clarendon Press, 1966).

also involves a progressive detachment from the worldly or external Jesus, who must yield to the spiritual or interior gospel. In the final analysis, Origen is deeply scandalized by flesh and matter, which explains why he is profoundly embarrassed by the scene at Gethsemane and Golgotha.[6] For Origen, the goal of the Christian mystic is knowledge of the divine Word prior to and independent of the divine Incarnation. The soul inevitably passes beyond faith in the Incarnation, which constitutes only a preliminary stage in its eventual ascent to God.

By the same token, for Origen, natural contemplation signifies not so much a rumination about God's wonder in creation, but rather a perception of the transience of this world accompanied by the paramount desire to move beyond this world: "The human mind should mount to spiritual understanding, and seek the ground of things in heaven."[7] Accordingly, Origen regards ethics as a process or practice, which eventually subdues the body to the soul and frees the soul from bondage to the material body.

Thus, Origen's attitudes to the material world and to historical reality remain somewhat problematic from a Christian perspective. In his worldview, there is an irreconcilable, inner tension between the biblical theologian and the philosophical speculator. While he never explicitly declares that matter and history are insignificant, he evidently considers them an imperfection and a distortion of what is truly human. God is, of course, to be encountered in this world, but the form of this encounter is only a shadow by comparison with the knowledge of the spiritual, heavenly world.

Nonetheless, while the inheritance and influence of Platonist thought is apparent in his writing, there is no evidence that Origen categorically devalues the material world. After all, if one believes and claims that material things are an image—no matter how imperfect, inadequate or incomplete—of heavenly reality, then how can one possibly despise or deny the world? The weakness of Platonism lies more in its lack of historical compassion and concern; in the end, its world remains largely static. Origen, however, speaks of moving forward, of never stopping,[8] thereby succeeding in investing historical evolution and development with a unique story

---

[6]Origen, cf. *On Prayer* 29 PG 11.529 and *Commentary on John* I, 7–8 PG 14.32–6. See also *Against Celsus* VI, 68 PG 11.1401.
[7]Origen, *Commentary on the Song of Songs* III, 12 PG 17.268–9.
[8]Origen, *On Prayer* 25, 2 PG 11.496–7.

and matter with a special place within the context of the larger cosmos.

The question, of course, remains whether Origen's Christ is less than fully incarnate, whether his Christ has—to adopt colloquial jargon —ever "fully makes touch-down." In the end, though Origen is a brilliant and elusive thinker, as well as arguably the precursor of more than one aspect of the Christian mystical tradition, he is unwilling to encounter and embrace human life and material creation fully and meaningfully. Although later theology will develop multiple different and diverse emphases derived from his thought, these will nonetheless invariably be shaped within the fundamental framework provided by this early Alexandrian giant and genius.

Plotinus of Alexandria (*c.* 204–270): Christian Metaphysics

Perhaps the greatest philosopher of religion in the ancient world, Plotinus was a disciple of Ammonius Sakkas, another renowned teacher at the Catechetical School in Alexandria, though he did not begin his writing career until the age of fifty. It was again later, toward the middle of the third century, that Plotinus opened his own school in Rome. Plotinus is recognized as the most prominent representative of what since the nineteenth century has become known as Neoplatonist philosophy. His school of Neoplatonism did not just modify or amend Platonism; in fact, it drew from the entire classical tradition to produce a new synthesis.[9]

Despite contemplating the cosmos as a hierarchy where the heavenly bodies, including the created sun and stars, are regarded as spiritual bodies, Plotinus adopted a seemingly negative attitude toward matter in general. For him, matter is without form or shape; it is a "nothing," much like the chaos out of which creation came to

---

[9]See *Plotinus*, trans. A. Hilary Armstrong, *Loeb Classical Library* (Cambridge, MA: Harvard University Press, 1966). Cf. other works by Prof. Armstrong who was, in recent times, the most faithful disciple of Plotinus. The "hierarchical" structure of the universe developed by Plotinus was also articulated and advocated recently by the chemist-philosopher Michael Polanyi (1891–1976) and by the theologian Thomas Torrance (1913–2007).

be. Even so, Plotinus clearly sought to challenge his contemporary Gnostics, who considered the material world as evil or inferior. He claimed that no one could frankly look upon the world and conceivably deduce that its origin lay in some demonic power. Salvation, then, can never be identified with an escape from matter.

It should be remembered that, in spite of its rational and radical concepts, classical Greek philosophy ultimately secured a certain balance between spirit and matter, preserving a sense of awe and wonder with regard to creation. This certainly appears to be true both of Platonist as of Aristotelian thought. Indeed, these two philosophical currents serve in this way to complement one another, thereby potentially avoiding the parallel extremes of idealism and materialism.

I would argue that there exists in Plotinus the basis for a concept of theism and even for what we have come to know as process theology. Still, certain critics deny this and prefer to label Plotinus a pantheist. Admittedly, there are some passages in Plotinus that underline the supremacy of God over the world, while there are also other passages that undermine any distinction between God and the world. One would surely be justified in reading both tendencies in Plotinus, especially since he has a strong sense of the otherness as well as the affinity of God in relation to the world. The truth is that, in the end, this dialectical philosophy of Plotinus is inclined to consider creation as a world of opposites.

At the same time, however, Plotinus' world *tends toward* (the literal sense of uni-verse) and expresses a sense of oneness (uni-ty). The cosmos reveals an innate order and organization; it manifests an integral identity and repetition. Logic demands recurrence; things must return and recapitulate in order for unity to be recognized in diversity. Though Plotinus actually likes to ascribe priority and preference to the principle of unity, such multiplicity exists both within the world around us as well as within the world inside us.

Strictly speaking, Plotinus does not have a clear and concise doctrine of creation, at least in the way that Christian theology would come to assert this dogmatic teaching in the century following his death. In Plotinus, the "one" brings forth "everything" by a kind of overflow or emanation of its divine being. This kind of language is indisputably reminiscent of the wisdom literature in the Old Testament, but the biblical emphasis on God's transcendence is surely lacking.

A simple examination of biblical terminology renders this discrepancy quite clear. The "grounded" Hebrew term *barra* is the word denoting creation by God, whereas the more "metaphysical" term *assa* refers to the making of lesser stars or the products of human beings. An artist, for example, may create a work of art, but the result is also an extension or emanation of the artist. Perhaps in stressing creation, the Hebrew-Christian Bible does not entirely exclude emanation. After all, does the concept of "image and likeness" not preserve a sense of the divine in the created? Moreover, is not the notion of a de-divinized cosmos the cause of our current lack of empathy for the earth that we tread? While it may be true that Christianity formally rejected an "emanationist" model of creation, at the same time its classical patristic writers and more enlightened theologians patently retained some of its positive overtones, such as the presence of the one God in all places and in all people. How else could one possibly explain the presence of God in the universe, in creation and in human nature, as formulated so unmistakably and irrefutably in the opening chapter of the Bible?

The "one" infinitely and interminably seeks the communion of its being—of that which overflows and emanates; and, in turn, the created being is profoundly and perfectly fulfilled by returning to its divine Creator. The mind is able to grasp things in their final unity, however partially, holding together the indissoluble union of thought and matter. Furthermore, there is a soul that also embraces the body of the world, and each soul belongs to the one cosmic soul.

This means that, when one soul suffers, so do all others; so too does the world soul. At the same time, each soul retains and never surrenders its individuality or integrity. Indeed, there are grades or degrees of soul-ness and soul-full-ness. Moreover, even God, who is beyond all human souls and transcends the soul of the world, personally shares in the suffering of the world and communicates divine compassion to all creatures.

Dionysius the Areopagite (Fifth–Sixth Centuries): Cosmic Theology

Highly esteemed in Eastern and Western Christianity alike, the writings of Dionysius are first mentioned early in the sixth century.

While the authenticity of his writings was challenged almost from the very outset, it is only in the twentieth century that serious doubts actually arose. Dionysius flourished around the year 500 and was, as we know now, probably of Syriac origin. The perpetrator of this historical confusion and author of the Dionysian *corpus* is of course not the disciple of the Apostle Paul mentioned in the Book of Acts; but he is undeniably the most faithful disciple of the Neoplatonist synthesis of the Alexandrian Plotinus in the later Christian tradition.

Of all ancient writers, Dionysius attempted the most complete synthesis of the biblical and philosophical traditions, of the Hebrew and Hellenistic worldviews. In contrast, however, to Plotinus who felt the need for higher beings to create lower ones through a process of emanation, Dionysius believed that the higher level actually transmits life and imparts communion to those below. Despite any politically incorrect overtones of the term hierarchy, there is no denying the fact that there are gradations in the universe itself: animals, vegetables, molecules, atoms, and so on. Abandoning the pejorative consequences of anthropocentrism does not necessarily mean a move toward some indiscriminate egalitarianism. After all, the Christian Gospel itself recognizes that there is a definite hierarchy of values on earth as in heaven: "Are you [i.e., human beings] not of more value than they [i.e., the birds of the air]?" (Mt. 6:26)

In the Dionysian hierarchy, the higher order is responsible for charging meaning and life into the lower order, while the latter is at the same time never undermined or trivialized by the former. Both, furthermore, contribute to the richness and beauty of divine life. There is a real sense of what today we might label as "bio-diversity." That is to say, there is a certain creative dynamism in reality and the world, which in turn envisages a reciprocal relation or communion between the various levels of being and is conscious of the inward relations of all outward things.

Nonetheless, for Dionysius, there is also an undeniable emphasis on the transcendence of God, who is not only at the summit of the hierarchical scale, but also over and outside of it. God's being is the very being of all that exists. This is why, like Plotinus, Dionysius is accused of overemphasizing transcendence to the point of implying a doctrine of pantheism. Nevertheless, Dionysius adds that God, out of divine passion (eros) for creation, moves outside of the divine nature in an act of ecstatic (ec-stasis) self-emptying (kenosis) toward the world: "The Creator of all ... moves outside of himself in an act of extreme erotic love ... [and approaches the world] burning with great goodness and love and eros."[10]

God, so to speak, crosses the "threshold"—to adopt the imagery and terminology of French Jesuit philosopher Teilhard de Chardin (1881–1955)—of divine nature in relating to creation. Dionysian cosmology and anthropology include an inner and innate concept of motion; perfection is never static but always involves transfiguration. At this point, Dionysian ecstasy introduces a spirited, perhaps even spiritual note into the understanding of the relationship between God and world. Neoplatonist and Christian elements thus coincide in an active and dynamic transcendence of a living and loving Creator God, who is neither unmoved nor aloof from creation.

In this sense, Dionysius becomes the archetypal theologian of a di-polar God that is discerned and defined by contemporary process theologians:[11] A God beyond all being, whose nature, however, it is to be with and in all being, whose self-fulfillment is expressed in the act of self-emptying. This act of loving self-humiliation is an essential, and not just an exceptional dimension of God (see Phil. 2:7-8). It marks the self-limitation of a divine Creator, who fashions creation in an exercise of freedom and extension of love.

John Scotus Eriugena (c. 810–877): Cosmic Reality

In ninth-century Ireland, Scotland, and Wales, monasteries still preserved a vivid and vibrant theological thought. It was there that

---

[10]Dionysius, *On the Divine Names* 4, 12 PG 3.712.

[11]Process theology was the school of religious thought prevalent in America in the early 1970s. Its exponents were disciples of the English mathematician-philosopher A. N. Whitehead, who in his *Process and Reality* (New York: Macmillan, 1929) and *Religion in the Making* (New York: Macmillan, 1926) maintained that the concept of "process" rather than the concept of "substance" is the key to a proper understanding of the world and of God. Other contemporary process theologians include R. Edwards (*Reason and Religion* [Eugene, OR: Wipf and Stock, 1972]), N. Pittenger (*Process Thought and Christian Faith* [New York: Macmillan, 1968]), and C. Hartshorne and W. Reese, eds. (*Philosophers Speak to God* [Chicago, IL: University of Chicago Press, 1963; also Amherst, NY: Humanity Books, 2000]).

John Scotus Eriugena received his education before traveling to France where he taught philosophy. With his knowledge of Greek, he was able to translate the writings of Dionysius into Latin. During his life, he was not in fact very popular; his students assassinated him, while the Western Church posthumously condemned his writings in 1210. More recently, however, there has been renewed interest in his works; and he is even regarded as a forerunner of certain aspects of modern religious thought.

Eriugena's language echoes that of Dionysius and Plotinus. Though none of them should be sweepingly dismissed as pantheists, the label is perhaps more accurate in Eriugena's case. For Eriugena speaks of a universal nature or a universe that consists of all nature, including God and every creature. However, God is not identified *with all of nature* but only *with part of nature*—namely, with the part that creates and is not created. Creating is the defining characteristic of God; God is not merely a part of nature but also exists apart from nature. In this way, Eriugena strives to hold together the two poles of divine transcendence and divine immanence, without seeking to undermine either. Inasmuch as it is impossible to express this paradox consistently, Eriugena resorts to paradoxical language. For him, therefore, God and the world are not two separate realities but belong together as a single whole. God is everything and God is everywhere; or, simultaneously and paradoxically, God is never separated from anything anywhere.

Moreover, Eriugena carefully preserves the otherness of God, the conviction that God is the Creator or cause of all things; hence, we can readily affirm the existence of God. However, there is a new logic that must be applied when referring to God: if one attributes a particular property to God, then one must also affirm its opposite. What is for us normally a contradiction is in reality a conviction when referring to God. This is what in the fifteenth-century Nicholas of Cusa (1401–1464) will describe as the "coincidence of opposites." Nothing can be said properly of God, because God transcends all understanding. Nonetheless, from the order of things, God may be seen to be wise, or "more than" (plusquam) wise. Likewise, from the very motion of the world, God is seen to be its life or very source.

God, then, is not the one who is defined but rather the one who defines. God is motion at rest and rest in motion, while all things move from God and toward God. However, at the same time, there is sufficient reflection of God in creation to permit us to speak metaphorically about the divine being. God is not estranged from the world, but Eriugena goes a step further when he claims that every visible and invisible creature can, at least potentially, be called a revelation of God and become a theophany. Where, at the beginning of the Christian era, Philo the Alexandrian Jew (*c.* 20 BCE–50 CE) referred to God as leaving behind divine traces in creation, Eriugena advances this notion to interpret the very works of God as constituting divine verity in the world. In effect, creation itself is a mode of divine existence.[12]

Nicholas of Cusa (1401–1464): Cosmic Synthesis

Nicholas of Cusa claims to have discovered the writings of Dionysius only after an experience of personal and mystical illumination. Whatever the case, he is clearly indebted to his Eastern predecessor. In his works, however, there is a sharpening of the traditional dialectical language about God.

A mathematician by formation, Nicholas was fascinated by the concept of infinity. For him, God contains and transcends all conflicts and contradictions. God is the coincidence or concordance of opposites, because the divinity embraces everything, including every difference and diversity. All dichotomies and divisions are somehow synthesized in God, who is the interconnection of all consciousness. As for us human beings, we can only wonder at how great God is. Nicholas claims that the more learned one is, the more ignorant one feels.[13] This doctrine certainly echoes Dionysius, for whom knowledge is the result of being blinded by an excess of light. Blindness or blissfulness is the experience of unity, whereby we become aware that separation is but an illusion. Similar notions are found in fourth-century theologians, for example, in Athanasius of Alexandria, who discerns a sense of concord in the apparent discord of the world:

---

[12]The idea of the consequent nature of God is expounded more fully by contemporary process theologians. By contrast, Eriugena is normally considered more a philosopher than a theologian. Perhaps this is why he does not seriously consider the reality of sin or evil. It may also account for the fact that his writings bear the imprint of Gnosticism, rather than the weight of traditional incarnational theology.

[13]See Nicholas of Cusa, *On Learned Ignorance*, trans. Jasper Hopkins (Minneapolis, MN: A.J. Benning Press, 1981).

Here is a pure and simple realization: beings of opposite natures can unite in a concord of harmony. There is a harmony, for instance, among the seasons: spring follows winter, summer follows spring, and autumn follows summer ... It is impossible, then, not to realize that there must be a superior being ... that gives unity to their multiplicity and orders their existence ... In the universe there is no disorder, only order; no disharmony, only concord.[14]

Nevertheless, as the reason for all things, God always remains absolute. Everything exists and subsists in God, who is the absolute "quiddity" (or thing-ness) of the world. God penetrates all things inasmuch as constituting the center of all; and, at the same time, God is the circumference of all things inasmuch as eluding all differences. In his later work, entitled *The Vision of God*,[15] Nicholas' image of a divine and omnivoyant face, whose eyes follow us everywhere, combines the polarities of God's universality (which does not swallow up time or particularity) and God's concreteness (which is not swallowed up by eternity or infinity). Nicholas writes of God as the face of all faces, which in turn is beheld in every human face. In this sense, the absolute face of God is discovered on the face of the entire world.

Despite efforts to personify the God of his philosophy, Nicholas of Cusa is usually criticized for the validity of mathematical examples that he adopts in his writings. He has ultimately devised a theological system out of mathematical speculation. In the end, it was the negative or apophatic theology of the Eastern tradition that would fully safeguard—at least, for that tradition—the transcendence of a living God, who is only adored and worshiped as the Creator of all things out of nothing. Apophatic theology is the structure and procedure that assisted Eastern writers to avoid the absolutization of any conception or terminology when describing or defining God.

Two Fundamental Paradoxes

Creation "Out of Nothing"

According to the Judaeo-Christian tradition, the world was created "out of nothing," namely from no other principle and for no other

---

[14]Athanasius, *Against the Pagans* 36f. PG 25.72.
[15]The subtitle of this book is *The Icon*; it was written in 1453.

reason than for God's unconditional love. The teaching that God created some-thing out of no-thing is, at least from an Orthodox theological perspective, again closely related to the element of asceticism or self-restraint. On every occasion of divine revelation and economy—for instance, at the moment of creation and the moment of Incarnation—God exercises a degree of self-limitation and self-restraint, which serve as a spiritual model for those adhering to the Judaeo-Christian covenants. These dimensions are a central part of the discussion that follows. Therefore, it may be helpful at this point to consider the notion of creation out of nothing in order to appreciate its place within and impact upon the history of theological thought.

In terms of the development of Christian doctrine, the teaching about creation "out of nothing" (ex nihilo) is not actually part of the Genesis story. It is in fact a doctrine that emerged during the intertestamental period, the earliest reference being found in the book of Maccabees (2 Macc. 7:28), and therefore unavailable to the writers of the Hebrew Scriptures. Indeed, it is entirely unknown to the world of classical philosophy during the pre-Christian and early Christian times, unfolding rather slowly and even uncertainly within Christian theology predominantly in response to questions raised by classical Greek cosmology. Tertullian expresses this vagueness already in the second century:

> I say that, although Scripture did not clearly proclaim that all things were made out of nothing—just as it does not say either that they were made out of matter—there was not so great a need to declare that all things had been made out of nothing as there would have been, if they were made out of matter.[16]

The doctrine of creation out of nothing assumes a degree of prominence in the subsequent Christian tradition,[17] where it is introduced to safeguard creation as an act of freedom rather than

---

[16]Tertullian, *Against Hermogenes* XXII, 2. Cf. *The Ante-Nicene Fathers*, vol. 3 (Grand Rapids, MI: Eerdmans, 1957), 489–90.

[17]See, for example, Hermas, *Shepherd*, Book II, Mandate I PG 2.913; Theophilus of Antioch, *To Autolychus* II, 4 PG 6.1052; Irenaeus, *Against Heresies* II, x, 4 PG 7.736; Origen, *On First Principles* I, iv [*The Ante-Nicene Fathers*, vol. 4 (Grand Rapids, MI: Eerdmans Publishing, 1951), 256]; Basil, *Homily on the Hexaemeron* VII, 7 PG 29.180C; John Chrysostom, *Homily on Genesis* II PG 57.28.

necessity, as a product of love and not nature, and as a result of will and not essence. By the early fourth century, there is general agreement on this concept, among orthodox and dissenters alike. For example, at the Council of Nicaea (325), the first ecumenical council that marks a watershed in the history of Christian thought, Athanasius and Arius—adversaries on so many other issues, especially with regard to the Incarnation of the divine Word—share a clearly articulated and widely accepted doctrine of creation out of nothing.[18]

Indeed, Athanasius refers to earlier Christian authorities as well as to Scripture in order to distinguish between the Trinitarian relationship of the Father to the Son (which he describes in a word as *gennesis* or birth) and the relationship of the Son within the Trinity to the world (which he describes in a word as *genesis* or "creation").[19] One problem that arises from such a definitive, ontological distinction between God and world is that there is no room for an intermediate zone between the two. The only exception, as already observed, is the sacrament of the Eucharist. Thus, the implications and conclusions of this crucial doctrine are dramatic not only for theology (as the understanding of God), but also for cosmology (as the understanding of the world) as well as for mystical theology (as the encounter between the two and the experience of God in the world).

In certain pagan creation myths, both matter and the divine beings assume pre-eternal and eternal existence. The Christian church, by contrast, claims and proclaims that God alone is the eternal being, "maker of all things visible and invisible"—to quote the Nicene-Constantinopolitan Symbol of Faith or Creed. The distinction is that God is omnipotent and independent, while the world is limited and dependent, always understood in reference to and in communion with God, without whom it remains incomplete. As previously intimated, the inherent danger of the Christian doctrine of creation is the temptation to press the sovereign independence of God to the point of separation from the world. No one today

---

[18]On the fourth-century patristic understanding of creation and doctrine of creation *ex nihilo*, see John Behr, *The Formation of Christian Theology: The Nicene Faith, Part 1* (Crestwood, NY: St. Vladimir's Seminary Press, 2004), 44–5 and 179–90.
[19]Athanasius, *On the Divine Incarnation* 2–3 (Crestwood, NY: St. Vladimir's Seminary Press, 1982), 26–9.

is seriously threatened by any form of "deism"—by a God entirely unconcerned and unengaged with the world. Today, people prefer to speak in terms of "theism"—of a God profoundly related and relevant to our world. Yet most theologians are reluctant to press this relatedness too far, lest they be criticized of "pan-theism." Some like to speak of pan-en-theism in order to ensure or safeguard a fundamental distinction between God and world. However, the term panentheism is neither always clear in meaning nor always consistent in usage, at least inasmuch as it is found among thinkers and theologians of varied convictions.

The question, of course, arises as to the precise content of the nothing (nihil) from which God creates. Is it some emptiness, a void or vacuum deprived of God? Or is it that which is no-thing inasmuch as it represents the energies of God?[20] The Western mystic Eriugena noted that *nihil* is simply another name for God, an alternative description for the ultimate abyss of divinity. And the notion is not unfamiliar to the Eastern mystics, which is perhaps where Eriugena received it in the first place. Thus, in his work *On Divine Names*, Dionysius the Areopagite refers to God as being "at one and the same time in the world (encosmic), and around the world (pericosmic), and above the world (hypercosmic) ... as being everything and nothing ... Nothing contains and comprehends God ... and nothing exists that does not share in God."[21] The same understanding is also found in the spiritual teaching of a more contemporary Orthodox saint, John of Kronstadt: "The Lord fills all creation ... preserving it down to the smallest blade of grass and grain of dust in his right hand, and not being limited either by the greatness or smallness of things created; he exists in infinity, entirely filling it, as a vacuum."[22]

Therefore, the nothing from which God creates neither denotes nor implies an absence of God. It is in fact another way

---

[20]Cf. P. Sherrard's argument in *Human Image: World Image*, already adumbrated in his earlier *The Greek East and the Latin West* (Cambridge, UK: Cambridge University Press: 1959). For the rabbinic tradition, "no place is empty of God." See Rabbi Nachman of Bratslav (1772–1811), *Zohar* III, 225a.

[21]Dionysius the Areopagite. The translation is mine, from *The Divine Names* I, 6 PG 3.596, and XIII, 1–2 (977). See also XIII, 3 (980–1). For the works of Dionysius, cf. *Pseudo-Dionysius: Complete Works*, in The Classics of Western Spirituality (New York: Paulist Press, 1987).

[22]John of Kronstadt, *My Life in Christ*, 140.

of understanding and underlining the very presence of God. The contemplative searches and finds God—discerning and discovering, as Shakespeare notes in *As You Like It*, "tongues in trees, books in brooks, sermons in stones, and god in every thing." Such is the depth of the spirituality of the "sponge" advanced by Gregory Palamas, who adopts the image of a porous sponge to describe the way that God's energies permeate human and material nature. Modern physics, too, supports such a view of matter as nothingness. Seen through the eyes of a physicist, the human body itself is 99.99 percent void, and even the little that appears to be dense matter is itself empty space. The entire human being is made out of nothing. So we might consider creation *ex nihilo* as a kind of "quantum" theology or "quantum" spirituality holding together the absence and presence of God in the world.

Transcendence and Immanence

While individual theologians and philosophers have struggled for centuries to reconcile the paradox of divine immanence and divine transcendence, how has Eastern theology approached this contradiction or mystery?

The Eastern Christian classics do not perceive in Scripture any sharp demarcation between grace and nature or any pronounced distinction between spirit and matter. Nor is there any marked difference between Scripture and creation; the two are complementary. We are called to discover the signature or signs of God in created nature. In the words of St. Ephraim the Syrian (*c.* 306–373): "Wherever you turn your eyes, there is God's symbol; whatever you read, you will God's types ... Look and see how nature are scripture are linked together."[23]

The fundamental dichotomy, then, in Judaeo-Christian literature is not between created nature and uncreated grace, but rather between two levels within created nature itself—namely, between the fallen and unfallen condition of human nature, or the sinful and redeemed states of human living.

---

[23]See Sebastian Brock, *The Harp of the Spirit: Poems of St. Ephrem the Syrian* (Cambridge, UK: Aquila Books, 2013).

Of course, contemporary Western theology no longer espouses the notion of God as eternal substance, a concept first proposed by classical Greek philosophy and later espoused by medieval scholasticism. However, the Eastern Christian tradition modified the Hellenistic concept of God as immobile essence, even if never to the point of embracing its opposite—namely, a God conceived as becoming. Any systematic examination of the notion of God in Scripture, as well as in Eastern liturgy and spirituality, reveals a God in constant motion between these two poles.

In an attempt to reconcile divine immutability or stability with divine becoming or historicity—that is to say, God's involvement in the human heart and within human history—Eastern theology is inevitably attracted toward a model of difference and unity. Tracing back at least as far as the fourteenth century with renowned theologian, St. Gregory Palamas (1296–1359) as its most influential representative, this model relates the immutable divine essence to the uncreated energies of God. The latter manifest the infinite possibilities and inexhaustible richness of the former, as well as the acts that express these infinite possibilities. The energies of God—what Hebrew Scriptures frequently refer to as God's glory (kâbôd)—charge the created world with reality and transparency, while allowing it at once to reveal and conceal the divine mystery. Thus, the Christian God transcends all opposition and contradiction; God rests comfortably in the dialectic of grace and dwells compellingly in the paradox of love.

The distinction between divine essence and divine energies defines the relationship—both intimate and separate—between Creator and creation. In other words, nothing exists or survives outside the embrace of God. Everything is directly related to God and dependent on God, inasmuch as all of creation is a reflection of and contains the trace of the divine Creator. At the same time, God's essence remains totally transcendent and undetermined. This is the theological conundrum prescribed and preserved in the teaching of Gregory Palamas, although it is already apparent much earlier in the Christian tradition.[24] Thus Palamas writes:

---

[24]See my article "Divine Essence and Energies," in *Phronema* 5 (Sydney: St. Andrew's Theological College, 1990), 15–31, where the distinction is discerned already in the Cappadocian Fathers of the fourth century. Also see my article "Essence and Energies: Dynamic Anthropology and Cosmology," in G. Moses and N. Ormerod, *Human Beings and Nature* (Sydney: Sydney College of Divinity Philosophical Association, 1992), 28–34.

On the one hand, the divine super-essentiality is never called multiple; on the other hand, the divine and uncreated grace and energy of God is, being indivisibly divided, like the sun's ray, which warms and lightens and vivifies and increases its own splendor in what it enlightens, and shines forth in the eyes of the beholders; in the way, then, of this faint image the divine energy of God is called not one, but multiple, by the theologians; and thus Basil the Great declares: "What are the energies of the Spirit? Their extent cannot be told, and they are numberless. How can we comprehend what is beyond the ages? What are the energies of that which precedes the intelligible creation?" For before the intelligible creation and prior to the ages (for the ages themselves are intelligible creations), no one has ever said, or considered, that there is anything created. Therefore, the powers and energies of the divine Spirit, which are, according to the theologians, multiple, are uncreated, indivisibly distinguished from the entire Essence of the undivided Spirit.[25]

British philosopher, translator, and writer, Philip Sherrard (1922–1995) aptly summarizes this paradox of divine transcendence and divine immanence:

For if only the total transcendence of God is affirmed, then all created things, all that is in change and visible, must be regarded as without any real roots in the Divine, and hence as entirely negative and 'illusory' in character; while if only the total immanence of God is affirmed, then creation must be looked upon as real in its own right, instead of as real only because it derives from and participates in the Divine; and the result must be a pantheism, and a worship of creation rather than of the Creator, which must ultimately lead to the notion that God is superfluous, and hence to an entirely materialistic conception of things. The full Christian understanding demands, thus, the simultaneous recognition of both the total transcendence and the total immanence of the Divine, the affirmation of the one at the expense of the other being the negation of this understanding

---

[25]Gregory Palamas, *In Defense of the Holy Hesychasts*. See the translation in Philip Sherrard, *The Greek East and the Latin West* (Limni, Evia: Denise Harvey Publisher, 1992), 37–8.

and the supreme doctrinal error; and it was for this recognition that Christian theologians had to find an adequate doctrinal expression.[26]

Process theologians have made overtures toward this essence-energies doctrine in their own distinction between the primordial and consequent nature of God. In response, however, Orthodox theologians might retort that the personal distinction of God-in-Trinity should never be undermined, while the distinction between the primordial and consequent sides in God must never be reduced to a philosophical exercise. For Orthodox spirituality, the essence-energies distinction remains real at all times, even in regard to the state of human deification and cosmic transfiguration. Moreover, while process thought revived the concept of panentheism (the teaching that God somehow includes or incorporates the world, while not being exhausted or effaced by the world), Orthodox theology would emphasize that the inherent risk there is that God, inasmuch as (closely or almost) identified with creation, ceases to evoke a sense of adoration and wonder.

I would submit that the Orthodox doctrine of divine essence and divine energies has much to offer in an age when the relationship or reconciliation between God and cosmos must vigorously be affirmed and maintained. This is the way that Byzantine theologians sought to advance their conviction that the world is part of God but not the whole of God. It is also the way that they fought to overcome the perpetual and perilous temptation of theology to detach God from the world.[27] This is because the essence-energies distinction makes possible cosmic transformation, while at the same time rendering viable the personal transformation required to accept responsibility for the whole of creation.

The God contemplated by Christian mystics in the early church as well as in the middle ages was a God elusive yet familiar, both transcendent and immanent; it was a God "afar" and at the same time "at hand" (Jer. 23:23 and Mt. 3:2). This is a God worshiped in heaven and venerated on earth. In the chapters that follow, I shall explore how such a God is conceived and celebrated in the Eastern spiritual tradition, beginning with the ascetic experience in the desert.

---

[26]Philip Sherrard, *The Greek East and the Latin West*, 36.
[27]See John Polkinghorne, *Science and Creation: The Search for Understanding* (Philadelphia, PA and London: Templeton Foundation Press, 2006), ch. 4 "Creator and Creation," 63–82.

3

The Desert Is Alive

The *Sayings* of the Desert Fathers and Mothers

The World of the Desert

The paradox of divine transcendence and divine immanence is evident not only in the intellectual tradition, but also experienced in the unfettered and unlettered, even unwritten wisdom of the desert. It is to this more practical and unpretentious school that I would like to turn. For the desert presents the starkest and sharpest symbol of creation in its search for the divine through the barrenness of the wilderness and wasteland as well as the earthiness of emptiness and aridity.

Ascetic writers of earlier centuries, notably the Desert Fathers and Mothers as well as their various monastic successors, rigorously pursued the complicated issues of how heaven relates to earth, precisely because they concretely experienced this double aspect as a powerful symbol of the union within themselves of matter and spirit, body and soul. The purpose of their journey in the desert was to encounter and experience God in an intimate and immediate manner. By the same token, the foundation of their life in the desert was to acknowledge and accept God's sovereign authority over heaven and earth, as well as God's sweeping claim over the whole creation. In the world of the *Sayings of the Desert Fathers*, also known by their Greek name *Apophthegmata Patrum*, the purely ascetic is constantly raised to the sacramental or mystical level.

After all, the way that the desert dwellers related to their natural and social environment reflected the wonder and worship that they reserved for God.

The *Sayings* themselves grew out of the experience of asceticism in the third through fifth centuries in Egypt, Syria, and Palestine. Originally an oral and fluid tradition, principally remembered and circulated among the monastics themselves, their written form evades precise dating, proving as rough and craggy as the desert landscape that surrounded the hermits. Even so, the *apophthegmata* transmit a sense of the beauty of creation, all the wit and witness of the sandy desert.[1] It is in the dryness of mundane, everyday circumstance that the Hebrew people sought and discovered God. It is here also that Moses encountered God, Elijah heard God, and Anthony spoke to God.

This is why, from the third century until around the end of the fifth century, the dry desert became the laboratory for exploring hidden truths about heaven and earth as well as a forging ground for drawing connections between the two. The hermits (men and women alike) living in that desert tested and studied what it means to be human— with all the tensions and temptations, all of the struggle beyond survival, all of the contact with good and the conflict with evil. And in this process, some of them made many mistakes; others made fewer mistakes. Whoever said that there is a clear and simple answer to the questions of life? Yet, all of them dared to push the limits, to challenge the norms. Their stories are more than just a part of the Christian past; they are a part of our human heritage, communicating eternal values and spiritual truths across centuries and cultures.

These inhabitants of the desert were men and women who chose to live outside the towns and villages of the ancient world, as far as possible from civilized life, often entirely aloof and alone. They had few, if any possessions, deliberately and voluntarily choosing to have as little as possible in order to be free for God. They lived in handmade huts or in caves, eating and drinking a sparse diet of bread, herbs, and water. Their clothing was that of the poorest of the poor: a simple garment, along with a sheepskin that could be

---

[1]Arsenius 1–2 in *The Sayings of the Desert Fathers*, trans. Benedicta Ward (London: Mowbrays, 1975), 8. For a general introduction to the spiritual teaching of the desert, see John Chryssavgis, *In the Heart of the Desert: The Spirituality of the Desert Fathers and Mothers*, revised (Bloomington, IN: World Wisdom, 2008).

used as a blanket or rug. They were neither scholars nor preachers, neither teachers nor clerics. They simply learned how to be still and silent, to know themselves and to know God, becoming themselves part of God's providential and redeeming work for the whole world. "One has to be alone, under the sky, before everything falls into place and one finds his own place in the midst of it all."[2] Yet, in their "self-forgetting attentiveness," the Desert Fathers and Mothers achieved what Evelyn Underhill describes as: "A profound concentration, a self-merging, which operates a real communion between the seer and the seen—in a word, in contemplation."[3]

This chapter explores the vocation of the desert ascetics to experience God intimately, thereby directly encountering the paradox of divine immanence and divine transcendence. Anthony the Great, conventionally acknowledged as the father of monasticism, and the other desert elders withdrew and detached themselves from the world, and yet became one with the desert, its animals, and plants out of a conviction that God created a world that he loved and cared for, a God who fills and fulfills all emptiness in the world inside us and around us. The ascetic three-stage journey of solitude (through withdrawal), silence (through self-will), and stillness (through encountering God) represented for them a movement away toward a movement within and to the very heart of creation. This enabled them to see the divine flame in all things, discerning and discovering the world as a burning bush of God's energies.

The Image of the Desert

It is fair to ask whether these early desert hermits recognized or overlooked the natural and aesthetic beauty of creation through their austere practices and harsh disciplines. What is the relationship of the desert dwellers with their environment and with the animals? In renouncing the world, did the Desert Fathers and Mothers disregard the world? Or did they in fact enjoy a new awareness

---

[2] Thomas Merton, *Conjectures of a Guilty Bystander* (New York: Image Classics-Doubleday, 1968), 294.
[3] Evelyn Underhill, *Mysticism: A Study in Nature and Development of Spiritual Consciousness*, originally published in 1911 (Oxford, UK: One World Publications, 2005). See Part II: The Mystic Way, Section 4 "The Illumination of Self."

of everything in the world—social, animal, and natural? Did they exemplify cosmic interconnection?

In the *Life of Antony*, Athanasius of Alexandria tells us that Abba Anthony (*c.* 251–356) saw the desert for the first time "and loved it."[4] The desert became home for Anthony and the other elders who lived there. It is there that they experienced their sense of communion with creation as well as their communion with their Creator. It is there, too, that they experienced a sense of continuity with the land as with their past. This is why Abba John the Eunuch said: "Let us imitate our Fathers. For they lived in this place with much austerity and peace."[5] Just as "the earth is the Lord's" (Ps. 23:2), so too the Desert Fathers were convinced that "no place belongs [to us]." Certainly "no place belongs to the demons."[6] The desert was a positive and beautiful place, where those who so desired were able to see God, to hear God, and to live with God.

Renunciation and detachment, however, also meant that the Desert Fathers and Mothers became as nothing, much like the sand of the desert dunes that surrounded them. Their detachment implied a sense of becoming one with the environment. Their holiness was part and parcel of a sense of wholeness. If *at-one-ment* with their neighbor was of the essence in the spirituality of the desert, so too was *at-tune-ment* to their environment, to the world, and to God. Abba Anthony said: "Renounce this life, so that you may be alive to God!"[7] And Abba John the Eunuch added: "My children, let us not pollute this place, since our Fathers have previously cleansed it from demons."[8]

The desert was commended for its wonderfulness and boundlessness. The barren environment was to be "admired," says the *Life of Antony*, but not "adored";[9] one was to wonder at, but not worship the beauty of the desert. Adoration was due to God alone as author and Creator of the world. The monastics

---

[4]Athanasius 50. See *The Life of Antony*, trans. Tim Vivian and Apostolos Athanassakis (Kalamazoo, MI: Cistercian Publications, 2003). For the Coptic life of Anthony, see *Journeying into God: Seven Early Monastic Lives*, trans. Tim Vivian (Minneapolis, MN: Fortress Press, 1996).

[5]John the Eunuch 4, *Sayings*, Ward, 90.

[6]Elias 7, *Sayings*, Ward, 61.

[7]Anthony 33, *Sayings*, Ward, 6–7.

[8]John the Eunuch 5, *Sayings*, Ward, 90.

[9]Athanasius, *Life of Antony* 76, Vivian.

were required to beware lest the desert itself turn into an idol. The desert is an icon, a unique revelation of God's Word, an infinite source of God's love; it must never become a source of individual pleasure or satisfaction for the sake of deprivation. Asceticism never seeks to undermine oneself or demean the world. It always remains a rigor and a discipline worthy of the land and upholding one's own worth.

Respect for the natural beauty of the world leads to reverence before the divine beauty of God. This conviction is what informs the desert attitude toward the surrounding natural and animal environment. Indeed, there is an abundance of information about the connection that the desert dwellers enjoyed with their animal coinhabitants of the desert.

> One of the Fathers used to tell of a certain Abba Paul, from Lower Egypt, who lived in the Thebaid. He used to take various kinds of snakes in his hands ... The brothers made a prostration before him, asking: "Tell us what you have done to receive this grace." He said: "Forgive me, Fathers, but if someone acquires purity, then everything is in submission to that person, just as it was for Adam when he was in paradise before the transgression of the commandment."[10]
>
> Abba Anthony also said: "Obedience with abstinence gives people authority even over wild beasts."[11]

Anthony surely understood the truth of this statement. He had persuaded the animals in his region to live at peace with him and no longer to disturb him.[12] In fact, the notion of being like Adam, before he fell from the graceful condition enjoyed in paradise, is the ideal to which the desert dwellers aspired. It was said of Abba Pambo that his face was like that of Moses, who received the image of the glory of Adam when his face shone. Pambo's face shone like lightening, so that he was like a king sitting on a throne. The same was contended about Abba Silvanus and Abba Sisoes.[13]

---

[10]Paul 1, *Sayings*, Ward, 171.
[11]Athanasius, *Life of Antony* 36, Vivian.
[12]Athanasius, *Life of Antony* 50, Vivian.
[13]Pambo 12, *Sayings*, Ward, 166.

One also reads of the peaceful relationship that monastics have with wild animals[14] or the love that ascetics have for the beauty of the wilderness.[15] It is helpful here to recall the prophet Isaiah's vision of the peaceful kingdom:

The wolf shall live with the lamb, the leopard shall lie down with the kid, the calf and the lion and the fatling together, and a little child shall lead them. The cow and the bear shall graze, their young shall lie down together; and the lion shall eat straw like the ox. The nursing child shall play over the hole of the asp, and the weaned child shall put its hand on the adder's den. They will not hurt or destroy on all my holy mountain; for the earth will be full of the knowledge of the Lord as the waters cover the sea. (Isa. 11:6-9)

A similar relationship with creation and animals is recorded throughout the history of spiritual heroes. It is *a relationship that transcends place*: we find it in the writing of Isaac the Syrian (seventh century) as in the life of Francis of Assisi (1181–1226). It is also *a relationship that transcends time*: we observe it in the hermits of early Palestine as well as in the nineteenth-century life of Seraphim of Sarov.

There is of course far more to this than a mere emotional attachment to animals. It may be helpful once again to recall the emphasis on detachment in the desert. The connection with land and animals is neither superficial nor sentimental; it is distinctly and deeply theological. It stems from the inner conviction of these hermits that God created this world, which for them implies that God loves the world and cares for everything in the world. The desert elders were, in the most intense and intimate manner,

---

[14]See *Life of Anthony* 50 PG 26.916-7. One also may recall similar stories in the lives of many other saints such as St. Mamas or St. Gerasimos, but especially St. Francis of Assisi and St. Seraphim of Sarov. For these accounts in the life of St. Francis, see Marion A. Habig, ed., *St. Francis of Assisi: Writings and Early Biographies* (Chicago, IL: Franciscan Press, 1972), 494–5. For the life of St. Seraphim, see Valentine Zander, *St. Seraphim of Sarov* (Crestwood, NY: St. Vladimir's Seminary Press, 1975), 61f. See also Helen Waddell, *Beasts and Saints*, reprinted (Grand Rapids, MI: Eerdmans, 1996).

[15]See Evagrius, *Practical Chapters* and *Anatolium* 92 PG 40.1249. Anthony compared a monk outside of the desert to a fish out of water: Anthony 10, *Sayings*, Ward, 2.

"materialists." Everything—including the simplest and slightest particle of matter—really mattered! In God's eyes, both wild animals and wild nature are important and have their place in a spiritual worldview; birds and trees are not excluded from sacred transformation.

If the purpose of fleeing to the desert was to reestablish a lost order, then reconciliation with all of creation and the reconnection of the entire world with God was critical. These elders may sometimes appear eccentric; but *their eccentricity signifies moving the center, re-centering the world on God*. The world is reduced to a wasteland unless it, too, comes alive in an authentic human being, who in turn becomes the eyes and conscience of the world. Nikos Kazantzakis speaks poetically of a holy mania:

> Listening intently, I heard the spirit, which stands by every blade of grass to help it grow and accomplish its duty on earth. Here in my impregnable solitude, I sensed that even the most insignificant of God's creatures—a grain of wheat, a worm, an ant—suddenly recalls its divine origin, is possessed by a God-inspired mania and wishes to mount step by step in order to touch the Lord. The wheat, the worm or the ant touch God and stand at his side along with angels and archangels; it, too, is an angel, an archangel.[16]

If we miss the stage of the desert, we also cause a split between the world and God, between the universe and the heart; ultimately, we create a split within ourselves. As the saying goes: if you don't go within, you end up going without. When we overlook the world of the spirit, then we also end up neglecting the spirit of the world; and when we disregard the world of our soul, we in fact end up ignoring the soul of the world. Such is part and parcel of the living mystery of God's creation.

In this way, the restoration of the human soul through Christ's redemption is revealed in the Desert Fathers and Mothers, who see the entire human race in the context of creation and who are at home with the whole of creation. There is, here, no sentimental attachment to animals or to nature; there is only a respectful cooperation and collaboration, even concelebration of the external

---

[16]Nikos Kazantzakis, *Report to Greco* (New York: Simon & Schuster, 1965), 446.

and the internal. Unsurprisingly, God intervenes naturally, by way of miracles or signs that reflect the powerful presence of the sacred. In this sense, the desert elders were neither eccentric nor original, but stood firmly within the tradition of the prophets and apostles. They simply lived out the inherited road of sanctity in uncharted ways.

People who choose the way of the desert on the one hand preserve silence like the early ascetics, but on the other hand they protest violently and publicly against an urbanization that reduces creation to a cycle of production and consumption, and ultimately to the waste of destruction. The way of the desert reminds us that "not everything was created for the sake of our bellies."[17] The harshness of the desert comes as provocation: it stands as a searing yet liberating haven between the sterility of a lukewarm religion and the tyranny of fundamentalism; it smashes the perception of prayer and silence as moments of relaxation and individual satisfaction; it pushes aside bourgeois and puritan ideologies that forge a connection between virtue and material success; it demands struggle and not just survival—whether financial, social, emotional, physical, or other; it disregards social descent, spiritual class, and native color; it ridicules the frantic pursuit of authority and security; and it unveils all forms of weakness even as it strives for personal transformation and transcendence.

The Desert Fathers and Mothers recognize that the transcendent is revealed in the most difficult and darkest moment of our struggle: God refreshes during the most intense heat of this fever. At the peak of this struggle with God (Gen. 32:24-31), discourse about God becomes (to adopt the daring terminology of the mystics) intercourse with God. This is a God born in barrenness, where there is an absence of pretentiousness and pride; this God fulfills in emptiness, where all space is abandoned to and abounds in divine presence.

The Way of the Desert

The desert culture is based on movement, and, at least in the writings of the more erudite mystics, on the flight from the body[18]

---

[17]Basil the Great, *Hexaemeron* V, 4.
[18]See John the Eunuch 3, *Sayings*, Ward, 90; and Evagrius of Pontus, *Praktikos* 52, Antoine Guillaumont, ed., *Praktikos* (Paris, 1971).

and its desire for material possessions.[19] Indeed, desert asceticism presents a curious ambivalence—the body is not simply decorative but substantive, never just incidental but essential: it toils, sweats, and expands. Still, there persists a temptation to regard created matter as evil. Though hints of this attitude certainly appear in desert literature, the central teaching is predominantly free of it, even in the most extraordinary and extreme of ascetic practices. Thus, despite a lifetime of harsh discipline, Anthony's body is in better condition than prior to his twenty years of solitude:

> The picture that is given us of Anthony, as he emerged from his solitude, is in no way of an ascetic emaciated by asceticism that is its own end: it is of a man calmed, brought into equilibrium, in whom everything human has become, as it were, transparent to the Spirit, docile to his influence.[20]

One might even say that Anthony is in harmony and equilibrium with the whole of his environment, indicating the ascetic's yearning for an equitable society and restored creation.

Furthermore, the flight to the desert should not be confused with a need to move elsewhere. Anthony's advice is for the need to stay in one's cell;[21] and the exodus to the desert is less a movement away from than a movement into the realm where one encounters God. In the cell, the hermit faces the most grueling temptations, in addition to the most intimate relations with God. However, in contemplating nature, the hermit becomes aware of things divine and of the world as a revelation of God's beauty.[22] The sacrifice of

---

[19]Evagrius, *Praktikos* 18 and 97, ibid. See also Peter Brown, *The Body and Society: Men, Women and Sexual Renunciation in Early Christianity* (New York: Columbia University Press, 1988), esp. 213–40.

[20]See Louis Bouyer, *The Spirituality of the New Testament and the Fathers* (New York: Seabury Press, 1982), 319. Cf. also *Life of Anthony* 14 (864) and 93 (973). For the transfiguration of the body, see also Anthony, Epistle 1, in Derwas Chitty, ed., *The Letters of St. Antony the Great* (Oxford, UK: Fairacres, 1977), 1–5. The biblical source is Deuteronomy 39:7.

[21]Anthony 10, *Sayings*, Ward, 2. See also Longinus 1. This understanding is also transferred and "translated" to the West by John Cassian: cf. for example, *Conférences* XXIV, 5 and VI, 15; cf. *Sources Chrétiennes*, vol. 42 (Paris: Cerf, 1955–9).

[22]On the spiritual awakening and attentiveness to the natural environment in the philosophy and practice of the early Christian tradition of the desert, see Douglas Christie, *The Blue Sapphire of the Mind: Notes for a Contemplative Ecology* (New York: Oxford University Press, 2013).

renunciation means little unless there is, first, a true esteem of the world as created by God. If sin is considered the failure to accept and assume the world as a gift from God, then denial of the gift of beauty can never be confounded with sacrifice or the sacred.

In this regard, asceticism essentially espouses, rather than opposes the fullness of life and beauty of the world. The Desert Fathers and Mothers do not provide us with a set of feats or facts, but rather present us with a story that affirms the whole of creation. Their greatest achievement was the transformation that they wrought upon the world around them. Ascetic struggle betrays the authentic hermit not as acrimoniously loathing, but as intensely loving, recognizing in creation the unique trace of sacredness. As Abba Anthony said: "Renounce this life, so that you may be alive to God."[23] Any movement in the desert culture entails advancing as pilgrims—in spite of sharp thorns and jagged stones—forward and upward into deeper and ever-deepening levels of self-knowledge and divine knowledge.

Another vital aspect of desert spirituality is its apophatic or negative dimension. The intense heat and flat barrenness of the desert at first seem to lead nowhere. Yet, the vast emptiness and desolate vacancy uncover another peculiar, even refreshing aspect of the desert, namely its imageless silence. No matter how divine the image discovered in solitude may be, the desert demands that the hermit always moves beyond this and all other images. The process of stripping or letting go is necessary to a proper relationship with God, world, and oneself. It is essential for a realization that in God (the transcendent) alone do we discover our world (the immanent) and ourselves (self-transcendence). The intellect assuredly needs the chastening stillness of the desert.

In this context, detachment means traveling light—and one can often manage with much less than imagined. In the desert, there are no defense mechanisms, no toys for distraction. One must look within and face directly the pain and passion of life in all its intensity. As the well-known contemporary "Twelve Step" programs might put it: No pain, no gain. Anthony experienced this already in the

---

[23]Anthony 33, *Sayings*, Ward, 6–7. Indeed, in the ascetic tradition, one who renounces the earthly and yet fails to be satisfied by the heavenly is regarded as most miserable: see the contemporaneous *Macarian Homilies* XLIX, 1, trans. A. J. Mason (London and New York, 1921).

fourth-century desert: "Whoever has not experienced temptation cannot enter the kingdom of heaven ... Without temptations no one is saved."[24] This apophatic element is perpetually fostered in the desert tradition, where the monk is denuded of all things[25] and at all times a beginner.[26] The apophasis of distance and silence provokes the unconditional action of God. Retreating into the desert makes allowance for the boundless grace of God. And the revelation of God imposes a corresponding silence in order to listen to and love God.

Glimpses of a New Heaven and Earth

The desert's sacramental dimension lies in its stark, abased remoteness. Standing as a sign and safeguard of authenticity, the desert is prized precisely because it is inaccessible, ultimately impervious to outside interference. It reflects—crudely and austerely, but most immediately and effectively—a direct encounter with nature and God. There are no frills, no comforts—little wonder then that simplicity and forthrightness are singled out as virtues in both work (labora) and prayer (ora).

So the ground that we tread can no longer be the object of possession, of uncharitable rights,[27] of exploitation. Instead, humanity must submit to the dynamism of the land, reverently bowing before the sacredness of place. The Desert Fathers and Mothers surrender before the sacredness of the surrounding land, respecting and cooperating with the earth, convinced that both humanity and earth belong to heaven, that the contract between heaven and earth (cf. Isa. 24:4-7) must be renewed. There is, among them, an uncompromising recognition that every detail and dimension of the created world belongs exclusively and unreservedly to God. The monks are called to cultivate the desert wasteland until

---

[24]Anthony 5, *Sayings*, Ward, 2; and Athanasius 56, *Life of Anthony* (PG 26.952).
[25]Benedicta Ward, ed., *The Wisdom of the Desert Fathers* (Oxford, UK: Fairacres, 1975) no. 11, 3.
[26]F. Nau, ed., *Apophthegmata*, Anonymous Supplement, no. 243 (in *Revue de l' Orient Chrétien* 14, 1909, 364). See also B. Ward, ed., *Wisdom*, no. 111, 34.
[27]Poemen 77, Nau, *Apophthegmata*.

it blossoms (cf. Isa. 35:1); after all, God speaks not just through the desert dwellers but also through the desert itself.[28]

However, the language of the desert ascetics is in many ways alien to our contemporary culture. As noted by Desert Mother Amma Syncletica, it entails struggle: "It is said, 'Our God is a consuming fire' (Heb. 12:24); so we must kindle the divine fire in ourselves through tears and hard work."[29] By becoming enflamed and consumed, these ascetics reveal the flame of God's energies that consumes all creation. By rendering transparent the treasure in their earthen vessel (2 Cor. 4:7), they illumine the density of the vase of the desert.[30] In their image of God and view of the world, a real transparency or sacred transformation takes place; by restoring the shattered world, the mysterious presence of the living God is gradually discerned. By imploring, in the seclusion of the desert, for the restoration of the whole polluted cosmos, they establish a new heaven and a new earth (Rev. 21:1).

The Desert as Indispensable Stage

It is hard to imagine imitating the behavior and ideals of the early Desert Fathers and Mothers, though one can occasionally discover in their ascetic lives and eccentric sayings a genuine source of inspiration. Perhaps it would be more appropriate to refer to the myth of the desert—a way of life that entails a symbolic depth, an inner meaning, and a secret or sacrament that must be explored or explained.

The desert is a powerful image and cannot be lightly dismissed precisely because it constitutes an essential and indispensable stage through which the soul must pass individually and collectively. Unfortunately, as stated by noted writer, Wendell Berry, we have either romanticized or else resisted the notion of wilderness:

> Apparently with the rise of industry, we began to romanticize the wilderness—which is to say we began to institutionalize it within

---

[28]See Theodoret, "*Philotheos Historia*," in *Sources Chrétiennes* 234 (Paris: Cerf, 1977), 268 PG 82.1332.

[29]Amma Syncletica 1, *Sayings*, Ward, 193.

[30]Sisoes 14, *Sayings*, Ward, 180. The desert is described as a "vase" or vessel, through which the entire world is transfigured.

the concept of the "scenic." Because of railroads and improved highways, the wilderness was no longer an arduous passage for the traveler, but something to be looked at as grand or beautiful from the high vantages of the roadside. We became viewers of "views." And because we no longer traveled in the wilderness as a matter of course, we forgot that wilderness still circumscribed civilization and persisted in domesticity. We forgot, indeed, that the civilized and the domestic continued to depend upon wilderness, that is, upon natural forces within the climate and within the soil that have never in any meaningful sense been controlled or conquered. Modern civilization has been built largely in this forgetfulness.[31]

People have in fact always preferred the non-desert-like, coastal, and marginal areas. Earthy areas are commonly accepted as belonging to the lowly and poor; the affluent prefer city balconies and vistas. Life in the city is, therefore, often an escape from the land to the abstractions of wealth and power. I am not suggesting a return to the desert in ways reminiscent of the Rechabite lifestyle or "Benedictine option."[32] Instead, I am alluding to a return to the concept of desert as a way of discovering our true place in the world and of recognizing our responsibility for the world. For just as the ruthless urbanization of the countryside and the heedless exploitation of natural resources have cosmic implications for the contemporary world, so too the desert has borne the crucial consequences of our history and spirituality. Through the desert experience, one learns—or, rather, re-learns—what in the Orthodox hymnography is defined as the reality of matter, "the truth of things."[33] The desert came alive in its monastic dwellers during the third, fourth, and fifth centuries, and we have something vital to learn from them about our relationship with the earth.

---

[31]See Wendell Berry, *Standing on Earth: Selected Essays* (Ipswich, UK: Golgonooza Press, 1991), 22. On the notion of wilderness, cf. Vincent Rossi, "Inspiration: Who Comes Out of the Wilderness?," *GreenCross* 2, no. 2 (Wynnewood, PA, 1996), 4–6. See also Alan Jones, *Soul Making: The Desert Way of Spirituality* (New York: Harper & Row, 1985).
[32]Title of a book by Rod Dreher, *The Benedictine Option: A Strategy for Christians in a Post-Christian Nation* (New York: Sentinel, 2017).
[33]Hymn for the Feast of St. Nicholas of Myra, December 6.

A Journey of Solitude, Silence, and Stillness

The Flight of Solitude

In broad terms, ascetics embarked on a three-fold journey—
involving the way of solitude, silence, and stillness—to reach their
ultimate goal of encountering God. They moved away from society
and into the desert to be alone, in a place of quiet, to find stillness
in their hearts and be at one with God in order to attain cosmic
reconciliation.

The desert, the symbolical backdrop for this sacred journey, is
variously described in Scripture and the Christian classics. It is seen
as a specific place, an area separated from and deprived of God[34];
a location, outside of the city, where one is exiled and executed like
Christ[35]; an area where one confronts the demons[36] or converses with
God.[37] However, it might be more helpful to picture the desert not
so much as a mystical place but above all as a mysterious way[38] that
includes all the intensity and inspiration of a sacrament. In this respect,
the desert is the yearning for the transcendent that becomes more
desirable than any worldly fulfillment and contentment (see Ps. 62:1).

The desert speaks in a coarse, albeit realistic manner; its voice
may not necessarily be eloquent, but it is certainly life-giving. Formal
structures and supports crumble in the desert; there remain only a
veiled God and a promise. The flight to the desert is a search for
God in the mundaneness of daily life, in the monotony of routine.
The flight is less an escape from society or the world, as it is a
pressing and powerful attraction toward God,[39] who retreats to the
heart of the desert. The descent into the heart is more than a vague

---

[34]See Origen, *Commentary on John* 18 PG 14.232 and Chrysostom, *Homily 17,3 on
Ephesians* PG 62.125.
[35]See Palladius, *Lausiac History* 1 PG 34.1010. See also Acts 7:58.
[36]See Lk. 8:29; Evagrius, *Practical Chapters* 48 PG 40.1245; and John Climacus,
Ladder 25 PG 88.893A. See Dan. 11:31 and Mt. 24:15.
[37]See Clement of Alexandria, *Paedagogus* 2, 10 PG 8.532; Chrysostom, *Against
Anomoeans* 10, 2 PG 48.532 and Evagrius, *De rerum monachorum* 6 PG 40.1257.
[38]See Clement of Alexandria, *Stromateis* 7, 12 PG 9.505, Chrysostom, *De
compunctione* 2, 3 PG 47.144, and Nilus, *Treatise to Eulogius* PG 79.1093.
[39]See Basil, *Longer Rules* 5, 2 PG 31.921.

or romantic nostalgia for the boundlessness or abyss of divinity. The nomadic element of those who wander in deserts, in mountains, in dens, and in caves of the earth (Heb. 11:38) ultimately reflects a worship of the absolute. The departure from our narrow limitations and the resulting spiritual contact with the infinite is a call beyond, an invitation to transcendence and transfiguration.

Many have gone to the desert, whether figuratively or literally. In his account of the monks in Egypt, Rufinus writes: "This is the utter desert where each monk remains alone in his cell ... There is a huge silence and a great quiet there."[40] Abraham was alone; Moses stood in solitude; and Elijah took the lonely journey to the desert. However, because these and others were called to meet and speak to God, in fact they were never less alone than when alone. The inhabitant of the desert, while a stranger and pilgrim on the earth (Heb. 11:13), feels at home with God and nature.

The silence described here is not absence or apathy; it is animated and ardent. It implies a depth filled with life and replete with energy. It reflects the sound and color of the ocean, bustling with activity and diversity (cf. Ezek. 1:24). It reverberates the din and darkness of the forest, buzzing with richness and array. In the desert, the contemplative encounters the same insight and intimacy, the same grace of transcendence and furnace of transformation:

> Solitude is the furnace of transformation. Without solitude, we remain victims of our society and continue to be entangled in the illusions of the false self. [In the desert, we] affirm God as the only source of our identity.[41]

So it is the innate, inward, and intense desire for God that forces the monastic to take to the mountains, somewhere between heaven and earth: Moses' Sinai and Anthony's two mountains, Olympus in Asia Minor and the column of the Stylite, Meteora, and Athos. Every mountain is a symbol of the Tabor of the heart. Rather than withdrawing from society, the desert hermit inevitably creates a new focus of order: ever alert, guarding the walls[42] or frontiers between

---

[40]*History of Monks in Egypt* PL 21.443 and 444.
[41]Henri Nouwen, *The Way of the Heart: Desert Spirituality and Contemporary Ministry* (San Francisco, CA: HarperCollins, 1991), 25–6.
[42]Palladius, *Historia Lausiaca* 18 PG 34.1041–4.

this life and the next, eagerly expecting the last days and taking by violence the heavenly kingdom (Mt. 11:12). This explains why, in the life of the desert, the essential content of fasting is to be free in order to feed on the Word of God without distraction; the inner meaning of silence is to hear this same Word; and the deeper reason for sleeplessness is the constant expectation of the Bridegroom in the middle of the night (Mt. 25:1-3).

The Quiet of Silence

The desert, as John Chrysostom preaches, is the mother of quietude.[43] Silence is a way of interiority, the willingness to explore the center of life, the heart, and to journey in silence to quiet the passions, temptations, and distractions that prevent us from intimate communion with God. The desert, however, is also a baptism of fire—a way of purification and regeneration.[44] In its frightening starkness, it purges the inhabitant from demons, who try to distract and sidetrack us from worship of God in as countless ways as the grains of sand.

In the desert, silence and death go hand in hand; in fact, to be utterly silent can feel like death. Sitting in one's cell resembles lying in the grave because there one experiences the death of the old self. One must die in order to live; and one must lose in order to find. In a world of conflict and death, the struggle for survival introduces a dimension of violence in society, where one learns to kill in order to persevere. This absurdity of death in the context of hope is another critical facet of the desert. There, the concept of communion is part and parcel of life,[45] while vulnerability and loving surrender of one's own and one's self become a constant reaffirmation and realization of Christ's words: "Take, eat, this is my body; take, drink of this my blood" (see Mk 14:22-24).

---

[43]John Chrysostom, *Homily 50, 1 on Matthew* PG 51.513.
[44]See Athanasius, *Life of Anthony* 65 (933–6), and *Life of Symeon the Stylites* 12 PG 93.1658.
[45]See Norman Russell, trans., *The Lives of the Desert Fathers* (Oxford, UK: Mowbray; and Kalamazoo, MI: Cistercian Publications, 1981), 106, 149. This book, a translation of the *History of Monks in Egypt*, contains eyewitness accounts of stories and teachings from the early, formative monastic tradition. See fn. 53.

As in the liturgy, what precedes the Eucharist is personal conversion (metanoia), a total change from the cultivation of the ego through a quieting of the passions. The desert dweller achieves this in an act of abandonment before the cross.

In this process of transformation, the emphasis is not so much on one's own imperfection and ugliness as on the perfection and beauty of God. Beyond any emphasis on ascetic feat or individual sin, the ulterior message of the Desert Fathers and Mothers is one of pervasive light and inexpressible joy. This accounts for the repeated images in the desert literature of light and life, of joy and angels. These ascetics are not gloomy and obsessed, but accessible and very much alive: John of Lycopolis has a bright and smiling face, despite years of ascetic feats; Didymus possesses a charming countenance, despite his unappealing habit of treading on scorpions with bare feet.

Even in their charming humor, they portray less an exhibition of escapism than an expression of humility,[46] whereby they reduce the tension between nature and grace, clay and fire, creation and Creator. John S. Dunne relates a rabbinical story of a student who asks why there are no longer in our age people able to see the face of God; the rabbi responds: "Because nowadays no one can stoop so low."[47] Stooping low enables us to see the face of the earth,[48] where the light and joy of the heaven spill over to penetrate this world. No wonder Abba Benjamin can exclaim: "Be joyful at all times."[49]

Along this journey of quieting the passions, the desert dwellers represent broken humanity before its Creator. They understand that they are nothing and possess nothing by right or privilege. Instead, they acknowledge that every minute particle of the world belongs solely and totally to God, a recognition borne out in silent adoration of God as in humble veneration of others. In the words of Pachomius, "If you see a person pure and humble, that is a great vision. For what is greater than such a vision, to see the invisible God in a visible human being."[50]

---

[46]Evagrius, *Chapters on Prayer* 96 PG 79.1188. See also Nau, *Apophthegmata* 7.
[47]John S. Donne, *The House of Wisdom* (London: SCM, 1985), 20.
[48]See Mt. 23.12; *Apophthegmata* John Colobos 22 and PL 73.966.
[49]Benjamin 4, *Sayings*, Ward, 37.
[50]F. Halkin, ed., *Greek Life of Pachomius* (Brussels: Société des Bollandistes, 1932), vol. 1, ch. 48.

The desert is as much a school for humility as it is a school of love. Aware of their own limitations, the Desert Fathers and Mothers show compassion for the weaknesses of others as well as for the vulnerability of all creatures.[51] In their solitude and humility, even while living apart from all, they comprise a part of all. The desert rule was to place hospitality and charity before any rules of fasting or prayer.[52] What counted in the desert was the principle of love, not the great individual fast or the feat of endurance:

> We should ask of a man not whether devils are subject to him, but whether he possesses love, says the Westerner John Cassian who learned so much from the Egyptian hermits.[53]

This love is the ultimate authority of the desert hermit, who is no longer under law but actually passes laws.[54]

The Stillness of Love

Solitude and silence issue in encounter with God through stillness that in turn issues in prayer.[55] External loneliness and wordless quiet are insufficient and infertile, unless they guide us to inner quiet and personal contact with God as the aim of all spiritual and ascetical struggle. The desert's formlessness and wordlessness are themselves ways of speaking to the Creator in a dialect of unpretentious beauty and genuine love, a way of communication and communion between God and humanity.

The only meaningful hierarchy is one that converges in God: all things are yours, and you are Christ's, and Christ is God's (1 Cor. 3:22-23). Belonging to another world does not undermine, but rather serves to underline the integrity of this world. Regrettably, distorting our proper focus has mutilated this order: "The land has

---

[51]Moses 2, Nau, *Apophthegmata.*

[52]See Poemen 92, 109, Nau, *Apophthegmata*, and many other similar passages.

[53]John Cassian, *Conferences* 15, ch. 7. See also Russell, *History of Monks in Egypt*, 148; and Macarius 32, Nau, *Apophthegmata.*

[54]See Isaac the Syrian, *Mystic Treatises* 23, Greek text (Athens: Spanos Editions, 1976), 91, and similar passages in *Symeon the New Theologian: The Discourses*, in Classics of Western Spirituality (New York: Paulist Press, 1980).

[55]See Arsenius 2 and Anthony 11, Nau, *Apophthegmata.*

been infected by its inhabitants; for they have … broken the eternal alliance" (Isa. 24:4-7).

Historians sometimes point out that the early monastics withdrew to the desert in order to avoid taxation or military service. What they fail to see is that these hermits were first and foremost conscripted in heaven, paying their dues in blood and tears to the Lord of heaven and earth. The prologue of the *History of Monks in Egypt*[56] describes them as loyal children awaiting their father, as an army expecting its emperor. They were alert, keeping watch, paying the dues even of those who had never so much as suspected the need for any tribute. As the Letter to the Hebrews asserts, "The world was not worthy of them" (Heb. 11:38)—which is perhaps why they took to the desert in the first place.

The Desert Fathers and Mothers stand still, like candles burning in prayer, interceding even for those who have no one to pray for them. They are like trees on a busy city street, purifying and refreshing through their powerful and prayerful presence. Confronted with the emptiness and formlessness of the desert, these ascetics stand unimpeded in the presence of God.[57] John the Hermit stood still under a rock for three years of uninterrupted prayer, neither sitting nor lying down to sleep, but simply snatching some sleep while standing.[58] And Anthony of Egypt emerges from the deeper desert, or the inner mountain as he calls it, as from some inmost shrine, initiate into the mysteries and God-borne.[59] The desert elders are able to discover the divine flame in all things, to discern the world as a burning bush of God's energies, to become all fire:

> Abba Lot went to see Abba Joseph and said to him, "Abba, as far as I can, I say my little office, I fast a little, I pray and meditate, I live in peace and purity and purify my thoughts. What else can

---

[56]The *History of Monks in Egypt* recounts the story of seven Christian monks, who travel from Jerusalem to Egypt toward the end of the fourth century and encounter some of the early Desert Fathers. The text exists in several ancient languages, including Syriac and Greek. For an English translation, see Russell, *The Lives of the Desert Fathers*; and E. A. Wallis Budge, *The Book of Paradise*, 2 vols. (London, 1904).

[57]John Lycopolis 62, *History of Monks in Egypt*.

[58]Ibid., 23. See also Arsenius 15, Nau, *Apophthegmata*: "One hour's sleep a night is enough for a monk if he is a fighter."

[59]Athanasius, *Life of Anthony* 14 (864–5).

I do?" The old man stood up and stretched his hands towards heaven. His fingers became like ten lamps of fire and he said to him, "If you will, you can become all flame."[60]

We need *more* deserts and forests, not less; we need more wilderness and wildness, more marshes and meadows—unspoiled by development and unsoiled by clutter. We can never have enough earth and soil—unpolluted by selfishness and unadulterated by ambition. We can never have enough nature and wonder—undefiled by vanity and untainted by waste. Above all, we can never have enough of God's mercy and love, which unveil God's wisdom and beauty in the world.

---

[60]Joseph of Panepho 7, Nau, *Apophthegmata*. See also Joseph of Panepho 6–7 (*Sayings*, Ward, 88), Arsenius 27 (*Sayings*, Ward, 11), and Sisoes 9, Nau, *Apophthegmata*.

FIGURE 2 *Andrei Rublev, Holy Trinity (Troitsa) 1425–27 Tempera on wood. Tretyakov Gallery, Moscow, Russia* © PAINTING/Alamy *Stock Photo.* ***See p. 127***

4

Divine Sophia

The Wisdom of the Word and Beauty of the World

The transcendence and transformation experienced by the Desert Fathers and Mothers resulted in a new way of thinking and living that brought them closer to the Creator and the creation. Yet, their ways constituted more than wisdom in the conventional sense; for them, true wisdom was attained through encounter with divine wisdom.

The personification of wisdom is broadly defined philosophically and theologically, but it unmistakably includes the issue of God's relationship with creation. Beyond the prophets and priests, for instance, the Jews recognized the potential and power of wisdom in God. Well before Christian philosophers embraced the concept, Jews perceived creation as a revelation of divine sophia. The wisdom of God—both *hokh' ma* in Hebrew and *sophia* in Greek are feminine terms[1]—is personified in the wisdom literature of the Bible: "I, wisdom, was the daily delight of the Lord ... rejoicing in the inhabited world and delighting in the human race" (Prov. 8:30-31). So the concept of wisdom is inextricably linked to a sense of wonder, perceived as an expression of fascination with the mystery of nature and a corrective to the folly with which we have treated creation. In this respect, wisdom became the popular philosophical

---

[1]The characteristics of sophia have been clearly personified as feminine from as early as biblical times, and it has today become popular to view sophia as the divine feminine par excellence.

pursuit of a number of contemporary theologians, especially feminist thinkers, but also of certain Orthodox intellectuals, most notably Russian theologian Fr. Sergius Bulgakov (1871–1944).[2]

This chapter examines the notion of sophia independently of any specific metaphysical system developed by any particular writer. While there is no uniform perception or formulation of sophiology in the Orthodox tradition, I shall explore certain broad dimensions of the sophiological theory relating to: (1) the centrality of Mary espoused in the West and Russia in contrast to the viewpoint in Greek thought, where sophia is exemplified in Christ; (2) the dialectical balance between dualism (as world denying) and pantheism (with its overemphasis on the world); (3) the concept of sophia in wisdom literature; (4) the implications of kataphatic theology and apophatic theology, as well as (5) the benefits of the wisdom acquired through spiritual direction.

The Ambivalence of Sophia

The concept of sophia is not an obscure, esoteric doctrine related exclusively to theosophy. Neither is it a sophisticated, abstract idea characteristic solely of Russian religious consciousness.[3]

---

[2]Bulgakov was Professor of Political Economy at Moscow University and, later, Dean of St. Sergius's Theological Institute in Paris. He belonged to a group of intellectuals who converted from Marxism to Christianity on the eve of the 1917 Russian Revolution. As early as 1912, he published his *Philosophy of Economy* where he first attempted a systematic formulation of his sophiology. Bulgakov was concerned to develop a worldview that was both consistent with the Orthodox tradition and also capable of meeting the challenge of contemporary technology. The formulations of Bulgakov regarding the significance and place of sophia in Christian theology and cosmology leave much to be desired—particularly with regard to his elaboration of its relationship to the traditional doctrines of the Holy Trinity (sophia either as an uncreated fourth person of the Trinity or else a created aspect of the world [pantheism]) as well as of the Incarnation ("God has created the world," wrote Bulgakov, "precisely for his Incarnation"). Yet, the contribution of this extraordinary thinker lies in his grappling with the critical issues of our time, specifically with the concept of God's communion with the created world.

[3]Cf. Frederick C. Copleston, *Russian Religious Philosophy* (Notre Dame, IN: Search Books, 1988), 81. For a fine article by A. Nichols on Bulgakov and sophiology, see *Sobornost* 13,2 (1992), 17–31. Certainly in Russian thought, sophiology is the convergence and culmination of several threads, such as the "Eternal Feminine" (Vladimir Solovyev, in *Lectures on Godmanhood*, 1878), the "Mother of God" (Pavel Florensky, in *The Pillar and Foundation of Truth*, 1914), together with the notions of "mother earth" (Fyodor Dostoevsky, in *The Brothers Karamazov*,

What is, in fact, connected to Russian philosophical thought is the identification—albeit only after the sixteenth century—of sophia with the Mother of God.

Such is the opinion of Vladimir Solovyev (1853–1900), Pavel Florensky (1892–1943), and Bulgakov himself. In the West, too, sophia is normally identified with the Mother of God. However, this is an incomplete representation of sophiology; in the Greek tradition, sophia is conventionally identified with Christ. In Greek theology, sophia is understood as the unity of heaven and earth, a unity most profoundly and uniquely held together in the divine-human person of Jesus Christ, as the eternal Word and Creator that lovingly assumes creation. This is the unity that draws and binds all things together.

This double emphasis or ambivalence—where the Russian tradition relates sophia to the Virgin Mother, while the Greek tradition relates sophia to the Incarnate Word—is by no means fortuitous. It is not by accident that early Russian churches are dedicated to the divine sophia in honor of the all-holy Virgin Mary, whereas the finest examples of Greek Byzantine architecture, including the Church of Haghia Sophia in Constantinople, are dedicated to Jesus Christ as the divine Word. Together, Christ and Mary reveal two corresponding and complementary aspects of the divine wisdom; together, they realize and reflect the sacrament of God's relationship with the world.

The church (as body of Christ) and Mary (as temple of God) are intimately and inseparably connected to the divine feminine perceived as sophia. As such, they unfold diverse and different aspects of divine love in creation and redemption. It would be naïve to identify sophia with the feminine aspect of the divinity in contradistinction with the logos as the male dimension of God. By contrast, divine sophia contains the qualities of creating, redeeming, and sustaining; it is conveyed in both feminine and masculine terms. Sophia and logos belong together, like male and female, earth and heaven. Just as the two icons on either side of the royal doors at the sanctuary of an Orthodox church reveal the inner and outer faces of God the Word: divine Logos and eternal Sophia.

1879–80) and "holy nature" (Vasily Rozanov, in *The Family Question in Russia*, 1903). See also George Fedotov, *The Russian Religious Mind*, vol. 1 (Belmont, MA: Nordland, 1975), 386–9.

Sophia and Mary

This cosmological role of Mary, as the parallel and premise of the cosmic event of Christ, is articulated by Philip Sherrard:

> This is the secret of the term Mother of God (Theotokos), as it is also the secret of the initial cosmogonic act. The Mother of God is the Virgin Mother or the unconditioned holy Wisdom— Sophia aeterna—through whom God reveals himself to himself by manifesting the virtualities of his divine Names, the prototypes of all created being latent in his unknown and transcendent Being. It is the revelation by means of which God acquires his Godhood.[4]

The Virgin Mother embraces created and uncreated in a manner corresponding to the way that Jesus Christ assumes divinity and humanity without confusion and without division.[5] Mary becomes the "Mater" from which all matter derives—Sherrard refers to her as universal nature, *natura naturans*—the matrix in whom all matter flowers:

> Although she is one, she exists in two modes, eternal and temporal, uncreated and created ... She is earth as a single immaterial feminine divinity, and she is earth as a manifold, material reality. She is herself the Body of the cosmic Christ, the created matrix in whom the divine Logos eternally takes flesh. She is the bridge that unites God to the world, the world to God, and it is she that bestows on the world its eternal and sacred value. She is the seal of its sacred identity.[6]

In order to appreciate how Mariology reveals the femininity of all creation, one must turn to the powerful symbolism of iconography and profound semantics of liturgy. In Orthodox churches after the late fourth century, Mary is depicted in the apse above the altar,

---

[4]Philip Sherrard, *Human Image: World Image. The Death and Resurrection of Sacred Cosmology* (Ipswich, UK: Golgonooza Press, 1992), 176f.
[5]The language is from the doctrinal definition of the Council of Chalcedon in 451 CE. See Norman Tanner, ed., *Decrees of the Ecumenical Councils*, vol. 1 (Washington, DC: Georgetown University Press, 1990), 86–7.
[6]Sherrard, *Human Image*, 181.

suspended somewhere between heaven and earth. She constitutes the bridge and link between the Creator, who contains all things (Pantokrator), and the world. In comparison to the inaccessible, transcendent God, Mary is the person immediately accessible and frequently invoked in daily devotion. Thus, in the popular Orthodox service of *The Akathist Hymn* (early seventh century), she is hailed as:

> [T]he throne of the King, as bearing the One who bears the universe ... as the womb of the divine Incarnation, and as the one through whom creation is refashioned ... as the heavenly ladder by which God descended, the bridge that leads the earthly to the heavenly (Stasis I). In her, the heavens rejoice with earth and the earth concelebrates with heaven ... She is the shelter of the world, broader than the clouds (Stasis II), the promised land, the land of the infinite God, the key of Christ's kingdom and the hope of eternal blessings (Stasis III).

She is not separated from the earthly and created; she is the rock that refreshes those who thirst for life; she is called the tree of life, a robe, a river, and a tower.

Through Mary, we learn something about who God is and why creation exists. We discover that God is love (1 Jn 4:8) and that the world bears the seed of the divine Word. As the living temple of God, Mary reminds us that we all comprise a temple (1 Cor. 3:16), that the human body constitutes a temple of the Spirit (1 Cor. 6:19), and that the whole world is an altar of the living God.

It is not by accident, then, that Orthodox iconography depicts Mary as the Platytera (who is more spacious than the whole of creation), while her image is found immediately beneath the Pantokrator (who holds all of creation). For the unceasing cosmological response to God's eternal initiative is the continual "yes" of the Virgin. Mary's word constantly and completely corresponds to God's Word, even as she conceives the Word in her womb and selflessly confirms the Word in her wisdom.

Mary can realize these mysteries because, again in the words of *The Akathist Hymn*, "[S]he has yoked together maidenhood and motherhood ... remaining a virgin, yet giving birth" (Stasis III). As virgin, she heals the brokenness of the world; as mother, she fulfills the barrenness of creation. As virgin, she signifies the integrity of life, not just celibacy; as mother, she personifies the affirmation of life, not just marriage. In this way, she brings opposites together. Little wonder, then, that Mary is esteemed by monastics and married persons alike.

Sophia and Cosmos

The world as revelation of divine wisdom and glory is a fundamental theme of Christian sophiology. Everything bears the seed of God, and it is the immanence of God in creation that lies at the center of wisdom theology. The very ground of this world is the wisdom of God and cannot be conceived apart from God. Thus sophia becomes the intelligible basis of creation. Indeed, it is through sophia, as manifested in Jesus and Mary, that we are able to comprehend creation and cosmic transfiguration.

According to Christian philosophy (as the love of wisdom) or sophiology (as the study of wisdom), everything temporal finds its true meaning and derives its ultimate value in the light of the eternal (or eschatological). The eternal image of divine sophia is what leaves in the temporal world the lasting imprint and image of God. According to an Orthodox hymn sung during the Feast of the Dormition of the Virgin Mother of God (August 15): "The wisdom of God is the creative and unitive power in all things."

Discerning in creation the wisdom of God is discovering the royal path between two extreme poles in our attitude to the world. On the one hand, there is a latent world-denying outlook (dualism); and on the other hand, there is a prevailing world-worshipping outlook (pantheism). The first burrows too sharp a separation between God and world; the result is a reduction of the latter. The second blurs the line of demarcation between God and world; the result is an exaggeration of the latter. Such attitudes are all too common among Christians leaning either toward an approach that despises the world or else toward an attitude that is subservient to the world. Both positions are detrimental to creation and dismissive of its Creator.

What is crucial in addressing dualism and pantheism is a reinterpretation of the doctrine of Incarnation, whose roots emanate from the innermost depths of God as communion and penetrate the very heart of heaven and earth. An incarnational basis also involves the transformative descent and abiding presence of the

Holy Spirit in the world. In this perspective, sophia proposes a fresh interpretation of the world and its destiny.[7] It becomes a dialectical balance between opposing extremes, an ascetic relationship with the world and God.[8] The change resembles the radical conversion of heart or reversal of mindset likened in the monastic literature to a constant violence against natural inclinations.[9] Paradoxically, if this "violence against nature" does not occur inside us, the inevitable result is the rape of nature around us. Somewhere or other, a cost must be borne for the world. Somewhere or other, a responsibility must be assumed for the world.

Sophia and Christ

Divine Wisdom is the revelation of the divine Word (Logos) as the all-embracing unity through whom all things were made (cf. Jn 1:3) and in whom all things exist (cf. Rom. 11:36). This is what constitutes a Christian worldview: The world is in God, despite the fact that it exists outside of God. The world belongs to God, in spite of being wholly other than God. Such a worldview is neither dualism nor pantheism, but Christian panentheism or immanentism: it recognizes that the identity and distinction—the unity and duality of sophia in God and in creation—rest on the same foundation.[10] In this way, sophia is directly connected to the Logos as the divine Word of God. Everything in the world speaks the same truth, says the same thing, and signals to the same end: from the "I am" of God's Word addressed to Moses in the burning bush to the great "I am" sayings of the Incarnate Word of Jesus recorded in the Gospels. As Maximus the Confessor writes: "God is everything"[11] and "nothing that exists is devoid of God."[12]

There is a cosmic interconnectedness of all things, which are profoundly connected to the divine Word (Col. 1:17 and Eph. 1:10);

---

[7]Cf. J. Pain and N. Zernov, eds., *A Bulgakov Anthology* (London: SPCK, 1976), 144–56.

[8]Ibid., 153.

[9]Cf. John Climacus, *The Ladder of Divine Ascent*, Step 1 PG 88.633.

[10]Pain and Zernov, *A Bulgakov Anthology*, 156.

[11]*Ambigua* PG 91.1257

[12]*Ambiguum* 7 PG 91.1092, in Blowers and Wilken, 66.

all things constitute a positive affirmation of all that is God's. An Orthodox hymn repeated three times at the Great Blessing of the Waters on the Feast of Theophany (January 6) declares: "The voice of the Lord on the waters cries aloud saying: Come all of you, and receive the Spirit of wisdom, the Spirit of understanding ... from Christ who is made manifest."

This Judaeo-Christian concept of sophia, as developed in the wisdom literature of the Hebrew Scriptures (notably in Proverbs, Wisdom, and Ecclesiasticus), is informed and influenced by Greek, Egyptian, and Persian thought. And the theological pinnacle of Hellenistic Jewish writing is reflected in the unknown author of the Wisdom of Solomon, whose most original contribution lies in a virtual identification of sophia and spirit: "I called on God, and the spirit of wisdom came to me" (7:7).[13] Sophia is unique and subtle (7:22), penetrating and permeating all things (7:23), ordering all things wisely and well (8:1). Wisdom is more than simply the all-pervading presence of God in the world. It is a gift from above, reflecting in its very immanence the transcendence of God: "While remaining in herself, she renews all things" (7:27). The author is very explicit: "She is a breath of the power of God, a pure emanation of the glory of the almighty ... an image of divine goodness" (7:25-26). Revealing sophia as the image of divine goodness, such personification relates divine Wisdom to the creative Word. Thus we read in Solomon's prayer: "O God ... you have made all things by your word, and by your wisdom you have formed humankind" (9:1-2).

In similar manner, New Testament writings depict Jesus as Wisdom; for he is the final Incarnation of the eternal Word and Spirit of Wisdom, the embodiment of divine truth and revelation. Thus, Orthodox iconographic representations of wisdom texts sometimes depict the Wisdom-Angel, or Christ as Angel (especially in earlier centuries), while at other times they portray the Wisdom-Christ. These symbolic representations express a naturalistic, almost humanistic approach, both of which were unacceptable to the sixteenth-century monk Euthymius: "The hypostatic Wisdom, as the Word and Power, is the Son of God. And if one dares to paint wisdom under an invented form, one will soon begin to dare

---

[13]Cf. John Breck, *Spirit of Truth: The Origins of Johannine Pneumatology* (Crestwood, NY: St. Vladimir's Seminary Press, 1991), esp. 79–98.

painting the Word by means of another invention ... What could be more absurd than that?[14]

It is the Christological definition of the Council of Chalcedon (451 CE) that provides the principal key to and justification for Christian sophiology. This definition speaks of the divine and human natures as united in the one person of Christ without confusion or change, without separation or division. Notice, writes Russian philosopher and staunch disciple of Bulgakov Lev Zander (1893–1964), how "the Chalcedonian formula merely contains four negative propositions and tells us how *not* to think of the relation between the divine and the human natures of Christ. The positive meaning of the formula, the Chalcedonian *yea* is ... the bequest of the patristic age to future generations, and it is our duty to work at it."[15] Traditionally and theologically, the Chalcedonian definition offered no final solution to the way that God relates to the world. This required, and continues to require, sustained interpretation.

Sophia as Mystery

The starting point of any sophiological philosophy is the basic appreciation of the world as communicating and conforming to the image of God. Thus the criterion must always be positive theology, not negative philosophy. Positive—or kataphatic—theology reflects the endeavor to reach God through creation and relates the revelation of God through creation. It regards God not as wholly incommunicable and transcendent, but as communicating through creation and drawing all creatures toward the divine. By contrast, negative thinking—or the apophatic way—implies negation rather than affirmation. It is the recognition that God lies above and beyond any and every image. It is the conviction that kataphatic images must be denied or stripped down in order for creation to penetrate behind and beyond the symbol to the ultimate

---

[14]Quoted in Leonid Ouspensky, *Theology of the Icon*, vol. 2 (Crestwood, NY: St. Vladimir's Press, 1992), 359. A theological connection between Wisdom (Sophia) and Word (Logos) was attempted by Solovyev in his *Lectures on Godmanhood*, esp. no. 7. For the iconographic tradition, see John Meyendorff, "Wisdom-Sophia: Contrasting Approaches to a Complex Theme," *Dumbarton Oaks Papers* 41 (1987): 391–401.

[15]Lev Zander, in Pain and Zernov, eds., *A Bulgakov Anthology*, xxiv.

reality. According to the positive theological method, those images sanctioned by Scripture are superior. However, according to the apophatic methodology, even symbols with no similarity to the divine can claim validity.

Sophiology adheres to the kataphatic method: God has depicted the divine image in creation; consequently, this image of God can be depicted and described.[16] For Bulgakov, the image of God in the world is heavenly humanity, namely Sophia as eternally divine and human;[17] hence the centrality of the doctrine of the Incarnation. As Bulgakov notes elsewhere: "God has created the world precisely for his Incarnation; it is not the world which, through the fall of man, has impelled God to become incarnate."[18] This broader, engaging approach to the Incarnation is characteristic of the Eastern Fathers and prevalent in Orthodox theology. The Incarnation is conceived as the expression of the eternal love of God, who wishes to be associated with creation in the most intimate manner.

The weakness of the sophiological worldview may lie in the way it tends to modify apophatic theology and undermine the transcendence of God. There always remains, in the expression and phenomenon of Incarnation, an untold reality and an unknown quality. To be negative is actually to make space and to allow for God, to defer and surrender to the boundlessness of God. This is the knowing that is an unknowing; it is the understanding that one cannot fully know.

Yet, while sophiology primarily adheres to the kataphatic method, the apophatic standpoint is not altogether absent from the wisdom texts: "Where then does wisdom come from? And where is the place of understanding? It is hidden from the eyes of all living, and concealed from the birds of the air ... But God understands the way to it, and knows its place" (Job 28:20-23). Negative language is essential for an appreciation of the way of wisdom; despite the volumes written about the ineffable and the transcendent, the content ultimately remains inapplicable to its object. The prologue to the Gospel of John should not serve to

---

[16]Sergei Bulgakov, *The Icon and Its Veneration*, in transl. Boris Jakim, *Sergius Bulgakov. Icons and the Name of God* (Grand Rapids, MI: Eerdmans, 2012), 82.
[17]Ibid., 83.
[18]In transl. Boris Jakim, *Sergius Bulgakov. The Lamb of God* (Grand Rapids, MI: Eerdmans, 2008), 139.

justify all that passes as theology. Apophatic theology provides a crucial corrective to undertaking academic inquiry without the presumption of exhaustive knowledge. Apophatic theology maintains a paradox at the center of its methodology. This paradox is what leads to the later distinction between divine essence and energies, although one must learn how to recover this approach from its reputation of irrelevance or obfuscation.

Orthodox theology has always exhibited a dipolar attitude toward creation, striving to respect and retain the tension between divine transcendence and divine immanence in relation to the world. The doctrine of a distinction between God's essence and energies calls for an observation and adoration of the divine mystery in all its complexity. The unknown God remains hidden and unchanged in its fullness, but is manifested in an infinite variety of loving acts; "Unknown, though well known" (2 Cor. 6:9). The energies are neither God's essence nor God's nature, because God is never bound but rather chooses to reach out in ecstasy (literally reaching outside: ek-stasis) to a nature of another order. The Greek word for "energy" (en-ergeia) signifies operation (ergon) or power (dynamis). Energies are distinguished from essence not because they are modified or less concentrated, but because they presuppose the existence of a free and personal God, whose goodwill is manifested in merciful grace.

A theology that fails to sustain and explain this paradoxical distinction between God's essence and energies is incapable of accepting any real relationship between ephemeral creature and eternal Creator. Such a theology advances no further than philosophical existentialism or social humanitarianism. The more God is humanized—the more one struggles to understand the mystery of Incarnation and the more one places creation on its proper level—the more majestic and mysterious the understanding of creation becomes. The most tangible rendering of God's love is the divine descent into relationship with creation, while absolutely retaining divine inaccessibility.

"God is" means "God is love" (1 Jn 4:8), which in turn implies that the "world is loved." The whole world is a burning bush of God's energies, pregnant with divine life. Time is a ladder established by God in order that creation may ascend toward heaven, and upon which God descends through divine energies to creation. At the same time, God is neither divine essence nor divine energy—God is not obliged to become in order to manifest divine fullness. Time and space, creation and the world, are generated by God's desire for human beings to become gods by grace and for the world to be transformed into sacrament.

In this perspective, the Incarnation must be viewed not so much as a phase, but as a culmination in a series of phases reflecting this double movement of descent and ascent. In one and the same person, human temporality and divine eternity are united and conformed in a way never previously realized. In Christ— in whom there is no interval between the offering of divine love and the response of human love—divine kenosis provokes and generates the virtues within humanity: humility, kindness, purity of thought, and love. The essence of all virtue is Jesus Christ (cf. 1 Cor. 1:30), who in condescending to descend and assume the human form of a slave (Phil. 2:7) reveals the value of humanity called to deification. The human person, whose image Christ makes his own, takes on the image of Christ and lives in Christ ... or, rather, Christ lives in them (cf. Gal. 2:20). Such a person reflects Christ, strives to become like Christ, and ultimately becomes Christ. Such a person holds together by grace the very same poles united by Christ—two natures in one person ... unconfusedly and unchangeably, inseparably and undividedly. This is why Symeon the New Theologian wrote of his elder, Symeon the Pious: "He possessed the whole of Christ, and was himself completely Christ ... Everything for him was Christ, as if clothed entirely with Christ."[19]

In the fundamental distinction between divine essence and divine energies, Orthodox theology perceives the very presupposition of all knowledge of God and the world, without which it would be very easy to resort to a rational connection between cause and effect as the only possible relationship between Creator and creation. The acceptance of this distinction denotes a nuanced understanding of God and world in terms of personal relationship and personal participation. Communication and communion further introduce the issue of relationships with others, particularly with one who imparts wisdom.

---

[19]Symeon the New Theologian, *Hymns*, vol. 1, ed. *Sources Chrétiennes*, no. 156 (Paris: Cerf, 1969), 245.

Sophia as Direction

A spiritual director enables us to view the world in a balanced way, avoiding the naive optimism that underlines the original perfection of creation (Pelagianism), as well as the destructive pessimism that emphasizes the original corruption of creation (Augustinianism). The relationship with a spiritual elder should serve as a bridge between Creator and creation, relating the transcendent God with the immanent world. Even as the human person is called to know and to become God, this dynamic reality is facilitated through the spiritual guide, who inspires and indicates the way to deification.[20]

Of course, the experience of cosmic reconciliation between God and world—as overcoming the fundamental errors of dualism and pantheism alike—mandates direct education and experience. One needs to know and discover personally the insight derived from loving God and the world with all one's heart and as oneself (cf. Mk 12:30-1). Yet, one cannot come to know by oneself. Just as a child learns to speak from someone else, so too the language of wisdom is always received and taught by someone else. The spiritual elder (geron in Greek, staretz in Russian) is one such initiator and indicator, who imparts the knowledge of truth, instructing us to contemplate God in the world and perceive the world with different eyes.[21]

From his personal experience of the Staretz Ambrose, Russian author Fyodor Dostoevsky offers a contemporary description of the wise elder.[22] Such elders merited the title "spirit-bearer" (pneumatophoros) because they strove to be led and to lead as compassionately as possible through the charismatic guidance of the Holy Spirit, rather than through individual authority or ambition. The spiritual guide assists in the rebirth and regeneration of the Christian into the life of the Spirit. This process entails the great understanding of radical conversion (metanoia).[23] The relationship

---

[20]Cf. Gregory the Theologian, *Apologetic Oration* II, 73 PG 35.481.

[21]See Symeon the New Theologian, *The Discourses*, in The Classics of Western Spirituality (Mahwah, NJ: Paulist Press, 1980), 58.

[22]Fyodor Dostoevsky, *The Brothers Karamazov*, trans. Andrew R. MacAndrew (New York: Bantam Classic, 1970), 35. On spiritual guidance and the role of the spiritual elder, see John Chryssavgis, *Soul Mending: The Art of Spiritual Direction* (Brookline, MA: Holy Cross Orthodox Press, 2000).

[23]See *Shepherd of Hermas*, Book II, Mandate IV, ii, 2 PG 2.920.

with the spiritual elder becomes a paradigm of the relationship with God, a preparation and attunement of one's capacity to be open to the grace of God in the world.

In this respect, the spiritual elder transmits wisdom, Christ himself, in a relationship with his or her disciples. Such a person seeks to give nothing of oneself, but rather only Christ who lives within (cf. Gal. 2:20). "To everyone, I give only what God tells me to give," said St. Seraphim of Sarov, a beloved staretz of the Orthodox Church.[24] In this sense, the spiritual elder exists alongside the apostles. Although not ordained through the episcopal laying on of hands, the spiritual elder is a prophet who receives the charisma of discernment directly from the Spirit of God—the difference between the apostle and elder lying in the degree of wisdom, not in the quality or potential of being.

This means that the personified sophia remains charismatic and personal. The wisdom of a spiritual guide is vital in progressively educating and gradually maturing other persons capable of discerning the beauty of God in the world. As Vladimir Solovyev would say: "The entire worldly and historical process is the process of the realization and incarnation [of the eternal feminine principle] in a great diversity of forms and degrees."[25]

Sophia: Let Us Attend!

The concept of sophia as beauty and understanding is the vision of a transfigured world beyond the damage or distortion of the temporal world. It is a sacrament that transcends the sphere of this world but is also discerned within this world. Sophia signifies the archetypal image of creation (the ideal world created in and by the Logos) and the active heart of this world (the same body of Christ, the incarnate Logos). The world thus comprises an extension in matter and time of the embodiment of the eternal Logos, just as the church is a prolongation of the body of Christ. It is hardly surprising that it took centuries of conversations, conflicts, and councils before the

---

[24]Seraphim of Sarov, cf. Valentine Zander, *St. Seraphim of Sarov* (Crestwood, NY: St. Vladimir's Seminary Press, 1984), 32.
[25]Vladimir Solovyev quoted in Georges Florovsky, *Ways of Russian Theology: Part Two* (Belmont, MA: BVA, 1987), 245.

early church could define the relationship of the eternal Logos to the incarnate Christ.

Even the final doctrine of Chalcedon bequeathed a conscious and open-ended ambiguity, a deliberate questioning of the relationship between the uncreated Word and the created world. Such, then, is the cosmological function of sophia: It is a bridge between God and world, belonging to and uniting both realities at once. As the creative and unitive Word of God, it is also the divine Wisdom whose seeds and traces are found in the multiplicity and diversity of creation. It is the uncreated beauty of God revealed and reflected in the beauty of creation. "One in God, she is many in creation," is how Florensky described sophia.[26]

This provides a valid alternative to the dichotomies with which we are confronted—between God and world, or between dualism and pantheism. For sophia is not simply the transcendence of God in contrast to the world; it is the immanence of God in connection to the world. This safeguards the "otherness" of God, while overcoming the inherent dangers of God's "affinity" to the world; for between Creator and creation, there is both distinction and identity. Sophia is the divinity of God and the createdness of creation. Yet, it is much more than this: for it is also the createdness of God and the divine spark within creation. Sophia preserves the luminosity and numinosity of God and creation alike. In this regard, sophiology represents much more than some aesthetical or mystical experience of the world's beauty; it reveals the world as a place of encounter with and experience of the personal God.

Sin and abuse have obscured but not obliterated this reality. Through the grace of the divine-human Word and Wisdom of God, there always remains the potential for recognizing the beauty of sophia within and beyond the shattered image of the world. This divine Word and eternal Wisdom is incarnate in Jesus Christ and, by extension, present in the church as body and bride of Christ. "Truly ... that is wisdom ... That is understanding" (Job 28:28). God is present in everything and recognized everywhere. In the words of Gregory Palamas:

---

[26]Pavel Florensky, *The Pillar and Ground of the Truth* (Moscow, 1914; repr. London: Gregg, 1970), 326. For an introduction to Florensky's world, see R. Slesinski, *Pavel Florensky: A Metaphysics of Love* (Crestwood, NY: St. Vladimir's Seminary Press, 1984).

God is also in the universe and the universe is within God—
the one sustaining, the other being sustained by him. Thus all
things participate in God's sustaining energy, but not in his
essence. Hence, the theologians say that divine omnipresence
also constitutes an energy of God.[27]

Such an understanding of the distinction between divine essence
and divine energies safeguards for sophiology both the freedom
and gratuitousness of divine love, as well as the dependence on
God by a creation that retains freedom and choice. The gift of
the divine energies presupposes permanent cooperation, intimate
communion, and cosmic interconnection. Participation in the divine
energies merges any distance and heals any division between God
and world, while at the same time retaining a distinction between
the two. In the final analysis, the divine sophia is perceived in the
unresolved dialectic of discontinuity and continuity, of rupture and
relation, of dissociation and association. The gift of divine wisdom
is transmitted in the affirmation of the unknowable essence of God
and the experience of the knowable energies of God that penetrate
and permeate the whole world.

Thus before every person and animal, before each bird and insect,
before all trees and mountains and rivers, the words of the deacon
during the Orthodox liturgy echo through the ages: "*Sophia*: Let us
arise! Let us attend!" It is a call, as Nicolas Cabasilas comments, to
"open all the doors of the mind and heart to the wisdom of God"[28]
in order to hear and proclaim the sacrament of creation.

---

[27]Gregory Palamas, *Topics of Natural and Theological Science* 104, in G. E. H. Palmer, Philip Sherrard and Kallistos Ware, *The Philokalia*, vol. 4 (London: Faber and Faber, 1995), 393.

[28]*Commentary on the Liturgy* 26 PG 150.421. See Robert Taft, *The Great Entrance: A History of the Transfer of Gifts and Other Preanaphoral Rites of the Liturgy of St. John Chrysostom* (Rome: Pontifical Oriental Institute, 2004), 403–16.

5

Ecology and Mystery

Creation as Sacrament

The Earth as Sacred

In the Orthodox Divine Liturgy, the call by the deacon to "arise and attend" occurs after he elevates the Holy Gospel before entering the royal gates of the altar. But it is not only the wisdom of the scriptural readings that the faithful are called to hear; the deacon's call is an exhortation to stand and honor divine Wisdom, Christ himself, encountered in the sacrament of the Eucharist. In this act, the Orthodox Church offers an opportunity to move beyond the literal, to transcend the immanent, to experience the book of divine wisdom, and to taste the Lord in sacrament of bread and wine.

A central feature of the sacramental ethos of the Orthodox Church is the perception of creation as sacrament, a unique and fundamental image in contemporary religious experience and the crux of my proposal in this book about the way we should relate to creation. While the concept of sacrament remains largely inaccessible or impenetrable—literally a sacred mystery—to the modern mind, it has less in fact to do with a transcendent divinity than it has with an immanent creation. Alternatively, it has more to do with the manifestation and revelation of the heavenly in the earthly. This is why St. Paul speaks of the "mystery hidden before all ages" now revealed in Christ (1 Cor. 2:7).[1] A contemporary

---

[1] See also Eph. 3:9 and Col. 1:26.

theologian observes that the divine Incarnation reveals creation as "secretly sacramental."[2] Perceiving creation as sacrament has to do with the truth and wisdom of God manifested in Christ crucified and revealed in time.

The conviction is that "the earth and all its fullness" (Ps. 23:1) presents an undeniable theological truth, a truth that "springs from the ground" (Ps. 85:11). Indeed, if there exists today a vision capable of transcending and transforming national and denominational divisions, social and political tensions alike, it may well be that of our world conceived as sacrament.

Unfortunately, however, we have been conditioned to consider the sacraments in a narrow, reductionist manner: a fixed number, so that all else assumes a non-sacramental tone; minimal requirements for the validity of sacraments, so that all else becomes un-canonical in nature; and an over-emphasis on the hierarchical structure of the church or the ritualistic nature of liturgy, so that all else falls outside the concern of salvation and concept of sacredness. We need to recall the sacramental principle, which ultimately demands a recognition that nothing in life is profane or unsacred. There is a likeness-in-the-very-difference between that which sanctifies (the Creator) and that which is sanctified (the creation), between uncreated and created. The Divine Liturgy of John Chrysostom, celebrated every Sunday in Orthodox churches throughout the world, affirms this conviction about God in relation to creation: "You are the one who offers and is offered, who receives and is distributed, and to you we offer glory."

This chapter expands the understanding of sacrament by exploring creation as a palpable mystery, a vast "incarnation" of cosmic proportions. Such a theology of creation is based on the fundamental intuitions that the world is fundamentally good, while remaining subject to evil and requiring redemption through the Incarnation, Crucifixion, and Resurrection of Christ. Attention will also be given to the notion of God creating the world out of nothing (ex nihilo), the distinction between essence and energies, and the relationship between God and world as a journey from divine image to divine likeness. Central of course to any theology that associates sacrament and creation is the Incarnation of the divine Word, who relates and reconciles the world to God.

---

[2]Olivier Clément, *On Human Being: A Spiritual Anthropology* (London: New City, 2000), 115.

A Theology of Sacrament

The divine mystery revealed in Christ is the foundation and substance of all sacraments, which unveil something greater and deeper than whatever we see in the world. The word "sacrament" (from the Latin sacramentum) may signify either the result or the means of consecration. The word was originally adopted in the third-century Latin West as the equivalent to the Greek term "mystery" (mysterion) that denotes a reality hidden while at the same time revealed through initiation (myesis). In this sense, since everything is a reflection of the divine, the actual number of Christian sacraments—or mysteries, as they are known in the Orthodox Church—can never be limited to the seven conventional rites of baptism, chrismation, the Eucharist, marriage, confession, unction, and ordination, which are traditionally administered by a bishop or priest.

While the clergy administer these rites, the mystery of changing bread and wine into the body and blood of Christ, the mystery of the cleansing of sin, and the mystery of uniting a couple in marriage occur by the action and operation of the Holy Spirit. They are God's way of entering, embracing, and transforming our lives. To regard and relate to the world without reference to the Holy Spirit is to worship an abstract God incapable of becoming or being involved with the human heart and history. Only an unreserved acknowledgement and affirmation of the Holy Spirit allows us to appreciate how God is able to "move outside" of divinity and enter into creation without either disrupting divine unity or abandoning divine transcendence.

Thus, in all its transcendence, a sacrament always remains an historical event, demanding material expression in which God becomes manifest in time and space. For instance, the Eucharist is God's manifestation in bread and wine, where the world becomes the historical and material sacrament of God's presence, transcending the ontological gap between created and uncreated. The world articulates and relates in very tangible terms this co-inherence and cooperation between divine and human in history, denoting the presence of God "incarnate among us" (Jn 1:14). In this way, the sacramental principle becomes the way that we perceive the world around us as sacred, a tangible mystery revealing and reflecting the invisible divine: the spiritual in matter and the eternal in time. It is a mystery concealed and comprehended in the flowers and the forests, the rocks and the mountains, as well as the rivers and the oceans. All of these look to God (Ps. 145:15); all creatures groan together in expectation (Rom. 8:22). For those who have ears to hear (Mt. 11:5) and eyes to see (Mt. 13:16), all of the earth makes a joyful noise, breaking out into song and praise. The sea roars, the floods clap, the hills sing (Ps. 98:4-8).

The notion and reality of sacrament must also be considered in the context of matter and time, while the struggle to reconcile a spiritual view of sacraments with the dominant secular view goes back many years. American farmer and writer Wendell Berry articulates the contemporary tension between the mechanistic and the spiritual worldviews with a striking, albeit mundane image:

> The figure representative of the earlier era was that of the otherworldly man who thought and said much more about where he would go when he died than about where he was living. Now we have the figure of the tourist-photographer who, one gathers, will never know where he is, but only, in looking at his pictures, where he was. Between his eye and the world is interposed the mechanism of the camera—and also, perhaps, the mechanism of economics: having bought the camera, he has to keep using it to get his money's worth. For him the camera will never work as an instrument of perception or discovery. Looking through it, he is not likely to see anything that will surprise or delight or frighten him, or change his sense of things. As he uses it, the camera is in bondage to the self-oriented assumptions that thrive within the social enclosure … He poses the members of his household on the brink of a canyon that the wind and water have been carving at for sixty million years as if there were an absolute equality between them, as if there were no precipice for the body and no abyss for the mind … He is blinded by the device by which he has sought to preserve his vision. He has, in effect, been no place and seen nothing; awesome wonders rest against his walls, deprived of mystery and immensity, reduced to his comprehension and his size, affirming his assumptions, as tame and predictable as a shelf of what nots.[3]

---

[3]Wendell Berry, *The Unforeseen Wilderness: Kentucky's Red River Gorge* (San Francisco, CA: North Point Press, 1991), 16–17.

Berry's description points out how neither the otherworldly man focused on the afterlife nor the tourist sporting a camera can appreciate "the mystery and immensity" of God's creation. How, then, can we reconcile and integrate the material and the mystical? Already by the first century of the Christian era, Judaism was profoundly infiltrated and influenced by Hellenism. The encounter of these two influential cultures and powerful worldviews had already emerged following the rapid spread of Hellenism in Palestine and Alexandria, particularly in the time of Alexander the Great. Yet, the Greek mind and the biblical spirit were not totally compatible. The former sought truth in the harmony and beauty of the world, even if the material and historical were merely an image—and a poor one at that—of the spiritual and the eternal. The latter searched for God in the immediacy of the present, even if God was "the one who is and who was and who is [yet] to come" (Rev. 1:4). By contrast, the early Christian community was deeply marked by an eschatological orientation, by a sense of fervent expectation and anticipation of the immediate and ultimate revelation of God in history. This is why the early Christians implored *maran'atha* ("Come, O Lord!") when celebrating the Eucharist.

Subsequently, the creative synthesis of a Greek interest in the cosmos and a Jewish sense of God's immanence shaped the liturgical and monastic developments of the early Christian tradition. In worship, the Eastern Church Fathers underlined the Eucharist as a foretaste of the final kingdom, an act whereby material creation is transfigured by Christ. In asceticism, the Eastern Church Fathers played a crucial role in reconciling the church with the world (presenting the community of believers as citizens of society, as in Mk 12:17) and separating the church from the world (promoting Christian believers as citizens of heaven, as in Heb. 13:14).

There is another distinction that becomes evident in the theological discourse of the formative Christian era. From the time of Tertullian (d. *c.* 225), theology in the Western part of Christendom was characterized by a deep sense of history and a deep concern with the historical. The emphasis was placed on God working in time, as we understand it, and on an Aristotelian concept of time that marked beginning, middle, and end. This resulted in a preoccupation with the institutional, namely the more material or moral aspects of Christianity. By contrast, Eastern theological thought has been concerned with the meta-historical, namely the more "spiritual" or "mystical" dimensions of the Christian life. The worldly or material were seen in light of the kingdom of heaven and the eternal nature of time.

Indeed, the spirituality of the East has always searched for some ultimate theological reason and justification behind historical occurrences and circumstances. Facts and figures are interpreted in terms of the Holy Spirit; power is understood from the perspective of the sacrament of Eucharist; the world around is considered in relation to the kingdom above. This illuminating teaching about the "last things" or the "last times"—the technical term is "eschatology"—has consistently been at the forefront of theological and spiritual reflection. To the minds of the early Christians, the "end" was integral to the immediate concern for life:

> If the farmer waits all winter, so much more ought you to wait the final outcome of events, remembering who ploughs the soil of our souls ... And when I speak of the final outcome, I am not referring to the end of this life, but to the future life and to God's plan for us, which aims at our salvation and glory.[4]

Unfortunately, throughout the history of Christian doctrine, many theologians assumed that the "last things" or "last times" implied an apocalyptic or escapist attitude to the world. It took a long time for theologians to cease treating eschatology as the last, perhaps unnecessary, chapter in a manual of Christian theology. Eschatology is not the teaching about the last things that follow all other things; it is the teaching about the relationship of all things to those "last things." In essence, it concerns the "last-ness" or "lasting-ness" of all things. This is how Gregory of Nyssa understood the abiding beauty of this world, which was never intended as an end in itself: "After all," as he wrote, "the conclusive harmony in the world has not yet been revealed."[5]

Gradually, however, the Omega came to be interpreted as giving meaning to the Alpha. The eschatological vision of the present began to be perceived as a way of liberation from the evils of stifling provincialism and narrow confessionalism, while the sacrament of the Eucharist was seen as the only perspective of reality inasmuch

---

[4]Cf. John Chrysostom, *On Providence IX*, 1, *Sources Chrétiennes*, vol. 79, 145f.
[5]Gregory of Nyssa, *On the Creation of Man* 23 PG 44.209.

as rooted in the eternal present. Indeed, the ultimate purpose of all that exists—the end of all things—is the Eucharistic offering of all and return of all to the Creator. And that is also the beginning, the original principle of the entire creation. In order to appreciate this, we require:

> An attitude of mind sustained by a constant awareness of an End intensely present and powerful in the here and now of our historical existence and which imbues this existence with meaning. When and where we are ready or bold enough to think and live consistently to the end, we reach out every time to that final boundary where our lives are transcended into life eternal, to the Lord of Time, and in so doing we are living eschatologically: our History becomes not merely a series of happenings but the disclosure and consummation of divine and human destiny, that is, apocalypse ... Human existence remains a temporal existence; its temporal character, however, contains the seed of the Kingdom: it is destined to end from within through self-transcendence and thus "prepare" the coming of the Kingdom. It must end from within as well as from without. The end from without cannot but be destruction, but the End from within is "construction" or "reconstruction" and transfiguration. "Verily, verily I say unto you, that there are some of them that stand here, who shall not taste death, till they have seen the Kingdom of God come with power."[6]

This sense of time as eternally present is very significant for grasping the notion of the world as sacrament. For it is in the sacraments that the world not only looks back in historical time to the moment of creation and to the event of the Incarnation, but also simultaneously looks forward in sacramental time to the redemption and restoration of all things—all humanity, all creatures and all creation—in Christ on the Last Day. In the sacraments, everything visible assumes an invisible dimension; everything created adopts

---

[6]Eugene Lampert, *The Apocalypse of History* (London: Faber and Faber, 1948), 14 and 164. See Alexander Schmemann, *For the Life of the World*, esp. ch. 2, 23–46. The importance of an eschatological, as well as a cosmological vision of history is underlined by Metropolitan John (Zizioulas) of Pergamon in his article "The Book of Revelation and the Natural Environment," Synaxi 56 (in Greek: Athens, 1996), 13–21; for an English translation, see *Creation's Joy* I, 2–3 (Cumberland, RI, 1996).

an uncreated perspective; and everything purely mundane becomes deeply mystical, rendered both timely and timeless.

Sacraments in the Church

This is precisely why the Orthodox Church does not limit the sacraments to seven, preferring instead to speak of every moment and aspect of life—from birth through death—as profoundly and profusely sacramental. Even the funeral service was once classified as a sacrament in Orthodox liturgy. For the sacraments do not work in some magical manner; rather, they function secretly and silently permeating the hearts of those open to the possibility of encounter with God.

In this respect, the seven traditional rites should themselves also relate to creation in a sacramental way. Baptism is more than just a formal initiation to some exclusive society or closed community. It is a re-creation of humanity and the world in the light of Christ. Through the water of baptism, we are immersed into the Cross and Resurrection of Christ (Rom. 6:4), "planted together" (Rom. 6:5) and forever with Christ. In a world where water is carelessly wasted and polluted, the sacrament of baptism reflects the profound action of the Spirit of God brooding over "the face of the world" in the first moments of Genesis (Gen. 1:1).

By the same token, the sacrament of chrismation is more than a confirmation of personal membership in the body of Christ. It recognizes "the seal of the gift of the Holy Spirit" in all human beings, in all corners of the world, and in all elements of the universe through a cosmic interconnection. We are, therefore, called to recognize the face of God "in all places of God's dominion" (Ps. 103:22), in the face of each person, as in the face of the natural world. The word "chrismation" derives from the Greek *chrisma*, which means anointing; and the "anointed one" is the Christ, the Messiah (in Hebrew). Our goal is to be "in Christ" and Christ-like, anointing and healing all of creation.

As we repeatedly highlight in this book, the sacrament of the Eucharist is pregnant with endless possibilities for this deepening sense of communion. It is an invitation to conform to the body of Christ. The Eucharist is never simply a spiritual reward for rigorous ascetic discipline or pious conduct. Instead, it challenges individuals and communities to work for a just society, where basic food and water should be plentiful for all and where everyone should have enough.

The sacrament of confession likewise provides more than simply some opportunity to express remorse for and acquire removal of guilt. Forgiveness provides the grace for healing and the space "for ... giving," for sharing through forgiveness. It focuses attention on others and on God's creation, not only on ourselves and our own. It is a way of reconciliation with the body of Christ. In this respect, it is a way of reintegration into the body of society and the world.

In the sacrament of marriage, two people are invited to experience love and celebrate communion despite the reality at times of brokenness, the pain of separation, and the risk of isolation. How unfortunate that this sacrament has been reduced to a social contract, merely reflecting a romanticized notion of love in the sense of convenience or complacency. On the contrary, marriage is a symbol of the desire for unity between Creator and creation, God and humanity, body and soul, time and eternity, heaven and earth.

The sacrament of holy unction is another healing sacrament. This Orthodox rite is celebrated throughout—and not simply at the end of—life as the outpouring of "the oil of gladness" on the scars of the soul and the wounds of the world. It aims at healing the breach or brokenness between body and soul, mending the shattered parts of the heart and the world, while reconciling heaven with all creation.

Finally, the sacrament of ordination is not merely a formal declaration of exclusive privileges granted to select members of the hierarchy. Priesthood is the royal vocation of all people.[7] Through ordination, the body of Christ receives renewed vitality: The whole world becomes a cathedral, while every person is ordained for the kingdom and no place remains unhallowed.

When we discern the sacramental principle in the world—the presence of God in every person and every place—then we can rejoice and celebrate the fullness of life and the joy of creation.

---

[7]On the priestly way as a model of creation care, see Chapter 6: "On Earth as in Heaven," especially in "A Liturgical View of Creation;" and Chapter 8: "Responding to Denial and Disdain," especially in "The Concept of Stewardship."

A Theology of Creation

Nature, it must be said, speaks a truth scarcely heard among theologians. In our minds, we have eliminated or excluded the role of creation as central to salvation. However, if God is revealed in created nature, then God is present "in all things" (Col. 3:11). There is an invisible dimension to all things visible, a "beyond" to everything beneath heaven. All creation is a palpable mystery, an "incarnation" of cosmic proportions, as if the Word of God was inscribed across the body of the world—in letters perhaps so large that they elude us. Augustine's celebrated phrase about himself in his *Confessions* might be aptly expanded to proclaim that God is "the most intimate interior and the supreme summit" of the whole world.[8]

As already underlined, such a broader, holistic outlook that accepts the land and the world as crucial and essential for a relationship with God bespeaks a unique reverence for the Holy Spirit; it illustrates a close connection between wholeness and holiness. If one can visualize the activity of the Spirit in nature, then one can also perceive the consubstantiality or cosmic interconnection between humanity and nature; then, one would no longer envisage humanity as the crown of a creation, which it is charged or entitled to subdue. Affirming the action of the Holy Spirit safeguards the intrinsically sacred character of creation, its sacramental dimension. A contemporary Greek ballad, whose verses echo the liturgical aspiration to connect heaven and earth, laments the spiritual tension between human attachment to the earth as our mother and human yearning for heaven as our aspiration:

> Heaven, how can I give you my consent?
> Heaven, you are such a distant friend.
> How can I embrace the affection of another lover?
> How can I reject the earth that is my mother, my life,
> The charming light of my life?[9]

---

[8] Augustine, *Confessions*, Book III, vi, 11.
[9] "The Ballad of Yuri" (1983). Lyrics by Nikos Gatsos and music by Manos Hatzidakis.

Briefly put, were God not present in the density of a city, in the beauty of a forest, as well as in the sand of a desert, then God would not be present in heaven either.

Fundamental Intuitions

A Christian vision the world as sacred and sacramental entails three fundamental intuitions about creation. If any one of these is isolated or violated, the result is an unbalanced and destructive vision of the world.

The first intuition is that the world is innately good and naturally beautiful inasmuch as created by a loving Creator.[10] From the beginning of time, creation has personified the biblical words: "And God saw that it was good" (Gen. 1:25). In the Septuagint translation of the Hebrew Bible, the Greek word for "good" (kalos) means "beautiful" and derives from the verb "to call" (kaleo), implying that the world is called by God to become beautiful. The world's vocation is beauty. Nothing is intrinsically evil,[11] except the refusal to see God's work as beautiful. The entire world was created for delight and admiration. In the words of John Chrysostom: "Creation is beautiful and harmonious, and God has made it all for your sake. He has made it beautiful, grand, varied, and rich."[12]

In a naive acceptance of this worldview, one might surrender to the world on its own terms and embrace a spirituality that assumes the conditions and criteria of this world. However, the reality of evil suggests an incalculable cost in the process of cosmic transfiguration. The glory of Mt. Tabor cannot be separated from the suffering of Mt. Calvary; the two hills are complementary as creation "groans" and "travails" in search and in expectation of deliverance (cf. Rom. 8:22).

---

[10]For this three-fold vision, cf. Alexander Schmemann, *Church, World, Mission* (Crestwood, NY: St. Vladimir's Seminary Press, 1979), 77, and *Liturgy and Tradition* (Crestwood, NY: St. Vladimir's Seminary Press, 1990), 98–9. On creation, liturgy and transformation, see David Goa, *A Regard for Creation: Collected Essays* (Dewdney, BC: Synaxis Press, 2008).

[11]Cf. Niketas Stethatos, *Spiritual Paradise* 3, *Sources Chrétiennes* 8, 64f.

[12]John Chrysostom, *On Providence* VII, 2, in *Sources Chrétiennes* 79, 109f.

The second intuition, then, involves an understanding that the world is subject to evil. This more negative principle affirms that creation is fallen, that the world lies within the realm of the prince of evil. Modern thinkers are uncomfortable with any notion of the fallenness of creation, as if it somehow incurs blame on animal or inanimate creation. Yet this principle relates to the radical and realistic consequences of the fall of Adam, as original sin is described in Orthodox theology. The results of the fall are also felt on the level of the created order. This should not surprise us, writes John Chrysostom:

> Why should you be surprised that the human race's wickedness can hinder the fertility of the earth? For our sake the earth was subjected to corruption, and for our sake it will be free of it ... Its being like this or that has its roots in this destiny. We see proof of this in the story of Noah ... What happens to the world, happens to it for the sake of the dignity of the human race.[13]

This second intuition explains, at least in part, the reactionary dualism of the early Manicheans and Gnostics, according to whom the visible creation has not fallen from perfection, but is the work of an inferior deity. Of course, this is not always expressed so crudely. Sometimes, the natural world is regarded as a mere stage, where the larger, more important human drama is played out. Such an apocalyptic worldview dictates withdrawal or escape from the created order, accompanied by condemnation of human beings that wallow in this "inferior" creation and by a conviction about the salvation of only "the few." Such an attitude also isolates a narrow band of human experience as sacred, while all else is relegated to the realm of the profane. By contrast, the goal of the sacramental principle is to affirm that, while nothing is intrinsically nonsacred, everything is innately fallen. This implies that everything—natural and animal, as well as all inanimate and material—requires transformation.

The third intuition acknowledges the world as redeemed. The Incarnation, Crucifixion, and Resurrection of Jesus Christ generated a re-creation of the world. Nonetheless, this redemption can only

---

[13]John Chrysostom, *On Isaiah* V, 4 PG 56.61.

be fully appreciated in light of the other two aforementioned intuitions: createdness and fallenness. Otherwise, the emphasis on human progress and scientific development, along with any optimistic evolution of civilization, can lead to a post-Christian determinism that influenced Western technology and culture in recent centuries. The result is a renunciation of the central axiom, that liberation from sin and transformation of evil are wrought by God at the moment of creation in Genesis as well as in the moment of re-creation in the Incarnation. Human salvation and cosmic transfiguration can only be achieved through cooperation or cosmic reconciliation between Creator and creation, never by imposition of one over the other.

The "honest to God" and the "death of God" debates of the 1960s brought about a total devotion to the world and a fervent commitment to its concerns, but also a total resistance to any self-centered sense of individualism or pietism in religious thought and practice. Theologians of that period alerted us to the danger of disenchanting nature, of stripping it of mysterious charm. This disenchantment of the natural world provides the precondition for the later development of natural science, rendering nature accessible for human use.

Today's lack of regard for and detachment from creation could be signs of indifference toward the world as well as of refusal to engage with the fallenness of the world—the pain and suffering, pollution and ugliness. The Christian attitude toward creation involves a synthesis or dialectical approach that reflects the nature of reality as a world of opposites and tensions. The world is both good and fallen; and these contrasts are rooted in biblical revelation and in mystical experience. There, the world emerges as a sacrament, where the relationship of humanity to the environment is perceived in terms of communion.

Sacrament and Symbol

Ironically, it is the very paradoxical or antinomical character of creation understood as sacrament that preserves the balance between the world as good and as fallen, while dismissing the slightest suspicion of theism or pantheism. A sacrament can be a symbol both of divine transcendence and divine immanence, where transcendence implies more than divine aloofness and mainly active involvement. Sacraments reveal not only a dimension of depth, but predominantly all the abyss of mystery in God, recalling not so much an absent God, but God as present everywhere.

However, when we refer to a sacrament as symbol, we must disabuse ourselves of the notion that symbols are just reminders or signs that point to something else and have an ulterior meaning. The ultimate significance of every symbol is its gratuitousness. A symbol almost resides in its "uselessness": it quite simply *means* and does not mean something *else*. This is a difficult concept to grasp in a world that expects what-you-see-is-what-you-get productivity and usefulness, in an age where everything is measured in terms of consumer value.

In this sense, creation as sacrament is also symbolic—like life, art, and poetry. A symbol is understood in its original sense of a "syn-drome"—an image that brings together (sym-ballo) two distinct or even different, although not divided, realities. Certain symbols are clearly more appropriate than others, particularly those that bear no apparent similarity with the archetype or original, since in those cases there can be no pretense or disguise about association to the archetype. The more veiled and distant the symbol, the greater the revelation (as apo-calypse or un-veiling) of the invisible God.

Consequently, the earth may be the very image of heaven: the ground reveals the abyss above, while the way we treat the world that we tread reflects our relationship with the God we worship. Our role is to dis-cover or un-cover—"at every hour and every moment, both in heaven and on earth,"[14] as well as "in all places of God's dominion" (Ps. 103:22)—the inwardness of the outward, just as visionaries and mystics have done through the centuries. The "end" is already inaugurated and foretasted here among us. A sacrament reveals life and the world as a movement from Alpha to Omega, as a transition from old to new, as "Pascha" or "pass-over" from death to life.

That is not to say sacraments cannot remain isolated from the world or invisible to people. Though open to the mysterious and

---

[14]Prayer of the Ninth Hour in the Orthodox daily liturgical cycle.

eternal, they nonetheless retain a material and temporal nature, articulating a divine glory present everywhere and tangible in all. It is we who frequently fail to see: "If your eye is healthy, your whole body will be filled with light" (Mt. 6:22). We are called to discern the paradoxical things in unity and not in contradiction, to bring about the same reconciliation of all things wrought by art, literature, and religion:

> Who but Shakespeare could bring the airy nothing of heaven into consonance with the heavy reality of earth, and give it a form that ordinary humans can understand? Who but the Shakespeare in yourself? ... When one is truly a citizen of both worlds, heaven and earth are no longer antagonistic to each other ... [It is] only the optical illusion of our capacity—and need—to see things double.[15]

Religion, too, should be included here precisely because the purpose of religion involves the task of "re-relating," of "rebinding" (per the Latin *re-ligio*). The aim of religion is to put all things back together, to heal the wounds of separation. Any religious insight into the natural environment connects and bridges by restoring and reconciling apparent opposites that cause suffering and torment— in therapeutical jargon, to heal the neurosis of dualism.

In Orthodox theology and tradition, the ultimate symbol or sacrament is of course the Eucharist, which constitutes—or, rather, celebrates—the perception and presence of heaven on earth. This is the context within which the Eastern Orthodox tradition proposes the spiritual and intellectual framework for a balanced affirmation of the sacredness of creation. In the words of Symeon of Thessalonika (d. 1429), the Eucharist constitutes "the mystery of mysteries ... the holy of holies, the initiation of all initiations."[16] Or, as Nicholas Cabasilas (d. *c.* 1391) commented earlier: "This is the final mystery. Beyond this it is not possible to go; nor can anything be added to it."[17]

---

[15]Robert A. Johnson, *Owning Your Own Shadow* (San Francisco, CA: HarperCollins, 1991), 108–9.

[16]Symeon of Thessaloniki, *On the Holy Liturgy*, ch. 78 PG 155.253.

[17]Nicholas Cabasilas, *The Life of Christ*, Book II PG 150.548.

The World Redeemed

Through the Divine Incarnation

As already noted, a sacramental consciousness—namely, the recognition of and respect for the sacramental principle—requires an awareness of the centrality of the Incarnation, Crucifixion, and Resurrection in their historical, spiritual, and cosmic dimensions. Eastern Christian writers always regarded the Incarnation as a normative spiritual movement than as an isolated moment. For instance, Gregory of Nyssa uses such terms as "sequence," "consequence," or—his favorite—"progression." This means that God at all times and in all things wills to work a divine incarnation. The Word assuming flesh two thousand years ago is only one— though arguably the last, the most unique, and most formative— in a series of incarnations or theophanies.[18] Divine self-emptying (kenosis: Phil. 2:7) is an essential, not an exceptional characteristic of divinity in the world. It is also an invitation to humanity and all creation to cosmic transformation: "He [Christ] emptied himself, so that nature might receive as much of him as it could hold."[19]

Furthermore, the Incarnation is considered as part of the original creative plan, and not simply as a response to the human fall. It is perceived not only as God's revelation to humanity but primarily as a revelation of the true nature of humanity and the world. This is the line of thought from Isaac the Syrian (seventh century) in the East to Duns Scotus (thirteenth century) in the West. It is also the theological focus of Maximus Confessor, who underlines Christ's presence in all things (Col. 3:11). Christ stands at the center of the world, revealing its original beauty and its ultimate purpose: "At all times and in all things, the Word of God wills and effects the mystery of his divine embodiment."[20]

The Incarnation is thus properly understood only in relation to creation. The Word made flesh is in fact intrinsic to the very act of creation, which came to be through the divine Word. Cosmic incarnation is almost—though the distinction may be

---

[18]See Maximus the Confessor, *Ambiguum* 33 PG 91.1285–8; and *Questions to Thalassius* 15 PG 90.297–300.

[19]Gregory of Nyssa, *On the Psalms* 3 PG 44.441.

[20]Maximus the Confessor, *Ambiguum* 7 PG 91.1084.

scholastic—independent of the historical Incarnation that occurred two thousand years ago. From the moment of creation, the Word assumes the world, which constitutes the body of the Word. The historical Incarnation is a reaffirmation of this reality, not an alteration of reality: "Christ ... was destined before the foundation of the world, but was revealed at the end of the ages for our sakes" (1 Pet. 1:20).

From the moment of creation, the world comprises the living body of the divine Logos. "God spoke a word [logos] and things were made, God commanded and they were created" (Ps. 33:9). In this sense, creation is a continuous process, where the energies of the incarnate divine Word are manifest throughout creation in time and space. Thus, the Incarnation assumes cosmological, and not simply historical significance. Already in the fourth century, Athanasius of Alexandria is unafraid to broaden these implications of the doctrine:

> And what is more strange, being Logos, he is not constrained by anything; rather he himself constrains everything; and just as being in the whole of creation, he is on the one hand outside everything according to essence but within everything with his powers, setting all in order, and extending in every way his providence to everything, and vivifying alike each and every thing, embracing all while himself not being embraced, but being wholly and in every way in his Father alone, so also in this manner is he in the human body, himself vivifying it, while he likewise vivifies all and is in everything being outside everything.[21]

In this perspective, Christ becomes the new Adam that realizes the sacrament rejected by us. The rejection constitutes the original sin of the old Adam, while cosmic reconciliation in Christ is the original blessing of the new Adam. If we reject the world of darkness and accept to live in the light of Christ, then everyone and everything become the embodiment of God in the world.[22] The divine presence is discovered in every detail and every particle of this world; the divine Word (Logos) converses intimately with

---

[21]Athanasius, *On the Divine Incarnation*, ch. 17, 45–6.
[22]See St. Cyril of Jerusalem, *Lectures on the Christian Sacraments*, Lecture II, 2 (Crestwood, NY: St. Vladimir's Seminary Press, 1977), 18, 59–60.

every word (logos) of creation because the divine Logos always and everywhere "wills to effect this mystery of divine embodiment."[23] Such a vision is already expressed in the Alexandrian tradition by Philo and Origen, who envisioned the eternal Logos as variously manifest in history and the world: "There exist diverse forms of the Logos, under which he reveals himself to his disciples, conforming himself to the degree of light in each one, according to the degree of their progress in saintliness."[24]

Maximus Confessor refers to the *logoi* of creation as "conceived" in the Logos of the Father, constituted by the Son and instituted by the Spirit in time and space. We could speak of the uncreated createdness of all things, preexisting in God's will and brought into existence:

> He is mysteriously concealed in the interior causes [logoi] of created beings ... present in each totally and in all plenitude ... In all diversity is concealed that which is one and eternally identical; in composite things, that which is simple and without parts; in those which had one day to begin that which has no beginning; in the visible that which is invisible; and in the tangible that which is intangible.[25]

Indeed, as Maximus affirms, the divine *logos* creates, permeates, and perpetuates all of the *logoi* in creation—spiritual beings and human beings, as well as animals, plants, and minerals:

> Through this Logos, there came to be both being and continuing-to-be, from him the things that were made came to be in a certain way and for a certain reason, and by continuing-to-be and by moving, they participate in God. For all things, in that they came to be from God, participate proportionally in God, whether

---

[23]Maximus Confessor, *Ambiguum* 7 PG 91.1084.

[24]Origen, cf. *Contra Celsum* IV, 16, in *The Ante-Nicene Fathers*, vol. 4, 503.

[25]Maximus, *Ambiguum* 7 PG 91.1085; also columns 1081 and 1329. See *On the Cosmic Mystery of Jesus Christ: Selected Writings from St. Maximus the Confessor*, trans. Paul Blowers and Robert Wilken (Crestwood, NY: St. Vladimir's Seminary Press, 2003), 55. A similar emphasis on the *logoi* of creation is also found in Gregory of Nyssa, *Apologia in Hexaemeron* 5 PG 44.73. See Anestis Keselopoulos, *Man and the Environment: A Study of St. Symeon the New Theologian* (Crestwood, NY: St. Vladimir's Seminary Press, 2001), 104.

by intellect [angels], by reason [humans], by sense perception [animals], by vital motion [plants], or by some habitual fitness [minerals].[26]

In the Cross and Resurrection

However, the words (logoi) of creation require deciphering, which is why the *Macarian Homilies* speak of interpreting the language spoken by creation.[27] For the Eastern mystics, everything in creation must undergo a crucifixion to achieve a resurrection; everything must die in order to rise (cf. Jn 12:24-25). Or, in the words of Maximus the Confessor, all created things must be nailed to the cross, "all visible realities need crucifixion and all intelligible realities require burial."[28] Elsewhere Maximus adds:

> The mystery of the incarnation of the Logos is the key to all the arcane symbolism and typology in the Scriptures, and in addition gives us knowledge of created things, both visible and intelligible. He who apprehends the mystery of the cross and burial apprehends the inward essences of created things; while he who is initiated into the inexpressible power of the resurrection apprehends the purpose for which God first established everything.[29]

Like Christ, everything entails and expects incarnation, crucifixion, and descent into to the deepest, darkest recesses of hell, before it can awaken to the light and arise in the life of Christ. It is what the Greek Fathers call "the little resurrection" (Evagrius of Pontus, d. 399), or "the resurrection before the Resurrection" (John Climacus, d. *c.* 649). The concept of a preliminary or diminutive resurrection is reminiscent of a recent Orthodox saint, who taught that taking delight in God's creation—marveling at the power of the ocean, admiring the beauty of a flower, or

---

[26]*Ambiguum* 7 PG 91.1080, in Blowers and Wilken, 55.

[27]*Macarian Homily* XXXII, 1. For an English translation of the *Homilies*, see *The Classics of Western Spirituality* (New York: Paulist Press, 1982).

[28]Maximus, *First Century on Theology* 67, in G. E. H. Palmer, Philip Sherrard, and Kallistos Ware, *The Philokalia*, vol. 2 (London: Faber and Faber, 1981), 64.

[29]Maximus, *First Century on Theology* 66, *Philokalia*, 127.

observing the magnificence of the stars—is "the little love" that attracts us to the grander love of the Creator.[30] Seraphim of Sarov also greeted his visitors with the Easter salutation: "My joy, Christ is risen!" At the same time, however, we should not overlook the long, hard years of physical struggle, solitude, and silence that precede any resurrection. The Eastern ascetic tradition, at least in its more authentic expressions, perceives the cross as an essential way of transforming the world rather than as a means of tolerating it.

The resurrection of matter—of the body as of material and animal creation—is part and parcel of the early patristic tradition. Justin Martyr (d. c. 165) and John Chrysostom, but especially Irenaeus of Lyons and Methodius of Olympus (d. c. 311), acknowledged and affirmed the sacredness of God's creation in its entirety, which was to be neither discarded nor destroyed but only rejuvenated and restored.[31] Athanasius of Alexandria also underlined this universal dimension: "Christ is the first taste of the Resurrection of all, ... the first-fruits of the adoption of all creation, ... the first-born of the whole world in its every aspect."[32]

The poetic tradition is more expressive and explicit. For Ephraim the Syrian in the fourth century:

At our resurrection, both earth and heaven will God renew, liberating all creatures, granting them paschal joy, along with us. Upon our mother earth, along with us, did he lay disgrace when he placed on her, with the sinner, the curse; so, together with the just, he will bless her too; this nursing mother, along with her children, shall he who is Good renew.[33]

And Symeon the New Theologian taught in the tenth century:

---

[30]The recently canonized Porphyrios, in Convent of Chrysopigi, ed., *Wounded by Love: The Life and Wisdom of Elder Porphyrios* (Limni, Evia: Denise Harvey Publisher, 2005), 218.

[31]See Justin, *On the Resurrection* VII, 8; Chrysostom, *On the Resurrection* 6; Irenaeus, *Against Heresies* V. 34, 2; and Methodius, *On the Resurrection* I. 6, 8.

[32]Athanasius, *On the Divine Incarnation* 20, 48–9; and *Against the Arians* II, 64 PG 26.281–4.

[33]Ephraim, *Hymn* IX, 1, in *Hymns on Paradise*, trans. Sebastian Brock (Crestwood, NY: St. Vladimir's Seminary Press, 1990), 136.

The bodies of the saints shall be made incorruptible in the general resurrection when, of a surety, the whole earthly creation, this visible and perceptible world, will be changed and united with the heavenly.[34]

In similar manner, the liturgical tradition combines the scandalous mystery of the cross with the luminous majesty of the Resurrection; the Crucifixion prepares the way of Resurrection, while the Resurrection presupposes the reality of Crucifixion. Together, the two visualize and materialize the redemption and sanctification of the world. Thus on Good Friday, the Orthodox Church sings: "All the trees of the forest rejoice today. For their nature is sanctified by the body of Christ stretched on the wood of the cross." And on Easter Sunday the celebration reaches a climax: "Now everything is filled with light: heaven and earth, and all things beneath the earth." No wonder St. Nikiphoros of Chios (1750–1821) would claim: "If you don't love trees, you don't love God."[35]

In the Resurrection of Christ, in that joyful abyss of the empty tomb and in the mystical encounters between the risen Lord and his disciples, the inner secret of all creation is revealed. In this sense, the Genesis account of creation can only be understood in the light of the Resurrection "that enlightens every person coming into the world" (Jn 1:9). In the light of Resurrection, one perceives the end and intent of God for all people and all things; one "rejoices and delights in God's presence" (cf. Prov. 8:31); one senses a new creation, a new earth, and a new joy. In the light of Resurrection, Jesus is recognized (cf. Lk. 24:31) as the meaning of the whole world, and not simply as the redeemer of individual souls. All creation belongs to God; and in God one discerns the destiny of all creation. For, "he came to what was his own" (Jn 1:11). He came "to make everyone see the plan of the mystery hidden for ages in God, who created all things, so that the wisdom of God in its rich variety might now be known ... in accordance with the eternal purpose that God carried out in Jesus Christ our Lord" (Eph. 3:9-11).

---

[34]Alexander Golitzin, ed., *St. Symeon the New Theologian, On the Mystical Life: The Ethical Discourses*, vol. 1 (Crestwood, NY: St. Vladimir's Seminary Press, 1995), 42.
[35]Constantine Cavarnos, *The Life of St. Nikiphoros of Chios* (Belmont, MA: Institute for Byzantine and Modern Greek Studies, 1986), 30.

Two feast days of the early Christian church that highlight the new life and new light of the Resurrection are Easter and Epiphany. Both feasts were the foremost baptismal occasions for those entering the church. In celebrating these feasts today, the Orthodox Church preserves the powerful images of renewal and regeneration in its liturgy, which abounds with images declaring that "the entire universe" and "all created matter" contribute to and constitute a cosmic liturgy:

> Now everything is filled with light, heaven and earth, and all things beneath the earth; so let all creation celebrate the Resurrection of Christ on which it is founded.[36]

> Today creation is illumined; today all things rejoice, everything in heaven and on earth.[37]

> Today the earth and the sea share in the joy of the world.[38]

It is not by chance that these two feasts also underline the creation of the world called to cosmic transfiguration "in the first days" (cf. Genesis 1), while understanding the significance of its re-creation "in the latter days" (cf. Heb. 1:2) in light of the restoration of all things "in the last days" (cf. 2 Tim. 3:1).

---

[36]Paschal Canon, 3rd Ode.
[37]Service for the Feast of Epiphany, *Sticheron* (January 6).
[38]Prayer during the Great Blessing of the Waters (January 6).

FIGURE 3 *Megas Ei Kyrie ("Great Art Thou, O Lord, and Marvelous Are Thy Works") by Ioannis Kornaros (1770), Toplou, Crete. Courtesy of His Eminence Metropolitan Kyrillos of Ierapytne and Seteia (Crete).* **See p. 128**

SECTION II

Principles and Practices

6

On Earth as in Heaven

Cardinal Symbols and Values

In a sacramental view of creation, particular symbols and values can offer a corrective path to the wrong road taken from "the beginning" that resulted in our current ecological crisis. In fact, "the beginning" is a good starting-point for any Christian—as, indeed, any Jew and Muslim—thinker when speaking about the environment. However, when we recall the Genesis story, we tend to focus on creation of the world by a loving God, but at the same time tend to forget our connection to the rest of creation. Whether this is a natural reaction or a sign of arrogance, the truth is that we overemphasize our creation "in the image and likeness of God" (Gen. 1:26) and overlook our creation from "the dust of the ground" (Gen. 2:7).

Indeed, there is a misconception of Genesis 1 that should be redressed in light of a commonplace misinterpretation of Genesis 2. The Old Testament command: "Be fruitful and multiply; and fill the earth and subdue it; and have dominion over ... every living thing that moves upon the earth" (Gen. 1:28) has for centuries implied a license to dominate and abuse the world according to selfish indulgence. Yet, how can such an explanation be reconciled in good faith with Paul's advice in the New Testament that we are to "use the world without abusing it" (1 Cor. 7:31)? The Genesis passage should be understood in the context of Adam's naming of the animals:

> Out of the ground the Lord God formed every animal of the field and every bird of the air, and brought them to Adam to see

what he would call them; and whatever Adam called every living creature, that was its name. Adam gave names to all cattle, to the birds of the air, and to every animal of the field. (Gen. 2:19-20)

The naming of animals signifies a loving and lasting personal relationship on the part of Adam with the environment, while also indicating a dialectical relationship between Adam and the Creator. The radical de-divinization of the world is the result of an inability to desire or acquire communion with God. The so-called dominion texts, falsely if not willfully construed as authorizing human control over the rest of creation, must be interpreted in light of human care and responsibility toward creation. We are called to care for the land (cf. Lev. 25:1-5), for domesticated animals (cf. Deut. 25:4), and for wildlife (cf. Deut. 22:6).[1] We fall short of this vocation when we treat the planet as a wasteland, when we fail to be the earth's conscience and voice, eyes and ears. Discerning the face of God in the face of the world[2] is part and parcel of being created "in the image and likeness" of God.

So our "heavenliness" should never overshadow our "earthliness." Most people are unaware that we human beings did not get a day to ourselves in the creation account. In fact, we shared that "sixth day" with the creeping and crawling things of the world (Gen. 1:24-26). As Elizabeth Theokritoff bluntly puts it, citing Gregory of Nyssa:

> Man ... made of the same stuff as the mosquito, receives the divine inbreathing for the sake of the whole creation "in order that the earthy might be raised up to the divine that the one grace might pervade the whole of creation."[3]

We do not have to talk about human beings in exceptionalist or hubristic terms; perhaps our uniqueness or distinction as human

---

[1]See, for example, Gregory Nazianzus, *Homily* 38, 11 PG 36.324. For the interpretation of these "kingship" passages in the Church Fathers, cf. Gregory of Nyssa, *On the Creation of Man* 2 PG 44.132; Basil of Caesarea, *On Psalm* 44, 12 PG 29.413; and Ambrose of Milan, *On the Gospel of Luke* IV, 28 PL 15.1620. For an extended discussion of the scriptural passages and contemporary concepts of dominion, see Elizabeth Theokritoff, *Living in God's Creation: Orthodox Perspectives on Ecology* (Crestwood, NY: St. Vladimir's Seminary Press, 2009), 70–9.
[2]Cf. Augustine, *On Psalm* 148, 15 PL 37.1946.
[3]Elizabeth Theokritoff, *Living in God's Creation*, 67. The passage from Gregory may be found in his *Great Catechetical Oration* VI. See James Herbert Srawley, *The Catechetical Oration of Gregory of Nyssa*, 1st paperback ed. (Cambridge, UK: Cambridge University Press, 2014).

beings lies simply in our peculiar relationship to nature. The creation story—just as the Noah story and the current narrative about climate change—tells us clearly that the salvation of humanity is inseparable from the survival of all living things. We enjoy a binding unity with God's world; it is both helpful and humble for us to recall this truth.

In recent years, we have been painfully reminded of this truth with the cruel flora and fauna extinction, with the irresponsible soil and forest clearance, as with the unacceptable noise, air, and water pollution. Of course, concern for the environment cannot be reduced to superficial or sentimental love. Creation care is a way of honoring our creation by God, of hearing the "groaning of creation" (Rom. 8:22). It is an affirmation the truth of that sixth day of creation. Anything less than the full story—anything less than the full truth—of that sixth day of creation is dangerous heresy.

Speaking of "heresy" in assessing the ecological crisis is not far-fetched at all. For whenever we speak of heavenly or earthly things, we are invariably drawing upon established values about ourselves and our world. The technical language we adopt or the particular species we preserve, all these depend on values and images that we promote, even presume. We tend to call our predicament an "ecological crisis." However, I would propose that the cause of the problem is rooted in the way we visualize and relate to our world.

And a sanctioned—or sacramental—way of appreciating and approaching the world lies in the distinct symbols and values of the Orthodox Church, which include: icons (the way we view and perceive creation), liturgy (the way we celebrate and respond to creation), and ascesis (the way we respect and treat creation). Orthodox icons, liturgy, and spirituality offer a fresh way of seeing and imagining the world as intended by God from "the beginning."

An Iconic Vision of Creation

With regard to the environment, *seeing clearly* is precisely what icons teach us to do.[4] Our generation, it may be said, is characterized by a sense of self-centeredness toward the natural cosmos, by a lack of awareness of the beyond. Icons move beyond what Aristotle

---

[4]Instead of seeing clearly the wonder of God, Basil the Great adopts the analogy of listening carefully to the wisdom of God. See his *Hexaemeron*, in Elizabeth Theokritoff, *Living in God's Creation*, 50–2.

envisaged as art. For classical Greek philosophy, art has nature as its model; or, in Aristotle's words: "Art imitates nature."[5] Even the renowned preacher of fourth-century Constantinople, John Chrysostom, recognizes nature as an exceptional teacher that exceeds human comprehension.[6] Art idealizes nature; art replicates or reproduces the world around us.

Aristotle describes "the poet as an imitator, like a painter (zographos), or any other artist (eikonopoios).[7] Nevertheless, he immediately amends this definition, adding: "The artist necessarily imitates three things: things as they were or are, things as they are said or imagined to be, or things as they ought to be."[8] With this qualification, Aristotle clearly approaches the culture of icons in the Orthodox Christian tradition. For, the world of the icon reveals an eternal dimension in all that we see and experience. It grounds the sensible reality in the truth of the cross and aspires to the transformation of nature. We might say, then, that the icon depicts reality "as it is said or imagined to be," "as it ought to be."

Nonetheless, we seem to have broken the sacred covenant between Creator and creation, between heaven and earth. And it is the icon that restores, that provides cosmic reconciliation. Much like the parables of Christ, the icon reminds us of another world—an alternate or alternative reality, where the will and way of God are paramount. The icon signals the heavenly kingdom, reveals the kingdom among us, while inviting us to recognize and realize the kingdom here and now. The icon aspires to the inner vision of all, the world as created and intended by God. And the iconographer strives to hold together this world and the next. For by disconnecting this world from heaven, we in fact desacralize both.

Any discussion of transcendence or transfiguration, at least from an Orthodox perspective, invariably invokes an introduction to the theology and mystery of the icon, as well as the doctrine behind and the vision beyond icons. The world of the icon not only presupposes a specific way of thinking and demands a particular way of living.

---

[5]Aristotle, *Physics* 194a, 22. For Aristotle, "imitation" (mimesis) is the essence and objective of all art.
[6]*On the Statues* XII, 7. In Philip Schaff, ed., *Nicene and Post-Nicene Fathers*, vol. IX (Peabody, MA: Hendrickson, 1994), 421.
[7]*Poetics* 1460b, 8
[8]Ibid.

It also proposes new insights into the world around us, infusing something of the eternal in everything we see.

It is precisely here that the doctrine of divine Incarnation, at the very heart of iconography, emerges. The Christ dimension is poignantly suggested in Orthodox icons of the enthroned Jesus, particularly in the truly magnificent mosaic of the late thirteenth century that survives in the Monastery of Chora (Kariye Camii in Istanbul). The icon of Christ over the door to the nave is entitled: "Dwelling-place (chora) of the Living."[9]

In this sacramental worldview, nothing and none can be excluded. Symeon the New Theologian poetically describes it as the cohabitation or co-indwelling of Christ in the world: "You make of all Your home and dwelling-place; You become a home to all, and we dwell in You."[10] Everything assumes a Christ dimension; everything becomes sacramental; everything depends on the receptiveness and openness of our heart. By the same token, everything is rendered unique, inasmuch as it has a particular place and singular purpose. This is why early Christian writers categorically confessed that "whatever God did not assume, God did not heal."[11] What God did not reach out and touch, did not come down and sanctify, cannot possibly be embraced by God. There is a saying attributed to Jesus that expresses this certitude of divine omnipresence: "Lift up the stone, and there you will find me, cleave the wood, and I am there."[12]

So icons declare that God is everywhere. And in the icon of Jesus Christ, the uncreated God assumes a concrete visage, a creaturely face, a "beauty that can save the world," as Dostoevsky puts it.[13] This is why in Orthodox iconography, faces are always frontal, depicting two eyes that gaze back at the beholder. The conviction is that Christ is in our midst, "Emmanuel" (Mt. 1:23); the assurance

---

[9]Robert Ousterhoust, *The Art of the Kariye Camii* (London: Scala, 2002), 25.

[10]Symeon the New Theologian, *Hymn* XV, 132–3. As with the concept of sophia, so also the notion of *chora* may equally be applied to the Virgin Mary (see *The Akathist Hymn*, Stasis I: She "contained [choresasa] the One who contains [chorei] the universe"). The concept of sophia is explored elsewhere in Chapter 4: "Divine Sophia." On the relationship between liturgy, iconography, and creation, see *Orthodoxy and Ecology: Resource Book* (Bialystok, Poland: Syndesmos, 1996), 72–81.

[11]Gregory Nazianzus, *Letter 101 to Cleidonius* PG 37.181.

[12]In J. Jeremias, *Unknown Sayings of Jesus* (London: SPCK, 1957), 95.

[13]F. Dostoevsky, in *The Idiot*, cited in Aleksandr Solzhenitsyn's 1970 Nobel Lecture: https://www.nobelprize.org/nobel_prizes/literature/laureates/1970/solzhenitsyn-lecture.html (accessed July 4, 2018).

is that the "undistorted image" of a human being can somehow restore and reveal the original splendor of the living God.

Many icons share similar appearances because the conventions for painting icons specify certain regulations and procedures. Accordingly, profile signifies sin, implying rupture. Faces are "all eyes," eyes wide open, profoundly receptive, eternally susceptive of divine grace. "It is only with the eye of the heart that one can see rightly," says the fox in Antoine de Saint-Exupéry's *The Little Prince*.[14] In the desert of fourth-century Egypt, Abba Bessarion said: "The monk ought to be as the Cherubim and the Seraphim: all eye."[15]

"I see" means that "I am seen," which in turn means that I am in communion. Love encourages us to see things differently, to see things from another perspective, from the perspective of another. Concern, compassion, and care enable us to focus on what really matters in the world. "Love compels us to see things differently, to love the landscapes we have looked at together,"[16] to regard things the way God regards the world, to view creation as "very good." People often think of ecology as merely flora and fauna. But it is much more than that. It is not just about the crops or the fish; it is mainly about the social nexus around them; it has to do with relationships, with connections, and compassion.

Nothing renders the mystery of life more sensible and more sensitive than a human face, which announces an infinite transcendence and a profound presence. Sanctity and salvation have a personal, social, and cosmic dimension. The human face embraces the level of freedom and the anguish of finitude; it grasps for the infinite and flees from the finite. The icon reveals all the tensions, conflicts, and contradictions through which one is called to transparency; every fall, every fault, and every failure is permanently inscribed on the wood of an icon.

In this way, the icon converts the beholder from a restricted worldview to a fuller, more global vision. The light of icons becomes the light of cosmic reconciliation. It is not the waning light of this world; it "knows no evening," to quote an Orthodox hymn on

---

[14]London: Picador Classic, 2015, ch. 21, 34–6.
[15]Bessarion 11, *Sayings*, Ward. Reference to "all eyes" is also found in Barsanuphius and John, *Letters*, 120 and 241.
[16]See Christos Yannaras, *Variations on the Song of Songs* (Brookline, MA: Holy Cross Orthodox Press, 2005), 67.

the feast of Pascha. And so icons depicting events that occurred in daytime are no brighter than icons depicting events that occurred at nighttime. For example, the icon of the sorrowful descent from the cross is no darker than the icon of the Ascension; the icon of the Nativity no brighter than that of the Crucifixion; the somber light of the Last Supper mirrors the supreme feast of light, the Transfiguration.

This is because the icon presupposes another way of seeing things; a "different way of life," as the Orthodox chant on Easter Sunday. The language of the icon is the language of silence and mystery, although it has so much to offer to a world inundated with information and idols. The icon reverses "perspective" as we know or imagine it, doing away with any "objective" distance between this world and the next. There is no double order in creation, no sharp line of demarcation between material and spiritual. For Philip Sherrard:

> [T]he art of the icon is ultimately so to transform the person who moves towards it that he no longer opposes the worlds of eternity and time, of spirit and matter, of the Divine and the human, but sees them united in one Reality, in that ageless image-bearing light in which all things live, move, and have their being.[17]

The icon thus constitutes the epiphany of God in the wood and communicates the existence of the wood in the presence of God. It is neither idealism nor idolatry.

In his definitive work *On Divine Images*, John of Damascus, the eighth-century champion of icons, claims: "I do not adore creation in place of the Creator, but I worship the One who became a creature."[18] Since it is through matter that God has worked salvation,[19] there is an appropriate honor due to material things. It is this salvific power of matter that we have lost and need to rediscover. As John of Damascus writes: "Because of the Incarnation, I salute

---

[17]Philip Sherrard, *The Sacred in Life and Art* (Ipswich, UK: Golgonooza Press, 1990), 84.

[18]John of Damascus, *On Divine Images*, Book 1, ch. 4, 15–16. See *St. John of Damascus, Three Treatises on the Divine Images*, trans. Andrew Louth (Crestwood, NY: St. Vladimir's Seminary Press, 2003), 21–2.

[19]John of Damascus, *On Divine Images*, Book 1, ch. 16, 23–5.

all remaining matter with reverence."[20] Like the unborn child in the womb of its mother, the icon presents to us the visible seeds of divinity in the world. Its art and beauty represent God's Art and Beauty in the creation of the world. In the words of a contemporary Athonite monk:

> The icon brings you a simple, peaceful and life- giving message, coming down from above ... It addresses itself to human nature universally, to human thirst for something beyond. Through the icon, an everlasting and unchanging reality speaks without words, a reality which, in the clarity of silence and in tranquility, raises up from the deepest level, that which unites everything.[21]

So the entire world is an icon, a ladder, a book where one can see, reach, and "read all of God's creation."[22] Within each of us, writes Origen, "there is a second universe: a sun, a moon, and also stars."[23] This is why, in icons, rivers assume a human form, as do the sun and the moon and the stars and the waters. They all have human faces; they all acquire a personal dimension—just like us; just like God. And if the world is an icon, then nothing whatsoever lacks sacredness. Indeed, if God is not visible in creation, then neither could God be worshiped as invisible in heaven. Whenever salvation is separated from the rest of creation, whenever sacraments are spiritualized or internalized, we lose the theological insight and cosmic integrity of the icon.

Whoever views the whole world as an icon experiences from this world the realities of the final Resurrection and the future kingdom. That person has already entered the life of Resurrection and eternity. John Climacus, the seventh-century abbot of St. Catherine's Monastery on Mt. Sinai, was convinced that, in the

---

[20]See the doctrinal formulation of the Seventh Ecumenical Council (Mansi, *Concilia* 13.269).

[21]Vasileios of Iveron, *Hymn of Entry* (Crestwood, NY: St. Vladimir's Seminary Press, 1984), 81. See also Richard Temple, *Icons and the Mystical Origins of Christianity* (London: Element Books, 1990), Gervase Matthew, *Byzantine Aesthetics* (London: John Murray, 1963), and Titus Burckhardt, *Sacred Art in East and West: Its Principles and Methods* (Middlesex, UK: Perennial Books, 1967).

[22]Evagrius of Pontus, *Praktikos*, 92, trans. John Eudes Bamberger (Spencer, MA: Cistercian Publications, 1970), 39.

[23]*Homilies on Leviticus* V, 2, in W. A. Baehrens, ed., *Die Griechischen Christlichen Schriftsteller*, vol. 29 (Leipzig: GCS, 1920), 336.

beauty of the shattered world, "we perceive everything in the light of the Creator God, and therefore acquire immortality before the ultimate Resurrection."[24] The result is a prefiguration of the restored image of the world, a configuration in this world of uncreated and created elements. Perhaps this is why an ancient text, the *Life of St. Stephen the Younger* (c. 764), speaks of the icon as a door.[25] For the world opens up to us and opens us up to a new reality, where the divine light permeates and illumines all things, articulates everything in divine praise.

A Liturgical View of Creation

What icons achieve in space, liturgy accomplishes in song: the same ministry of cosmic reconciliation between heaven and earth. If we are guilty of relentless waste, it may be because we have lost the spirit of worship. We are no longer respectful pilgrims on this earth; we have become ... mere tourists. At a time when we have polluted the air that we breathe and contaminated the water that we drink, we must learn to restore a sense of awe and delight in our relationship to the world.

However, by liturgical I do not imply ceremonial. I mean relational. When Orthodox Christians enter a church, they bow down before the altar, reverence the holy icons, and lower their head at certain points of the liturgy. The whole architecture and symbolism of the church becomes a hymn of entry into another reality, a heavenly kingdom: the musical chants, liturgical gestures, building bricks, mosaic pieces, candle flame, incense fragrance, and ordinary petitions pray altogether: "For favorable weather, for an abundance of the fruits of the earth, and for peaceful times." All of them contain and convey the elements of the Christian faith in a variety of ways, appealing to each person in a unique but tangible manner.

Preaching to a congregation in fourth-century Constantinople, Gregory the Theologian explained: "Through what is accessible and known, God attracts us; while through what is inaccessible and unknown, God is marveled by us and desired still more

---

[24]John Climacus, *Ladder of Divine Ascent*, Step 4, 58 PG 88.892–3.
[25]*Life of St. Stephen the Younger*, PG 100.1113.

ardently."[26] And after receiving the sacrament of the Eucharist, however, Orthodox Christians depart bowing to none, for the life of the world and the heart of the church are at that moment seeded and seated deeply within their hearts. Initiated into the mystery of the Resurrection and transformed by the light of the Transfiguration, we understand the purpose for which God has created all things.[27] An Orthodox hymn, sung during the Office of Matins, declares: "Everything that receives the experience of the Resurrection is filled with joy." Even the limitations of createdness betray not alienation from but attraction to God, and the whole world is rendered a precious gift—received from and returned to God. This is the climax of the Orthodox liturgy: "Your own from your own we offer to you, in all and for all."

Gradually, the experience of awe and wonder is replaced with the certainty of the knowledge and recognition of God in all creation. Human beings must be associated with, and never dissociated from, the created world; it is through the human person that the created world will be transformed and offered to God. Then, the world is freed from natural limitations and becomes a bearer of new life. In the words of Metropolitan John of Pergamon:

> We believe that in doing this "in Christ" we, like Christ, act as priests of creation. When we receive these elements back, after having referred them to God, we believe that because of this reference to God we can take them back and consume them no longer as death but as life. Creation acquires for us in this way a sacredness, which is not inherent in its nature but "acquired" in and through man's free exercise of his Imago Dei, i.e., his personhood. This distinguishes our attitude from all forms of paganism, and attaches to the human being an awesome responsibility for the survival of God's creation.[28]

---

[26]Gregory the Theologian, *Homily* 38, 7 PG 36.317. The ascetic dimension of such a worldview is almost taken for granted in the patristic tradition. A positive vision of the world both presupposes and produces purification. Thus Gregory adds that in our ardent desire for God through matter, we in turn are "purged" and "divinized."

[27]Cf. Maximus Confessor, *Gnostic Chapters* I, 66 PG 90.1108. On the priestly dimension of human nature, see Kallistos Ware, "The Value of the Material Creation," *Sobornost* VI, 3 (London, 1971), 154–65.

[28]John Zizoulas, "Preserving God's Creation," *King's Theological Review* 13, 1 (London, 1990), 5.

This priestly dimension or para-priestly character of the human person was previously affirmed by Leontius of Cyprus (556–634):

> Through heaven and earth and sea, through wood and stone, through relics and Church buildings and the Cross, through angels and people, through all creation visible and invisible, I offer veneration and honor to the Creator and Master and Maker of all things, and to him alone. For the creation does not venerate the Maker directly and by itself, but it is through me that the heavens declare the glory of God, through me the moon worships God, through me the stars glorify him, through me the waters and showers of rain, the dew and all creation, venerate God and give him glory.[29]

The truth is that we react to nature with the same sensitivity as we respond to a human being. This is why, in liturgy, we also pray "for the sick, the suffering, and for those in captivity." If we assume that we cannot treat people like things, it may be time for us to accept that we should not treat even things like mere things. If we recognize that it is immoral to exploit and illegal to abuse human beings, perhaps it is time for us to realize that it is equally immoral to exploit nature and illegal to abuse its resources. Or, as Russian philosopher-theologian Vladimir Solovyov (1853–1900) put it: "[N]ature or earth is not merely a thing ... an instrument for obtaining things."[30] After all, if all of our spiritual activities are measured by their impact on people, especially the poor, then they are also manifest in our treatment of the planet, especially its natural resources.

So liturgy is the language that commemorates and celebrates the innate and intimate connection between God, people, and things, between everyone and everything—what in the seventh century Maximus the Confessor called a "cosmic liturgy";[31] this is what in the same century Isaac the Syrian described as acquiring: "A merciful

---

[29]Leontius of Cyprus, cf. his *Apologetic Sermon 3 on the Holy Icons* PG 93.1604.

[30]Vladimir Solovyov, *The Justification of the Good: An Essay on Moral Philosophy* (Grand Rapids, MI: Eerdmans, 2005), 299–300.

[31]Pierre Teilhard de Chardin wrote in similar fashion, echoing Maximus Confessor's image of the "cosmic liturgy." See his *Mass on the World in Hymn of the Universe*, trans. G. Vann (New York: Harper & Row, 1972), 16: "Once again the fire has penetrated the earth ... the flame has lit up the whole world from within."

heart, which burns with love for the whole of creation—for humans, for birds, for the beasts, for demons—for all God's creatures." There is a dimension of art, music, and beauty in nature's liturgy. Which means that whenever we narrow life—even religious life—to ourselves and our own interests, we are neglecting our vocation to reconcile and transform all of creation. Our relationship with this world determines our relationship with heaven; the way we treat the earth is reflected in the way that we pray to God. Walking on this planet and kneeling in church are ultimately tantamount to the same thing.

An Ascetical View of Creation

Of course, it would be an understatement to say that this world does not always look or feel like heaven. In the wake of the Fukushima nuclear disaster in March 2011, or British Petroleum's oil disaster in April 2010, it was admittedly difficult to perceive what Dostoevsky called "the divine mystery in things." How, then, do we reconcile mystery with reality?

The answer again lies in creation—in a tree, or a sacred root, as John Chrysostom and John of Damascus are fond of interpreting the Cross.[32] This is why, in his Letter to the Colossians, St. Paul writes: "Through [Christ], God was pleased to reconcile to himself all things, whether on earth or in heaven, through the blood of his cross (1:20)." Reference here to "the blood of the cross" is a clear indication that a cost is involved. It reminds us of the reality of human failure and the need for cosmic repentance and cosmic resurrection. What is required is nothing less than a radical reversal of our perspectives and practices.

In preparation for and partaking of the Eucharist as well as in the priestly function itself, the symbols and signposts of sacrifice, asceticism, and gratitude are essential for a sacramental approach to life and the world. These three central aspects described by

---

[32]John Chrysostom, *On the Creation of the World* V, 7; and John of Damascus, *An Exact Exposition of the Orthodox Faith* II, 11. See also Origen of Alexandria, *On First Principles* IV. 3, 1, cited in Robert Grant, *Early Christians and Animals* (New York: Routledge, 1999), 49.

Norman Wirzba enable us to live more honestly and humbly within God's creation:

> Life is a miraculous, inexplicable gift. It exceeds all economies of exchange. As priests we stand within it, beggar-like, unable to fully or properly receive it, because whatever we would claim or take already exceeds our longing and comprehension. The best that we can do is make our lives into an offering to others, not for purposes of repayment (how could we ever know what sufficient payment would be?) but as the effort to overcome the sinful pride and aggression that otherwise distort or bring life to a halt. In this self-offering we often do not know what we are doing. Nor can we predict or control what the offering will accomplish. What we can do is open ourselves to the many dramas of life going on around us, trusting that our offerings will enrich the multiple memberships of which we are only one part.[33]

There is a price, then, to pay for our wasting. The balance of the world has been shattered, and the ecological crisis will not be solved with sentimental slogans or recycling programs. On the Feast of the Exaltation of the Cross (September 14) each year, Orthodox liturgy chants: "Every tree of the forest can rejoice, for their nature has been sanctified by Christ, who planted them at the beginning [of creation] and now hangs stretched out on the tree [of the cross]."[34] The "tree of the cross" reveals a way out of our ecological impasse by proposing self-denial as a solution to self-centeredness. The cross is not merely an emblem of faith or piece of jewelry; it is the very transformation of brokenness and failure. Perhaps this is why so many are still in denial about climate change—whether claiming it is a hoax or assuming that it can be corrected by other or better, more moral or more sustainable, ways. Societies embarrassed of failure should contemplate the cross; while the cross is considered a symbol of life and hope, it is quintessentially a sign of dead loss and sheer abandonment.

---

[33]Norman Wirzba, "A Priestly Approach to Environmental Theology: Learning to Receive and Give Again the Gifts of Creation," *Dialog: A Journal of Theology* 50, no. 4 (Winter, 2011): 356–64. [Here at 363–4]
[34]On the tree of the cross, see Cyril of Alexandria, *Against Julian* 3 PG 76.929.

In the Orthodox spiritual tradition, the cross translates into *ascesis:* a way of respecting and treating creation through resignation, repentance, and restoration. The way of the cross is self-sacrifice and self-discipline—a sacrifice and surrender—that ultimately results in liberation from egocentrism, a way of assuming responsibility for one's actions and one's world. It is sometimes helpful to look in the mirror and ask: Is what we have what we need? How do I reflect the world's thirst for oil or greed that is destroying the planet?

It is compelling that the earth constantly reminds us of our denial. Still, we stubbornly refuse to accept that our comfortable lives, dependent as they are on cheap energy, are in any way responsible for the Gulf of Mexico being polluted by millions of gallons of oil. And that was not an isolated tragedy: There were five unprecedented oil spills by Chevron and Exxon/Mobil in 2010 (including the largest recorded in China) and seven in 2011 (including the worst recorded in Northern Africa and New Zealand). How can we, as intelligent human beings, believe that a century of pumping oil-fired pollution into the atmosphere has no ramification?

Classical Christian literature speaks of the divine Incarnation as rendering humanity with new sight, new hearing, new scent, new taste, and new touch—as endowing us altogether with new spiritual senses[35] that enable us to perceive the deeper or distant mystery of things. In this light, human beings become another creation, a new creation, a recreation of the world by the divine Word. We are called to relearn how to notice and feel, how to hear and smell, as well as how to taste and touch. In order to perceive this world in the light of the next, we need to acquire new sense, spiritual senses, becoming entirely new people.

We can begin with the practice of ascesis, which entails learning to be free, uncompelled by ways that use the world; characterized by self-control and the ability to say "no" or "enough." Ascesis aims not at detachment or destruction, but at refinement and restoration. Take the familiar example of fasting in the Christian tradition, a discipline that transcends the narrow sense of restricting one's intake of food. Learning to fast is actually learning to share with joy and

---

[35]For the origin of the concept of spiritual senses in Origen of Alexandria, see especially his *Dialogue with Heracleides* in *Sources Chrétiennes* 67, 78–102, together with Karl Rahner, "Le debut d'une doctrine des cinq sens spirituels chez Origène," *Revue d'ascetique et de mystique* 13 (1934): 113–45.

gratitude;[36] it is learning to give and not simply give up. It is living for communion, and not merely for consumption. It is recognizing in other people faces—icons, we might say—and recognizing in the earth the face of God.

Before advocating or preaching about the environment to others, we might consider how we ignore this call ourselves. Everyone is guilty of consuming far more than we should, far more than we deserve, far more than someone in Mozambique or Madagascar. Returning to the practice of fasting, we might conclude that to fast is to see more clearly the original beauty of the world. It is moving away from what I want to what the world needs. Fasting means valuing everything for itself, not for myself. It involves regaining a sense being filled with God-liness.

Consumption and Communion

Fasting from food does, however, provide profound insights on ascesis. The two extremes of food consumption include the ascetic who eats temperately and the glutton who eats excessively—both risking abuse of the very bodies created by God. Asceticism involves not only self-control with regard to the amount or indulgence of food, but also entails self-awareness in order to achieve moderation for oneself and for the sake of the world.

Food—along with its corollary vices of greed and gluttony, as well as its concomitant symptoms of indifference and waste—comprises the single, most striking factor in ecological exploitation and economic inequity. The reason people go hungry today is not the number of people in the world. If there were fewer people but the way we distribute food remained the same, the poor would still go hungry. The problem is the way we distribute food through the market as private property, so that the people who are poor cannot afford it. Moreover, while religious communities are often afraid

---

[36]On fasting and joyful gratitude, see Basil of Caesarea, *Homily 4 On Giving Thanks*, in *Saint Basil the Great, On Fasting and Feasting*, trans. Susan Holman and Mark DelCogliano (Yonkers, NY: St. Vladimir's Seminary Press, 2013), 97–122. On fasting in an age of consumerism, see Andrew Walker and Costa Carras, eds., *Living Orthodoxy in the Modern World: Orthodox Christianity and Society* (Crestwood, NY: St. Vladimir's Seminary Press, 2000), especially Kallistos Ware, "Lent and the Consumer Society," ch. 5, 64–84.

to touch on the problem of overpopulation, it is in fact primarily a problem of education—especially women's education, whereby the latter can gain control of their fertility and nutrition.[37]

Food, then, is about far more than just eating or surviving. It is about relationships and communion. As Norman Wirzba says:

> Food is about the relationships that join us to the earth, fellow creatures, loved ones and guests, and ultimately God. How we eat testifies to whether we value the creatures we live with and depend upon. To eat is to savor *and* struggle with the mystery of creatureliness. When our eating is mindful, we celebrate the goodness of fields, gardens, forests and watersheds, and the skill of those who can nurture seed and animal life into delicious food. We acknowledge and honor God as the giver of every good and perfect gift.[38] But we also learn to correct our own arrogance, boredom and ingratitude. Eating invites people to develop a deeper appreciation for where they are and who they are with so that their eating can be a sacramental rather than a sacrilegious act.[39]

The sacramental dimension of feasting and fasting is acknowledged by philosopher and farmer alike. Thus, for Sergei Bulgakov, "food is natural communion—partaking of the flesh of the world."[40] By the same token, for Wendell Berry:

---

[37]See Raj Patel, *Stuffed and Starved: The Hidden Battle for the World Food System* (Brooklyn, NY: Melville House, 2012), especially chs. 5 (107–28) and 8 (221–58). On the ethical considerations of the global food and seed industries, see Franz-Theo Gottwald, "Genetically Modified Food: Ethical Implications along the Food Chain," in *Democracy, Ecological Integrity and International Law*, ed. J. Ronald Engel, Laura Westra and Klaus Bosselman (Newcastle upon Tyne, UK: Cambridge Scholars, 2010), ch. 15, 287–305, where Gottwald concludes: "[The] *integrity of creation* must serve as ethical barrier—profit does not justify everything feasible" (294). On the sacramental dimension of food, see Fred Bahnson, *Soil and Sacrament: A Spiritual Memoir of Food and Faith* (New York: Simon & Schuster, 2013).
[38]Cf. Jas 1:17.
[39]Norman Wirzba, *Food and Faith: A Theology of Eating* (New York: Cambridge University Press, 2011), 4. See especially chs. 1 (1–34) on a theological understanding of food and 5 (144–78) on a Eucharistic view of eating.
[40]Sergei Bulgakov, *Philosophy of Economy: The World as Household* (New Haven, CT: Yale University Press, 2000), 103.

To live, we must daily break the body and shed the blood of Creation. When we do this knowingly, lovingly, skillfully, reverently, it is a sacrament. When we do it ignorantly, greedily, clumsily, destructively, it is a desecration.[41]

There are two particular images of food and sustenance that bespeak a Christian response to the ecological crisis. In a Gospel parable, Jesus tells of a poor man, Lazarus, who sat at the gate of a rich man, "longing to satisfy his hunger with what fell from the rich man's table" (Lk. 16:21). The rich man never once invited Lazarus to sit with him. What is worse, the rich man probably did not even notice Lazarus, though he was so close to his table. I wonder sometimes whether we even notice what goes on around us. Yet, how can we respond if we do not notice, if we are unaware or uninformed? And how many people do we invite to sit at our table? What sort of issues—poverty, or peace, or the environment, or healthcare, or education, or social justice, or human rights—are we willing to embrace? How open or inclusive is the table at which we have chosen to sit in the first place?

In another iconographic representation, sitting under the shade of the oak trees at Mamre, Abraham received an unexpected visit from three strangers. The story is recorded in Genesis, Chapter 18 (see also Heb. 13:2), and describes the venerable patriarch of Israel spontaneously and sincerely sharing his friendship and food, extending such generous hospitality to these unexpected visitors that, in the Orthodox spiritual tradition and iconographic commentary, this scene is interpreted as symbolizing the Holy Trinity. In fact, the only authentic image of the Holy Trinity, of God as communion, in the Orthodox Church is precisely the depiction of this scene of encounter from rural Palestine.

In traditional Orthodox representations of "Abraham's hospitality," iconographers portray the guests on three sides, allowing an open space on the fourth side of the table. This is particularly conspicuous in the renowned icon by Andrei Rublev (c. 1360–1430), whose image is a celebration and communication of life.[42] The icon reveals the potential sacredness of the world not

---

[41]Wendell Berry, *The Gift of Good Land: Further Essays Cultural and Agricultural*, revised edition (Berkeley, CA: Counterpoint, 2009), 281.
[42]For a detailed description of selected icons of the Trinity, including the one by Andrei Rublev, see Paul Evdokimov, *The Art of the Icon: A Theology of Beauty* (Pasadena,

merely as promise, but also as vocation. With its open seat at the table, the icon of the Trinity serves as an invitation. Will we sit at the table with strangers?

In 2005, then Senator Barack Obama (addressing the National Association for the Advancement of Colored People's Fight for Freedom) noted: "It's one thing to know that everyone has a seat at the lunch counter, but how do we figure out how everyone can pay for the meal?" In order to begin to care for the hungry—as well as care for all those who are suffering—we must first give them a seat at the table. I recall the moving scene of Pope Francis during his official visit to Washington, DC in 2015, when he declined a meal with the US Congress, choosing instead to eat with the homeless in a neighboring park.

The icon of the greedy rich man unwilling to share dramatically contrasts with the icon of hospitality that inspires us to control our greed and to let go of our selfish desires, so that, everyone seated at the table may have equally full plates.

Rapacity and Resurrection

There is another icon that reinforces the ascetic principles of renunciation, repentance, and resurrection.[43] The "Great Blessing of the Waters" in an eighteenth-century image by Ioannis Kornaros (1745–1796) at the Monastery of Toplou in Crete, depicts at the very center a scene from the baptism of Christ, commemorated each year on January 6 at the Feast of Theophany. The language from that day's service—echoed in the baptismal rite of every Orthodox Christian—makes reference to the beauty of creation: "Great are you, O Lord, and wondrous are your works; no words suffice to hymn your wonders!"

In this elaborate and bustling icon, there is a panorama of detailed settings from city life in Nineveh and Samaria alongside

CA: Oakwood Publications, 1990). On the icon of Rublev, Pavel Florensky once exclaimed, "There is Rublev's Trinity, therefore there is God." Cf. V. Bychkov, *The Aesthetic Face of Being* (Crestwood, NY: St. Vladimir's Seminary Press, 1993), 42.
[43]The interpretation that follows is inspired by the address of Ecumenical Patriarch Bartholomew during the Black Sea Symposium in Bergen, Norway, on June 24, 2003, and cited in *On Earth as in Heaven*, ed. John Chryssavgis (New York: Fordham University Press, 2012), 204–9.

farmers working in their fields, boats crossing rivers, and "every kind of beast and bird, of reptile and sea creature" (Jas 3:7), "living things both small and great" (Ps. 104:25). The covenant between Creator and creation is displayed as a large rainbow toward the middle left. Symbolical depictions include the Trinity, the Nativity, and the Last Supper, while biblical narratives portray the creation and recreation of Adam and Eve, as well as the Incarnation and Resurrection.

In the lower left corner, nature is portrayed as a woman— the mother earth honored by many indigenous people, including the Aborigines of Australia and Natives of North America. Her extended open arms beckon and welcome all people and all things—embodying and embracing every instant and incident of the icon.

However, two distinctive scenes of note, found in the upper left of the icon, relate in a unique way to creation and asceticism: the killing of Abel by his brother Cain and Jonah's ejection from the mouth of a sea monster. When Cain sensed that God was more pleased with Abel's sacrifice than his, he murdered his own brother in a rage of jealousy. Cain's lack of self-control led to a punishment of cursed soil that would no longer give him strength (Gen. 4:12). The violent scene foreshadows the ravaging of the earth today by uncaring polluters and mercenary policies. Unless the world begins to appreciate and apply the ascetic principles of self-examination and self-control, the violence and destruction to the earth will persist.

What we need is repentance for our callous disrespect, the repentance depicted in the second icon of a large sea beast ejecting Jonah from his mouth. God ordered Jonah to ask the city of Nineveh to repent; instead, Jonah avoided the task, boarded a boat, was thrown overboard, and swallowed by a large sea monster. While inside the sea monster, Jonah recognized his error in disobeying God, repented, and asked for God's forgiveness; whereupon the fish vomited Jonah onto land, a dramatic symbol of repentance and resurrection. This dramatic story and icon reminds us of the inevitable and vital way of ascetic renunciation and resignation. It is possible to recognize that greed, selfishness, and violence transgress and trample on the covenant with our Creator, who seeks cosmic reconciliation and restoration with us as well as with all creation.

A Way Out of an Impasse

Not long ago, my elder son and I paid a routine visit to the optometrist. Alex is not as meticulous as he should be with his eye care. So as he received his new prescription, I overheard his reaction: "Wow! *That's* what I'm supposed to see?" When we look at our world, what do *we* see? Because the way we view our planet will invariably reflect how we relate to it. We *treat* our planet in a god-forsaken manner precisely because we *see* it in this way.

In his now classic article entitled "The Roots of our Ecological Crisis," medieval historian Lynn White Jr. already suspected this truth, noting that:

> The Greek saint contemplates; the Western saint acts. The Latins felt that sin was moral evil, that salvation lay in right conduct. The implications of Christianity for the conquest of nature would emerge more easily in the Western atmosphere.[44]

Creation care is not merely an intention or decision to act differently. Far too often, we are convinced that solving the ecological crisis is a matter of doing things differently, perhaps more effectively or more sustainably.[45] Yet, entrusting climate change to a more refined

---

[44]For more on White, see Chapter 8: "Responding to Denial and Disdain."

[45]Karl Barth understood this more than half a century ago. See Karl Barth, ed. G. W. Bromiley, *Church Dogmatics* IV/2 (London: Bloomsbury Academic, 1958), §64, 233:

> "Looking back, we may well ask with amazement how it was that the Reformation, and (apart from a few exceptions) the whole of earlier and especially more recent Protestantism as it followed both Luther and Calvin, could overlook this dimension of the Gospel which is so clearly attested in the New Testament— its power as a message of mercifully omnipotent and unconditionally complete liberation from corruption, death and wrong as the power of evil. How could Protestantism as a whole, only too faithful to Augustine, the "father of the West," orientate itself in a way which was so one-sidedly anthropological (by the problem of repentance instead of by its presupposition—the kingdom of God)? In other words, how could it become such a moralistic affair—so dull, so indifferent to the question of man himself, and therefore so lacking in joy? How could it possibly overlook the fact that it was depriving even its specific doctrine of justification and sanctification of so radiant a basis and confirmation by not looking very differently at the character of the self-revelation of God in the Son of Man as it emerges in the miracles of Jesus, in these works of God; by not considering the freedom of the grace which appeared in Him? And *in spite*

capitalism is likely to be as productive as asking the iceberg to fix the Titanic. The logic and method that led to the critical challenge we currently face cannot be the same logic and method that generate a solution to our ecological predicament, as pointed out by Greek theologian Christos Yannaras:

> This is what the environmental movements unfortunately do: they want to preserve the utilitarian logic of "development," simply changing its evaluation of what is more useful from an egocentric, human point of view, so that it is no longer a mindless "exploitation," but a well-reasoned (by rationalist and self-interested principles) "protection." It is the same logic as that which was taught in the catechetical schools in my youth: Don't go to brothels to avoid catching syphilis! Personally, I believe that the destruction of the ecosystem cannot be slowed down or halted unless there is a change of attitude in us toward nature.[46]

At the same time, however, it would be arrogant to presume that the "utilitarian logic" was manufactured by the rationalistic West or by Western Christianity, while a "changed attitude" is monopolized by the Orthodox East or the Orthodox Church. Orthodox Christians often regard their theology as somehow self-righteously

---

of its many saints and their many miracles, there is nothing much to be learned in this respect from Western Catholicism, with its almost exclusive concentration on the work of man in canon law, mysticism and a correct social and perfect monastic morality. From the Reformers we can at least know what free grace might be, and therefore learn, perhaps, to recognize its radicalism as revealed in the miracles of Jesus. But where the Reformers were opposed and the doctrine of free grace completely rejected, it seems that an almost hopeless barrier was set up to any advance in this direction. *It puts us to shame, however, that in its strange and contradictory fashion the Eastern Church has not ceased to see and to take seriously what has to be seen at this point—and seen in a way which is completely new for us troubled Westerners ... The time has now come finally to emphasize the connection which emerges in the New Testament passages between the actions of Jesus and the faith of the men to whom and among whom they occur. This is sometimes so distinct that if we are really to understand the general nature or direction of the miracles of Jesus we cannot possibly ignore it."* [Emphases mine]

[46]See Christos Yannaras and Norman Russell, *Metaphysics as a Personal Adventure: Christos Yannaras in Conversation with Norman Russell* (Yonkers, NY: St. Vladimir's Seminary Press, 2017), 120.

monopolizing salvation, as sanctimoniously encapsulating in their spirituality the solution to all global problems. Orthodox would do well to look *inside* their rich tradition to discern ways of responding to climate change; but they would also do well to look *outside* their tradition to discover ways of acknowledging and embracing that same tradition.

A notable and remarkable example is the recent release by Pope Francis of the Encyclical Letter *Laudato Si'* [On Care for Our Common Home], which is considered in the concluding chapter to this book. Other instances where I have encountered the honesty to address the need for sacrifice to replace selfishness and gratitude to substitute greed may be found in diverse, albeit isolated statements—as, indeed, in diverse, albeit important policies— in the Quaker tradition.[47] I have also been surprised to observe that the call for surrender or abandonment of—indeed, even the appeal to challenge or dispute—the lifestyles with which we have become accustomed and anaesthetized more than often arise in non-religious circles. The provocation to adopt simpler ways and customs is less frequently welcomed in traditional religions and institutional churches.

Thus, I was also pleased to come across an eloquent call for personal and societal transformation by James Gustave Speth.[48] The same emerged in remarks made by Naomi Klein, "a secular Jewish feminist," as she described herself during a conference at the Vatican, where Klein fearlessly claimed: "In a world where profit is consistently put before both people and the planet, climate economics has everything to do with ethics and morality. Because if we agree that endangering life on Earth is a moral crisis, then it is incumbent on us to act like it."[49]

---

[47]See Quaker statements in the United States from their annual conference in 1996 entitled *Simple Life* and the Third Assessment Report (January 2001) of the Intergovernmental Panel on Climate Change.

[48]James Gustave Speth, *The Bridge at the Edge of the World: Capitalism, the Environment, and Crossing from Crisis to Sustainability* (New Haven, CT: Yale University Press, 2008).

[49]The conference was organized by the Pontifical Council on Justice and Peace on July 1–2, 2015. How ironic that a "secular Jewish feminist" would resonate more closely with "Orthodox theology" than some ordained clergyman! See Chapter 8: "Responding to Denial and Disdain."

The truth is that we do not simply need climate action, "climate solutions that adhere to market logic."[50] It is not just a matter of emphasizing geo-engineering or antipollution measures, of fracking natural gas or genetically modifying crops, or even of increasing nuclear or solar power. The issue is neither securing a more moderate, more palatable consumerism; nor discovering a mitigated, more restrained development.[51] There is a more radical response—a far more revolutionary reformation—that is required. In this respect, perhaps we need more revolution than evolution or development. In the final analysis, we are not searching for ways to settle back into complacent lifestyles; we cannot possibly return to the ways that led us in the first place to the predicament that we are presently facing. How tragic it would be to conceptualize the future in the manner of Richard Branson boasting to journalists that, if only we could go green for a while, then "we can carry on living our lives in a pretty normal way—we can drive our cars, we can fly our planes, life can carry on as normal."[52]

Paradoxically, ecological correction may in fact begin with environmental in-action or mere awareness. It is a matter of contemplation, of *seeing* things differently. Progress is not just a matter of moving without stopping; it is slowing down, even stopping, in order to consider proper direction and appropriate action. First, we must *stop* what we are *doing*. Then we might gain new "in-sight" into our world. And peering through this lens, foreign policy and the economy actually *look* different, whereby we can abandon the urge for unbridled expansion and instead focus on the sustainability that we so desperately need. The ancient Greeks understood very well that *oikonomia* (economy) perceived as removing something from somewhere and replacing it elsewhere solely for profit is intrinsically nonsensical and unethical. Aristotle appreciated this and bequeathed it to Aquinas; thereafter, the world, East and West, somehow misplaced or displaced it.

---

[50]Naomi Klein, *This Changes Everything: Capitalism vs. the Climate* (New York: Simon & Schuster, 2014), 279.

[51]The Club of Rome already emphasized such solutions in 1972, when it commissioned the seminal book by authors Donella H. Meadows, Dennis L. Meadows, Jørgen Randers, and William W. Behrens III, *The Limits to Growth* (Falls Church, VA: Potomac Associates/Universe Books, 1972) on pollution, population, food production, and resource depletion.

[52]Klein, *This Changes Everything*, 232.

It is actually possible to see the world in ways other than through the glass of the market; there actually *can* be a green way of looking at the world apart from that of Alan Greenspan, former chairman of the United States Federal Reserve. We desperately need a different economy, a new economy. What we face today is nothing less than a choice about how genuinely human we want to be. In Deuteronomy, Moses proclaims: "Today, I am giving you a choice between good and evil, between life and death ... Choose life!" (Deut. 30: 14-19). We must develop a worldview that involves more permanent—not short-term, make-shift, or band-aid—solutions for creation. Such solutions should be based on ethical values and spiritual choices.

We shall return to the question of choices in later chapters. For now, it is sufficient to ask ourselves whether we can commit to the path proposed above concerning the way we view, celebrate, and treat creation—a path that reflects spiritual values and communicates generosity and gratitude, not arrogance and greed. Because if we fail to do so, then a significant patch of the Gulf Coast in the United States will have been lost in vain; and the Fukushima nuclear disaster precipitated by a tsunami will have gone unnoticed. Will their "prophetic" warnings be heard? Ongoing and escalating oil spills, chemical spills, and coal ash spills throughout America— along with endless and extreme wildfires, floods and earthquakes throughout the world—would seem to indicate otherwise. The science tells a different story.

7

Living Cosmology

Creation in Faith and Science

For some time now, specialists in the scientific community have analyzed data and issued prophetic warnings about the catastrophic consequences of abusing and neglecting our planet. Their data augments the urgings of those theologians who call for respect and care for God's creation. At the same time, a handful of scientists dispute the facts of the scientific majority, which is then used by some religious leaders to downplay the prophetic warnings. This tension and intertwining of faith and secular scientific thinking is not new. In fact, the relationship between religion and science over many centuries has proved one of the most fascinating and challenging areas of study and scholarship. One reason for this is that the conversation between religious belief and the natural sciences brings to the table two of the most fundamental and formative forces of society, both of which seek to explore the great mysteries of human nature.

It is in the nature of the universe to move forward between great tensions, between dynamic opposing forces. If the creative energies in the heart of the universe succeeded so brilliantly in the past, we have reason to hope that such creativity will inspire us and guide us into the future. In this way, our own generativity becomes woven into the vibrant communities that constitute the vast symphony of the universe.[1]

These are the closing words of *Journey of the Universe* that takes the reader on a systematic voyage—actually, a sacred pilgrimage—through the creation of the sun and stars, the complexity of life and death, and the connection between animals and humankind. It is the same inspiring tension that has survived the conflict between sacred and secular, the clash between religion and science, as well as the confrontation between heaven and earth.

Like the tension between sacred and secular, there has long been a clash between religion and science, two clearly distinct and often disparate disciplines looking for truth. This chapter briefly surveys the mystical and prophetic literature, in both religious and philosophical circles, that attempts to explain and reconcile those tensions with reflections on: the universal seed in Genesis by church Fathers, the logos of the ancient Greeks and early Christian writers, the distinction between the immutable essence and uncreated energies of God in Gregory Palamas, and the divine seed theory of Nikos Kazantzakis. These diverse writers are of course representative of an extensive, almost comprehensive body of texts that recognizes God as contained in the heart of every creature and as comprising the meaning of every feature of the natural world.[2] Their writings propose what Orthodox Christian thought likes to call a sacred—or sacramental—worldview.

A Tale of Two Truths

When medieval scholars maintained in their "tale of two truths" that science was called to observe the book of Nature while religion

---

[1]Brian Thomas Swimme and Mary Evelyn Tucker, *Journey of the Universe* (New Haven, CT: Yale University Press, 2011), 118. See also Jennifer Wiseman, "Universe of Wonder, Universe of Life," in *Reason and Wonder: Why Science and Faith Need Each Other*, ed. Eric Priest (London: SPCK, 2016), 74–85. On perspectives from theology, philosophy, and science, see also the two volumes by Andrew Torrance and Thomas McCall, eds., *Knowing Creation* vol. 1, and *Christ and the Created Order*, vol. 2 (Grand Rapids, MI: Zondervan, 2018).

[2]See, for instance, Ralph Waldo Emerson (1803–1882) in Andrew Linzey, ed., *Compassion for Animals: Readings and Prayers* (Eugene, OR: Wipf and Stock, 2017), 11.

was reflected in the book of Scripture, they were struggling with a longstanding debate regarding the inconsistency between science and religion as well as the incongruence between creation and church. In his book *Being as Communion*, Metropolitan John of Pergamon compares these two different approaches, and asserts:

> Science and theology for a long time seemed to be in search of different sorts of truth, as if there were not one truth in existence as a whole. This resulted in making truth subject to a dichotomy between the transcendent and the immanent.[3]

Indeed, this single truth about creation is proposed by many of the early church Fathers—both Eastern and Western—in a variety of interpretations ranging from the fundamentally literal to the spiritually symbolical. Thus, in his exceptional treatise *On the Six Days of Creation*, Basil the Great insists that the scriptural narrative is not a scientific explanation.[4] He strongly denounces those obsessed by the letter of the text, who overlook the spirit of Scripture, and describes them as preferring "technology to theology." For St. Basil, the book of Genesis should be considered not as history, but rather as meta-history.

Thus, the living universe invites us to an enlarged view of life, a more organic view of the world, not unlike that exposed with a wide-angle lens. By nature, it prevents us from using or abusing its resources; it prohibits a narrow, self-indulgent, self-serving way. Instead, the world becomes a celebration of the cosmic interconnection and interdependence of all things. What people conveniently overlook about the Genesis story is that the sixth day of creation is not dedicated exclusively to Adam (Gen. 1:26), but shared with "living creatures of every kind; cattle and creeping things; and wild animals of every kind" (Gen. 1:24). And when Noah

---

[3] John D. Zizioulas, *Being as Communion: Studies in Personhood and the Church* (Crestwood, NY: St. Vladimir's Seminary Press, 1997), 119. For a survey of the historical interaction and intercourse between science and religion, especially from the sixteenth through the nineteenth centuries, see the various studies by Alister McGrath. A brief, general introduction to the subject may be found in his *Science and Religion: A New Introduction*, 2nd ed. (Oxford: Wiley-Blackwell, 2010). For a positive assessment of scientific discovery and technological development in contemporary Orthodox thought, see Charles Miller, *The Gift of the World: An Introduction to the Theology of Dumitru Stăniloae* (Edinburgh: T&T Clark, 2000).
[4] *Hexaemeron* 1.2 PG 29.8; 1.11 PG 29.28; 6.2 PG 29.120; 9.1 PG 29.188.

saved the animals two-by-two, he was not simply saving specimens or preserving species; he was first and foremost conserving and sustaining an ecosystem! There is far more that unites us with than separates us from other creatures and the rest of creation—not only as human beings but also within the entire universe. This is a lesson we have only learned the hard way in recent decades.

A Universal Seed

Two ancient theories or theologies about the origin of the universe are fairly well known. Almost two thousand years ago—long before the Big Bang theory was generated by physicists as a single-point, ever-expanding worldview—there emerged the classical concept of the germinative principle or generative logos[5] and its far-reaching theological implications for ancient Greek philosophy and early Christian thought. Logos was the logic observed in nature by the classical philosophers, especially Aristotle; and to the early Christian thinkers, the rational design of nature is clear evidence of a God, who plans and implements the universe.

What most people may be less acquainted with, however, is the notion of the universal seed. The second verse of the book of Genesis relates how "the Spirit of God hovered over the waters" (Gen. 1:2). This is interpreted by Basil as the divine Spirit preparing the nature of water to produce all living beings, bracing the nature of water to produce the living universe—very much, as he observes, "like a bird broods on its eggs."[6] Similarly, in his *Third Commentary on Genesis*, John Chrysostom refers to a fertile power that was active and alive in the waters and in the world, ultimately empowering all living things to emerge.

It is this intrinsic potentiality of creation that reflects the inalienable openness of the Creator as well as the inherent randomness of the universe. Thus, all of life in the universe originates from a single ontological source or seed implanted by God in that original moment or "beginning." Basil continues:

---

[5]In Latin: *ratio seminalis*. Adopted by the Sophists and Stoics, the phrase was incorporated into Jewish philosophy by Philo (20 BCE–50 CE) and into Christian thought by Justin Martyr (100–165).
[6]Basil, *Hexaemeron* II, 6 PG 29.40f.

This short command ("Let the earth bring forth") is—in a moment—an elaborate system; so nature receives the impulse of this first command and follows its course without interruption until the consummation of all ages.[7]

The world and the waters were pregnant with every limitless variety of living species. Over the ensuing five days, God embellished the world, differentiating each creation by divine command and bringing forth hidden treasuries of forms stored within them. For Basil, this is precisely why the Greek (Septuagint) translation of the Hebrew text speaks of "one day" whereas the subsequent days are chronologically designated as "the second day," "the third day," and so on. Something unique and different happened on that seminal "day-one," that original word, that first "bang."

So the church Fathers shared a view of the world as containing a determinative force, through which God calls the immense variety of life forms to unfold—from the elements through the plants and from the animals to the human beings. Such a dynamic view of nature is undoubtedly compatible with the scientific theory of biological evolution.[8]

Unity and Diversity

However, there is yet another aspect of an Orthodox cosmology or worldview that is worth highlighting here, namely that creation is always perceived as an organic whole. All living creatures are branches of the same tree, organic shoots of the same primordial seed, maintained in existence through the divine energies in which all life participates. Every January, on the Feast of Christ's baptism, Orthodox Christians proclaim: "The nature of waters is sanctified ... the earth is blessed ... the heavens are enlightened." On that

---

[7]Basil, *Hexaemeron* V, 10. For the entire passage in English translation, see Philip Schaff and Henry Mace, eds., *Nicene and Post-Nicene Fathers*, Series 2, vol. 8 (Edinburgh: T&T Clark, reprinted 1996), 81.
[8]See Andrew Louth, "The Six Days of Creation According to the Greek Fathers," in *Reading Genesis after Darwin*, ed. Stephen Barton and David Wilkinson (Oxford: Oxford University Press, 2009), 39–55; and Peter Bouteneff, *Beginnings: Ancient Christian Readings of the Biblical Creation Narratives* (Crestwood, NY: St. Vladimir's Seminary Press, 2008).

day, they pray "That by the elements of creation, by angels and human beings, by things visible and invisible, God's most holy name may be glorified."[9] Christian cosmology is the other side of the same coin of Christology. That is why, in celebrating Christmas, Orthodox Christians sing: "A marvelous wonder has today come to pass; nature is made new and God becomes human."[10]

This binding unity is a direct result of the common evolution of all life that shares the same elements (carbon, nitrogen, trace metals, etc.), the same processes (cell division, replication and repair of DNA, etc.), even the same genetic code. In this respect, all species share in unity even as they evolve in diversity. The unity, this cosmic interconnection, helps us to perceive the relationship of all creatures as well as our relationship with the earth itself. The diversity helps us appreciate the essential importance of all creatures, all life, and all environments for the sustainability and survival of our planet.

No wonder, then, that the oldest surviving Christian liturgy prays: "Every material and spiritual creature proclaims the magnificence of God."[11] Indeed, during its most sacred moment of the Anaphora, the Jerusalem rite of the ancient Liturgy of St. James includes and involves "the heavens and all their powers; the sun and the moon, together with all the choir of stars; the earth and the sea, along with everything that is in them." Ecumenical Patriarch Bartholomew can resonate:

> This connection is even detected in the galaxies, where the countless stars betray the same mystical grace and mathematical inter-connectedness. We do not need this worldview in order to believe in God or to prove God's existence. We need it to breathe; we need it simply to be.[12]

Unfortunately, with time, there was a cosmic shift and separation between God and man, heaven and earth, cosmic liturgy and mathematical mechanics. Nevertheless, the Eastern Christian tradition persistently sought to modify the early Greek concept

---

[9]The Great Blessing of the Waters on the Feast of Theophany, January 6.
[10]Vespers for the Feast of Nativity, December 24.
[11]The Liturgy of St. James is still celebrated twice a year in the Orthodox Church.
[12]Ecumenical Patriarch Bartholomew, "Faith and Environment: An Inspirational Perspective" (Public lecture, Utrecht, April 24, 2014). See also Chapter 10: "The Green Patriarch—A Contemporary Worldview and Witness."

of God as immobile essence, even while struggling to embrace its opposite—namely, the concept of a God understood as becoming. Thus, the Orthodox interpretation of Scripture, liturgy, and spirituality reveals a God constantly reconciling all divisions by balancing the distinction between the immutability or stability of God with divine becoming or historicity—namely, with God's intimate involvement in the created world and the human heart.

In this context, Eastern theology prefers the model of a dynamic distinction between the immutable essence and the uncreated energies of God. The latter manifest the infinite possibilities and inexhaustible potentiality of the former. The divine energies—what the Hebrew Scriptures call God's "glory"—charge the created world with reality and transparency, allowing it at once to reveal and to conceal the mystery of God. In the fourteenth-century paradoxical language of Gregory Palamas:

> God is both existent and non-existent; he is everywhere and nowhere; he has many names and cannot be named; he is ever-moving and unmoved; in short, he is everything and no-thing … He remains wholly within himself and yet dwells wholly within us, causing us to participate not in his nature but in his glory and radiance.[13]

At the same time, God's essence remains totally transcendent—undefined and undetermined. "God cannot be grasped by the intellect," wrote Evagrius of Pontus; "if he could be grasped, then he would not be God."[14] Therefore, "[W]e do not know God in his essence, but rather from the grandeur of his creation and from his providential care for all creatures."[15] However, without divine energies there is no connection between God and the material

---

[13]Cited by K. Ware, "God Immanent yet Transcendent," in *In Whom We Live and Move and Have Our Being: Panentheistic Reflections on God's Presence in a Scientific World*, ed. Philip Clayton and Arthur Peacockc (Grand Rapids, MI: Eerdmans, 2004), 162. To quote Arthur Peacocke, "God would not be Creator unless the divine Being and the divine Becoming were facets of the same ultimate divine Reality." See his *Theology for a Scientific Age: Being and Becoming—Natural, Divine and Human* (Minneapolis MN: Fortress Press, 1993), 185.
[14]PG 40.1275.
[15]Maximus Confessor, *Centuries on Love* I, 96, *Philokalia*, vol. 2, 64.

universe, as affirmed in the twentieth century by a pioneer Orthodox thinker on the environment, Philip Sherrard:

> For if only the total transcendence of God is affirmed, then all created things, all that is in change and visible, must be regarded as without any real roots in the Divine, and hence as entirely negative and 'illusory' in character; while if only the total immanence of God is affirmed, then creation must be looked upon as real in its own right, instead of as real only because it derives from and participates in the Divine; and the result must be a pantheism, and a worship of creation rather than of the Creator, which must ultimately lead to the notion that God is superfluous, and hence to an entirely materialistic conception of things.[16]

Precisely because of the presence of divine energies in creation, nothing falls outside the embrace of God; everything is a reflection of the divine. The God contemplated by the Christian mystics of the medieval East was a God elusive yet familiar, both transcendent and immanent; it was a God, who was afar and at the same time at hand.[17] This is the God intimated by the distinction between essence and energies, who is worshiped in heaven while also venerated on earth.

A Divine Seed

It is a tragedy that, in spite of the destruction and the suffering that we have inflicted on our planet, we have not yet apparently learned our lesson. The world remains for us a human-centered reality: we are still obsessed with ourselves, our problems, even our

---

[16]Philip Sherrard, *The Greek East and the Latin West: A Study in the Christian Tradition* (originally London: Oxford University Press, 1959; Limni, Evia: Denise Harvey, 1995), 35–6.

[17]Western mystics confess the same worldview of a God worshipped "in heaven as on earth." Thus, when Julian of Norwich (1342–1413) received "something small, the size of a hazelnut, in the palm of her hand," she was told that it resembled the whole world and "everything that was made." "I marveled how this could be," she conceded, "for it was so small that it might suddenly fall into nothingness." Whereupon a voice revealed: "It lasts and shall last forever; for God loves it. All things have their being in this way." See her *Revelations of Divine Love*, ch. 5.

survival. And yet this is precisely what led us in the first place to this fateful predicament. Very little significance is attached to the reality that all things are coherent not just in their interrelatedness and interdependence, but also in their relation to and dependence on God. For the fourth-century poet and theologian of Constantinople, Gregory Nazianzus, "All things dwell in God alone; all things swarm to God in haste. For God is the end of all things."[18]

The ancient Greeks had a similar worldview, recognizing the divine presence in all things. Thales (624–546 BCE) exclaimed: "Everything is full of God."[19] And Basil the Great believed that even the slightest detail of creation bore the mark of the Creator:

> Look at a stone, and notice that even a stone carries some mark of the Creator. It is the same with an ant, a bee, a mosquito. The wisdom of the Creator is revealed in the smallest creatures. It is he who has spread out the heavens and stretched out the immensity of the seas. It is he who has also made the tiny hollow shaft of the bee's sting.[20]

The same truth—discovered by science and discerned in theology—is poetically expressed outside of the theological world by the controversial twentieth-century Greek author Nikos Kazantzakis (1883–1957), whose work was regrettably misunderstood and maligned, even banned by the Vatican and condemned by the Church of Greece. Yet Kazantzakis retains a powerful religious worldview of the divine seed in the world—a view that critics might argue is a reinventing of Christianity. For

---

[18]Gregory Nazianzus, *Dogmatic Poems* 29, in PG 37.508.

[19]Thales, *Fragment* 22.

[20]Basil of Caesarea, *Commentary on Psalm 32*, 3 in PG 29.329. In a presentation entitled "Nature's Bounty: Why We Need All Other Species on Earth," Enric Sala (explorer-in-residence of the US National Geographic Society) addressed a conference on "the intrinsic value of all creatures" at the Pontifical Gregorian University (March 6–7, 2018) about an invisible marine microbe known as Prochlorococcus, whose existence was only discovered in 1988. Prochlorococcus is the scientific name of a bacterium only a millionth of a millimeter in size. It is so small that it took microscopes powerful enough to be *invented* in order for humans to be able to *see* it. Yet it is one of the most abundant creatures on the planet, with twenty thousand of them living in a single drop of seawater.

Prochlorococcus draws its existence through sunlight in the shallow ocean to transform molecules in seawater into energy, releasing oxygen in the process. It is a

Kazantzakis, created nature is the only premise and promise for either salvation or destruction; it is not a finished product, but a moving ground, a process of continuous self-transcendence and transformation:

> Everything is an egg, and within it lies the seed of God, restlessly and sleeplessly active ... With the light of my mind and the fire of my heart, I beset God's watch—searching, testing, knocking to open the door in the stronghold of matter, and to create in that stronghold of matter, the door of God's heroic exodus ... For *we are not simply freeing God* in struggling with and ordering the visible world around us; *we are actually fashioning God*. Open your eyes, God is crying; I want to see! Be alert; I want to hear! ... For to save something [a rock or a seed] is to liberate God within it ... Every person has a particular circle of things, of trees, of animals, of people, of ideas—and the aim is to save that circle. No one else can do that. And if one doesn't save, one cannot be saved ... The seeds are calling out from inside the earth; God is calling out from inside the seeds. Set God free. A field awaits liberation from you, and a machine awaits its soul from you. And you can no longer be saved, if you don't save them ... The value of this transient world is immense and immeasurable: for it is on this world that God depends in order to reach us; it is in this world that God is nurtured and increased ... *Matter is the*

---

process similar to what plants do on land—namely, photosynthesis—by synthesizing sugars using sunlight as their energy source, with oxygen as a by-product. Yet terrestrial plants, our forests and grasslands, produce *less than half* of the oxygen we breathe. More than half of this comes from the ocean, from seaweed on our shores, microscopic plants in the ocean, and incalculable microbes. In brief, a little bacterium that we were unaware of thirty years ago, and other marine creatures unknown to most humans, give us every alternate breath that we take.

This tiny microbe alone would cost at least $200,000 trillion or 1600 global GDP to replace. Its value is vital, priceless, and irreplaceable. These bacteria have been in existence for hundreds of millions of years and their destruction is analogous to the destruction of the library of Alexandria. Is it ethical that we destroy them for the benefit of very few? Is there a connection between ecocide and genocide? In fact, we should stand with gratitude and humility before this microscopic Prochlorococcus, not only because of its extraordinary role in the global ecosystem, but also because our advanced technology could never replace its role, which is otherwise invisible to the naked eye.

"I wonder," Dr. Sala concluded, "what other invisible creatures do that we also take for granted?"

bride of my God: together they wrestle, together they laugh and together they mourn, crying through the nuptial chamber of the creation.[21]

The Dance of Creation

The great minds examined in this chapter struggled to integrate science and faith in understanding creation with rigor and respect. In these efforts, it has always been a source of great comfort to me that Orthodox spirituality retains a sacramental view of the world, proclaiming a world imbued by God and a God involved in the world—a sacrament of communion. God is the Lord of the dance of creation, which is perceived as a voluntary overflow of divine gratuitousness and grace resulting in cosmic transformation. Or as the seventh-century mystic, Maximus Confessor, puts it: the whole world is "a burning bush of divine energies," "a cosmic liturgy." Through an inspection of the world and an introspection of the heart, we arrive at knowledge of the creator.

The dimension of liturgy, of joyful praise in creation is God's gift to the world and does not at all depend on any of our environmental efforts or awareness. So unless we willingly entertain and joyfully enter into this interdependence of all persons and all things, we certainly cannot hope to resolve issues of economy and ecology. For we should respond to nature with the same delicacy, sensitivity, and tenderness, with which we respond to a person in a relationship. And our failure to do so is the fundamental source of pollution, a consequence of our inability to relate caringly toward the created world.

Such is the breadth and depth of the Orthodox Christian cosmic vision, one that is much larger than that of any one individual. I may be at the center of this vision or theophany, but I become aware that I am also but a detail of the living universe. Indeed, the world ceases to be something that I observe objectively, or exploit selfishly, and instead becomes something of which I am a part,

---

[21]Nikos Kazantzakis, *Askitiki: Salvatores Dei*, 5th ed. (Athens: no publisher, 1979), 85–9. Translation (and emphasis) mine from the original Greek. This book is currently included in the series Kazantzakis Editions (Athens, 2009). For the English edition, see *The Saviors of God: Spiritual Exercises*, trans. Kimon Friar (New York: Simon & Schuster, 1960).

personally and actively. No longer then should I feel as a stranger, whether threatened or threatening, but as a compassionate friend in and of the world. For whenever we reduce life to ourselves (to our concerns and our desires), we neglect this enlarged, cosmic vision of creation, our innate cosmic interconnection. In fact, whenever we narrow even religious life to ourselves (to our concerns and our desires), we ignore the vocation of faith to implore God for the renewal of the whole polluted cosmos and for divine grace to help humanity embrace its purpose to transfigure the whole world, starting with each individual.

It will take nothing less than divine grace to bring about the introspection and change required for personal transformation. Indeed, it will take nothing less than divine grace to help us to reconcile the continuing tension between faith and science, as well as resolve the crippling dissension between religious and political thinkers who debate one other in a cultural environment as toxic as the polluted air.

FIGURE 4 *Fourth Day and Fifth Day of Creation: Scene from the Bible, Byzantine mosaics of The Palatine Chapel in the Norman Palace, Palermo Sicily © Paul Williams/Alamy Stock Photo.* **See p. 140**

8

Responding to Denial and Disdain

The Devil's Advocate, Part 1

A Toxic Combination

Major changes in mindsets and worldviews—whether scientific or religious—are no more rapid in human societies than in natural settings. In fact, human beings are sometimes less prone to rapid conversion than geological fault lines or tectonic plates are to sudden shifts. This is especially true of religious institutions and political movements, where acceptance or adjustment is "traditionally" sluggish, if not frustratingly stagnant. It may also account for the burden of hope—sometimes unreasonable, perhaps unrealistic—placed on the shoulders of religious leaders, such as Pope Francis and Ecumenical Patriarch Bartholomew. It was possibly the reason why the June 2015 papal encyclical *Laudato Si'* ("Praise be to you"—"On Care for our Common Home") was received with such fervor—while at the same time challenged with such ferocity—in religious and secular circles alike.[1] Would it create a sudden shift in thinking about climate change? Could it convince deniers and disdainers that the problem was real and that religion should be part of the solution?

The pope's encyclical preceded the UN Conference of the Parties (COP 21) held in Paris in December 2015, where a record 175

---

[1]See my appraisal of the papal encyclical in the *Conclusion*.

parties (174 countries as well as the European Union) agreed that climate change is real, recognizing a consensus in "the science, the conscience, and the circumstance"?[2] Surely progress could now be made. After all, the science is long convinced, the technology progressively committed, and the economy increasingly capable.

Yet everyone knows the devil is in the details. The Paris climate conference attendees returned to their home countries to face the reality that politics and ideology remain deadlocked and convoluted. For example, in the United States, "culture wars" have regrettably branded any association with protecting the environment in the same vein as abortion, gun control, feminist and gay rights, positions generally supported by the Democratic Party with the Republican Party always on the "other" side![3] Regarding the environment, in general Democrats encourage government involvement, which includes regulations and laws. In general, Republicans do not; instead, they favor libertarian or market solutions that rest on such pillars as privatization and deregulation—with all their corollary consequences for lowering corporate taxation and reducing public spending. Despite the separation of church and state, these political ideologies have also come to affect thinking in church pews. Can correct religious thinking on the environment perhaps clear the air and help people evaluate creation care on its own merits, decoupled from the other issues mentioned above?

What seems to make the debate extraordinarily exasperating and exhausting is the toxic mix between religious ideology and political persuasion, which can often be reduced to anti-scientific conviction and anti-intellectual assertion. Moreover, what makes the effort especially difficult and delicate is the presumption that the core beliefs of libertarian ideology and the gospel message are somehow fundamentally compatible (if not identical), when in fact they are profoundly contradictory (if not irreconcilable).

---

[2]From an address by Laurent Fabius, French foreign minister, at a summit organized by the French government in preparation for the COP 21 international climate meeting held in Paris, November 30–December 11, 2015. Since December 2015, all 195 countries have signed the agreement, while 178 have become party to it. In June 2017, the United States announced its intention to withdraw, which would render it the only country on the planet outside of the agreement.
[3]See the article by Mark Stoll, "The Historical Roots of Evangelical Anti-environmentalism," *The Christian Century*, June 17, 2015.

Over the last twenty-five years, I have been privileged to work alongside Ecumenical Patriarch Bartholomew, who has proved a pioneer in the "greening" of churches around the world—including the Roman Catholic Church and the Anglican Communion, the World Council of Churches and the Conference of European Churches.[4] This has entailed addressing climate change from a theological viewpoint over a long period of time. This and the following chapter address and confront the distorted theology of climate deniers regarding stewardship and sin, free will and asceticism, as well as greed and compassion. My aim is to consider the arguments,[5] while countering an unorthodox evangelicalism that is far removed from the Orthodox Christian roots with which I am familiar, even if those roots convey "an inconvenient truth."[6] It is the theological attitude of climate deniers, rather than their political position, which should be challenged and changed; already from the tenth century, Symeon the New Theologian was convinced that "if we are to change our attitudes toward creation, we must correct our attitude toward God."[7]

The Concept of Stewardship

Despite the positive engagement with the issue of climate change today by Ecumenical Patriarch Bartholomew and other religious leaders, deniers question the role of Christianity in the debate, its involvement invariably regarded as interference. Sometimes, the

---

[4]In his ecological encyclical, Pope Francis recognizes "the striking example" of the Ecumenical Patriarch. See paragraph 7 of *Laudato Si'*.

[5]Fr. Michael Butler and Andrew Morriss, two ardent climate deniers, are as confident as they are categorical: "As Christians, we know why the world was created and why it was entrusted to our care." See their *Creation and the Heart of Man: An Orthodox Christian Perspective on Environmentalism* (Grand Rapids, MI: Acton Institute, Amazon Digital Services, 2013), 5. The authors are alarmed that environmentalism has been "captured" by the "left of center" agenda. Butler and Morriss admit their prejudice toward conservatism and commercialism, classifying environmentalism among the social plagues of liberalism and communism.

[6]The title of a popular book and educational series by Al Gore, *An Inconvenient Truth: The Planetary Emergency of Global Warming and What We Can Do about It* (Emmaus, PA: Rodale, 2006).

[7]See his *Ethical Discourses*, I, 7. Also D. Stăniloae, *The Experience of God: Orthodox Dogmatic Theology* (Brookline, MA: Holy Cross Orthodox Press, 2000), 2.

criticism is quite crude: Let religion stick to ethics and doctrine instead of interfering in the work of scientists and economists:

> The patriarch could be more effective if he stuck to principles of Christian stewardship of the environment and left the practical implications to those who have some expertise in these matters. Bartholomew has extended himself outside of his competency ... lest Christian thought become reinterpreted and subsumed as a mere component of contemporary social idealism.[8]

Frequently, however, the rationale is subtler: Short-term dominion and self-centered mastery over creation is considered to be grounded in Scripture (Genesis 2), as though it is our God-given role to reap and rape the earth without a long-term vision or worldview. In narrower confessional circles, this attitude regards all earthly activity in light of an imminent return of the Messiah, where everything that we care about and do is somehow caught up in that final rapture, fading into insignificance. This justifies the limitless acquisition of wealth, the reckless imposition of power, and the heedless oppression of others, especially the poor.

In response, Ecumenical Patriarch Bartholomew has never claimed scientific expertise, relying instead on the discovery and direction of world-renowned scientists. Nor has he castigated economic progress, recognizing instead that all socio-economic programs are flawed and unqualified to reach the ideal. His concern has rightly been on man's proper relationship to God's creation, in accordance with gospel precepts and patristic principles. The phrase normally adopted in this regard is "environmental stewardship," although it too should be approached with cautious discernment, especially since it is routinely acceptable even to climate deniers. It may be helpful to consider how the term "stewardship" has been devised and defined through the centuries.

The conventional Judeo-Christian view of stewardship begins with the Book of Genesis, where the vocation and covenant to cherish and care for creation is proposed as the principal reason for which God placed Adam and Eve in the garden of Eden (Gen. 2:15), namely "to till and keep it"—a phrase I like to translate (based more

---

[8]John Couretas, "Green Patriarch: No Nukes," Acton Institute Powerblog, Monday March 14, 2011.

closely and literally on the Greek translation of the Septuagint) as "to serve and preserve it." It has not, of course, helped in the least that we have also misconstrued the biblical term "dominion" (in Gen. 1:28 and Ps. 8:5-8) as "domination" in an unashamedly self-centered and self-serving manner; after all, "dominion belongs only to the Lord" (Ps. 22:28).

I sometimes wonder why deniers and disdainers do not complain or protest against more radical and extreme biblical commandments, such as the injunction to "sell all that one has in order to follow [Christ]"? Are they more concerned about reflecting Caesar than Christ, their hearts moved more by the markets than by the mystics? This may account for the sharp dissociation between their ideology and theology, but how do they interpret the revolutionary words of John Chrysostom: "The earth is God's (Ps. 23:2) signifies that our possessions belong to one common Lord and, therefore, belong to our fellow servants; for the possessions of the Lord are, all of them, common to all."[9]

Any dominion over creation implies ruling in accordance with the love, peace, and justice of the Creator. Whether for fear of pagan idolatry or out of a sense of arrogant selfishness, there is no doubt that, over the centuries and in our own lives, we have preferred to overemphasize the exceptional role of humanity. Anthropocentrism is an entrancing temptation to which we are all guilty of submitting at one time or another, and which has detrimentally burdened our perspective and practice: "The whole of creation has been groaning together in pain until now, inwardly awaiting its liberation by the children of God" (Rom. 8:22-23). However, will we be accountable for our neglect and abuse?

While there are numerous passages in the Old and New Testaments that provide insight into the principle and practice of stewardship—intimately relating its social and ecological aspects and ramifications—it is a message that acquires increasing urgency in light of our ultimate accountability on the day of judgment with Christ's parable about the faithful and prudent steward in Luke's Chapter 12 that concludes with the following warning: "Everyone to whom much was given, more will be required; and from those to whom much was entrusted, more will be demanded" (v. 48). This verse may not meet with general agreement on a political level;

---

[9]See Chrysostom, *Homily on 1 Timothy* XII, 3.

yet it is a statement that deserves close attention on a spiritual level: "Blessed is that servant whom his master will find so doing when he comes" (v. 43).

Like the servant in the parable, we too will be asked for accountability by the Master: "What is this that I hear about you? Turn in the account of your management" (Lk. 16:2). We will surely be judged for the abuse of the earth that has been entrusted to us "to preserve," as well as for the unjust distribution of its resources to our fellow human beings that we are called "to serve"—for the devastation of God's creation by human beings unjustly usurping the right to control and arrogantly assuming the right to manipulate it, as well as for the exploitation of the poor (and poor nations) by the rich (and rich nations).

This is why I have long been uncomfortable with the various implications or undertones of the term *steward*, which is the conventional rendering of the scriptural and seemingly sustainable lifestyle implied by the Hellenistic *oikonomos* and the Hebrew *ben-bieth*.[10] Both of these biblical expressions denote more broadly a state of "son-ship" and "servant-hood"—beyond the more literal and more conservative (but not necessarily conservational) sense of conquest and control.[11] Whenever we adopt the term "steward," it would behoove us to examine the underlying implication and

---

[10]See the sermons of Basil of Caesarea in *On Social Justice: St. Basil the Great*, trans. Paul Schroeder (Crestwood, NY: St. Vladimir's Seminary Press, 2009), esp. 46, 61–2, and 69–70; and the sermons of John Chrysostom in *St. John Chrysostom: On Wealth and Poverty*, trans. Catharine Roth (Crestwood, NY: St. Vladimir's Seminary Press, 1984), 50f.

[11]Why else would an evangelical, albeit political group such as the Cornwall Alliance, otherwise explicitly in favor of fossil fuels and the oil industry while at the same time glaringly silent on religious responsibility for creation care, have as their motto and mantra: "For the stewardship of creation"? Similarly, in *Creation and the Heart of Man*, Butler and Morriss claim that "there is no basis for assuming that God's intention for a mountain full of coal precludes the mining of that coal" (77). This resonates less with Orthodox theological and spiritual concepts than with religious and political convictions of Southern Baptists, such as former United States Environmental Protection Agency administrator Scott Pruitt, himself formerly a deacon at First Baptist Church in Broken Arrow, Oklahoma, who understood from the Bible—indeed, as he says, "God really spoke to him in his heart"—that he should oppose regulations restricting the mining of non-renewable energy resources: see https://baptistnews.com/article/god-wants-humans-use-natural-gas-oil-not-keep-ground-says-epa-chief/#.W0FYYl4nZ9K (accessed May 2, 2018). For an authoritative commentary on the oil industry in the United States, see John

intention, as well as the associated cost and sacrifice, of the context within which it is used.

Despite such scriptural references, most church-attending Christians today perceive stewardship still more narrowly, seeing it as a financial commitment to be fulfilled when a collection tray is circulated. However, the concept of stewardship goes beyond notions of monetary contribution and proprietary management. The modern rendering of the Greek word *oikonomia* (economy) is not very illuminating, providing a further linguistic and conceptual reduction of this classical and originally biblical word. Thus, we have narrowed the scope of the Bible's teaching and neglected the depth of our church's tradition concerning the place and role of human beings in the world, indeed at a time when these are more vital and critical than ever before.[12]

If we turn to the church Fathers, we will see that they attribute the highest importance to *oikonomia*, which in their eyes implied a broader and more inclusive concept of revelation and salvation, identified with God's vision and desire to care for and conserve creation, ultimately to serve and save the world. The word *oikonomia* literally signifies being responsible for or respectful of—carefully ministering and dutifully administering (nomos)—one's household (oikos). For the great theological teachers and spiritual masters, economy in fact refers to our very salvation by the all-embracing love of God for all humankind and to the universal compassion of the Creator for all creation.[13] All of God's actions relate to the world are caring and compassionate: the original genesis for the creation of the world, the divine Incarnation for the life of the world, and the final reconciliation for the judgment of the world.

The translation of the biblical term "stewardship"—or, at least, the interpretation of this term in many circles today—seems to retain

---

Chryssavgis, "An American Guilt Trip," *Public Orthodoxy*: https://publicorthodoxy. org/2018/10/18/an-american-guilt-trip/. For a theological criticism of the concept of stewardship, see John Zizioulas, *The Eucharistic Communion and the World* (Edinburgh: T&T Clark, 2011), especially ch. 7: "Proprietors or Priests of Creation" (133–41).

[12]For a comprehensive list of over two thousand scriptural passages highlighting creation care and ecological sensitivity, see *The Green Bible* (San Francisco, CA: HarperOne, 2008).

[13]See Athanasius of Alexandria, *Against Arians* II, 11 PG 26.169; Basil the Great, *Homily I on Psalm* 44 PG 29.400; and Gregory Nazianzus, *Oration* 29, 18 PG 36.97.

much of the controlling, prideful elements that lie at the very source of the ecological problem. Speaking of human beings as "stewards" or "custodians" can therefore prove both misleading and mistaken. In more traditional pastoral logic, "shepherd" or "farmer" may well be an alternative rendering; in more liturgical language, "mystic" or "priest" may more fittingly place humanity in the context of a world that praises God with its very being and at its very core, a world that we are called to serve and preserve, a world in which all things are in God's service and not ours.

In an earlier chapter, we have explored the importance of desert spirituality. However, the association of the concept of stewardship with the monastic tradition may still not be immediately apparent to readers. The desert is normally viewed as a way of renunciation—as a means of giving up rather than of giving, as a life of sacrifice than of sharing. In their radical abandonment of the world, the monastics of Egypt and Palestine learned about liberation from any attachment to worldly things in order to assume a more compassionate and communal way of living. Their understanding of stewardship is better encapsulated in the term "detachment" (apotage), which is more than merely material and spatial; it is, in fact, cosmic and spiritual. Detachment is not primarily the inability to focus on things, but rather the ability to focus on all things without attachment.

One of the finest desert instructions on stewardship as detachment comes from Abba Zosimas, who founded a community in Palestine during the first half of the sixth century and authored a series of spiritual *Reflections*. Zosimas was fond of saying, "It is not possessing something that is harmful, but being attached to it."[14] His fundamental axiom was that "we should possess things as if in fact we do not own them (1 Cor. 7:30-31)."[15]

The aim at all times and at all costs is to shift the focus from oneself as the center of the world, to abandon oneself to the authority of the Creator, in order to place oneself at the service of others. In this perspective, creation care becomes an act of faith—of assurance, reliance, and confidence. When the frightened disciples

---

[14]Zosimas, "On Detachment," in *In the Heart of the Desert: The Spirituality of the Desert Fathers and Mothers*, ed. John Chryssavgis, revised (Bloomington, IN: World Wisdom, 2008), 123. For a translation of the *Reflections* by Abba Zosimas, see Chryssavgis, *In the Heart*, 111–50.

[15]Chryssavgis, *In the Heart*, 124.

awaken Christ in the middle of a storm (see Mk 4:35-41), they expect him to comfort their fear and relieve their distress. Imagining God to be asleep, they call on divine intervention at a time of crisis instead of confessing God's jurisdiction over all of nature. To their surprise, Christ tells them to "be still" (Mk 4:39), to face the elements of the universe like a splash of grace on their faces, not to be afraid of being "drenched in deity," as C. S. Lewis might say.[16]

The genuine and faithful disciple always observes and always preserves the sacredness of creation. The humble and caring person always gives thanks for all things and gives to all others without exploiting nature for selfish reasons. The true steward of creation is always satisfied with and always shares the resources of the planet. Such a person stands at the intersection of a sacramental worldview and a sustainable way, subsisting as a vessel of gratitude and grace.

Recent Scholarship

Lynn White Jr. (1907–1987)

The debate about the meaning of stewardship is hardly new. The definition of stewardship and dominion was addressed in the 1960s by medieval historian Lynn White Jr., as well as by geography scholar Clarence Glacken.

In White's now classic article, "The Historical Roots of our Ecologic Crisis," many have misinterpreted his words criticizing the Judaeo-Christian faith communities for promoting the willful use and abuse of the natural environment:

> The present increasing disruption of the global environment is the product of a dynamic technology and science, which were originating in the Western medieval world against which Saint Francis [of Assisi] was rebelling in so original a way. Their growth cannot be understood historically apart from distinctive attitudes toward nature, which are deeply grounded in Christian dogma. The fact that most people do not think of these attitudes

---

[16]C. S. Lewis in his introduction to the cosmology of English priest and theologian Richard Hooker, in C. S. Lewis, ed., *English Literature in the Sixteenth Century, Excluding Drama* (Oxford, UK: Clarendon Press, 1954), 462.

as Christian is irrelevant. No new set of basic values has been accepted in our society to displace those of Christianity. Hence, we shall continue to have a worsening ecologic crisis until we reject the Christian axiom that nature has no reason for existence save to serve man.[17]

Lynn White is often decried and dismissed for his thesis that "Christianity bears a huge burden of guilt" for the ecological crisis.[18] What people tend, or perhaps choose, to overlook is how White acknowledged "that many contemporary Americans who are concerned about our ecologic crisis will be neither able or willing to counsel with wolves or exhort birds" like St. Francis of Assisi,[19] who "worshipped a God who was the God both of squirrels and of men."[20] To his credit, White explores the intellectual ideas and technological developments since the eleventh century, comparing Eastern and Western Christian thought as early as the fifteenth century:

Those who doubt should contemplate that most monumental achievement in the history of automation: the weight-driven mechanical clock, which appeared in two forms in the early 14th century. Not in craftsmanship but in basic technological capacity, the Latin West of the later Middle Ages far outstripped its elaborate, sophisticated, and esthetically magnificent sister cultures, Byzantium and Islam. In 1444 a great Greek ecclesiastic, Bessarion, who had gone to Italy, wrote a letter to a prince in Greece. He is amazed by the superiority of Western ships, arms, textiles, glass. But above all he is astonished by the spectacle of waterwheels sawing timbers and pumping the bellows of blast furnaces. Clearly, he had seen nothing of the sort in the Near East.[21]

---

[17]Lynn Townsend White Jr., "The Historical Roots of Our Ecologic Crisis," *Science* 155, no. 3767 (March 10, 1967): 1207.
[18]Ibid., 1206.
[19]Ibid., 1207.
[20]Lynn Townsend White Jr., "Continuing the Conversation," in *Western Man and Environmental Ethics: Attitudes Toward Nature and Technology*, ed. Ian G. Barbour (Boston, MA: Addison-Wesley, 1973), 61.
[21]White, "Historical Roots," *Science*, 1204.

Indeed, White distinguished between the approaches toward nature in Eastern and Western Christianity:

> When one speaks in such sweeping terms, a note of caution is in order. Christianity is a complex faith, and its consequences differ in differing con-texts. What I have said may well apply to the medieval West, where in fact technology made spectacular advances ... The key to the contrast may perhaps be found in a difference in the tonality of piety and thought which students of comparative theology find between the Greek and the Latin Churches. The Greeks believed that sin was intellectual blindness, and that salvation was found in illumination, orthodoxy—that is, clear thinking. The Latins, on the other hand, felt that sin was moral evil, and that salvation was to be found in right conduct. Eastern theology has been intellectualist. Western theology has been voluntarist. The Greek saint contemplates; the Western saint acts. The implications of Christianity for the conquest of nature would emerge more easily in the Western atmosphere.[22]

In many ways, White seems to gravitate toward an appreciation of the Eastern approach to a resolution of contemporary ecological challenges. Even today, very few scholars—including those who recognize the important contribution of Eastern patristic thought—fully comprehend just how the contemplative approach of the East is capable of shaping lifestyles and worldviews.[23]

While the charges of White against the Christian tradition are as relentlessly advanced by nonbelievers and neo-pagans as ruthlessly denounced by climate deniers and disdainers, what people often fail to realize is that White is actually quite supportive of Christianity and especially positive toward Orthodoxy, instead firmly indicting

---

[22]Ibid., 1205–6.

[23]Thus, for example, while Australian historian Peter Harrison spends a great deal of time explaining the early Christian notions of the divine origins of creation, "the book of nature" as divine Scripture, and even the three mystical stages (purification, illumination, and deification) of the contemplative tradition, he neither suggests nor suspects how such an approach can be translated into modern categories and practices. See his *The Territories of Science and Religion* (Chicago, IL: University of Chicago Press, 2015). For a more comprehensive approach, see Philip Sherrard, *Christianity: Lineaments of a Sacred Tradition* (Brookline, MA: Holy Cross Orthodox Press, 1998), esp. ch. 8, 180–99.

Christian concepts and practices that have not been properly demythologized and led to an abuse of nature. Regrettably, in an age like ours, when people on both sides of the political or religious spectrum contend over who is responsible and culpable, White is glibly relegated to a scapegoat against any authentic religious involvement in creation care.

Clarence Glacken (1909–1989)

The truth is that White was hardly exceptional among scholars of his time. His contemporary Clarence Glacken, a professor of geography, published his magnum opus[24] in the same year as White's definitive article saw the light of publication in *Science*. Glacken's *Traces on the Rhodian Shore* recounts the relationship of human beings with their environment by exploring the history of Western thought from the beginning of time until the beginning of the nineteenth century, from the dawn of classical times to the prelude of the contemporary era. After discerning some historical pattern and establishing some meaningful purpose in a complexity of sources and concepts, Glacken concludes his review around 1800, after which he feels that the fertile kinship between nature and culture becomes a futile domination by humanity over the world.

Human sovereignty over nature's resources may be championed today as original and authoritative, arguably as originating in the Judeo-Christian scriptures (Gen. 1:26-28), filtering through the Hellenistic age, and informing Western thought. In that respect, White would claim, "especially in its Western form, [that] Christianity is the most anthropocentric religion the world has seen."[25] However, as White continues,

---

[24]Clarence J. Glacken, *Traces on the Rhodian Shore: Nature and Culture in Western Thought from Ancient Times to the End of the Eighteenth Century* (Berkeley, CA: University of California Press, 1967). Indeed, Glacken was writing on the West coast in Berkeley, CA, in 1966, the very same year that White was speaking on the East coast in Princeton, NJ. I am grateful to Garry Trompf, Emeritus Professor of religion at the University of Sydney, for bringing to my attention the connection between White and Glacken. See G. Trompf, "Clarence Glacken," in *The Encyclopedia of Religion and Nature*, vol. 1, ed. Bron Taylor (New York: Thoemmes Press, 2005), 696–7, and G. Trompf, "Islands, the Humanities and Environmental Conservation," *Environmental Conservation* 45, no. 2 (2018): 101–9.

[25]White, "Historical Roots," *Science*, 1205.

The Christian dogma of creation, which is found in the first clause of all the creeds, has another meaning for our comprehension of today's ecologic crisis. By revelation, God had given man the Bible, the Book of Scripture. But since God had made nature, nature also must reveal the divine mentality. The religious study of nature for the better understanding of God was known as natural theology. In the early Church, and always in the Greek East, nature was conceived primarily as a symbolic system through which God speaks to men: the ant is a sermon to sluggards; rising flames are the symbol of the soul's aspiration. This view of nature was essentially artistic rather than scientific. While Byzantium preserved and copied great numbers of ancient Greek scientific texts, science as we conceive it could scarcely flourish in such an ambience. However, in the Latin West by the early 13th century natural theology was following a very different bent. It was ceasing to be the decoding of the physical symbols of God's communication with man and was becoming the effort to understand God's mind by discovering how his creation operates.[26]

Patristic Perspectives

In fact, however, anthropocentrism is a relatively new phenomenon in the history of ideas. The archetypal and authentic myth in our relationship to creation is fundamentally and essentially theocentric. In the Genesis story (Genesis 1), creation is never god-forsaken or objectified. The sky (vv. 1–5), the sea and the soil (vv. 6–12) are not gods. They are not infested with eternity; nor again are they inhabited by deities. They are creatures, like Adam and Eve (vv. 26–27) who, according to St. Basil, resemble gardeners attending to and tending the beauty and balance of nature.[27]

Here, too, East and West seem to differ in their interpretations of dominion over nature. It is clear that early patristic sources indicate and illustrate the need to establish and retain a connection between spiritual conversion and ecological conservation. However, the

---

[26]Ibid., 1206.
[27]That is how Basil the Great of Caesarea describes the role and responsibility of humankind in his *Hexaemeron*. See especially Books II, 3 and V, 1.

way in which this connection was established varies in the Eastern tradition from that in the West, particularly in monastic or ascetic circles. The philosophy of "work" (labora) in the Benedictine Rule allows for greater manipulation and exploitation of environmental resources, whereas the life of "contemplation" (theoria) in the Desert Fathers and Mothers is frequently accompanied by legends of wild animals and natural elements working with and for the desert dwellers. The first involves an assumption of rights over the natural environment, while the second implies a principle of respect for all creation. After all, the animals and the earth "teach" and "tell" us that "the hand of the Lord is the life of every living thing and the breath of every human being" (Job 12:7-10). This is why we discover almost an overindulgence of excessive hagiography in the East, with stories about the lives of wilderness saints and the taming of wildlife creatures.

It is not just the approach but also the attitude toward nature that differs in Western theology from that in the East. For instance, in his treatise *On the Soul*, Tertullian of Carthage will adopt the image of man as a governor that controls and drives nature, whereas—in a similar period and part of the world—Origen of Alexandria would elect a term like "the Creator's partner" or "creation's protector" to describe man's relationship with nature in his treatise *Against Celsus*.[28] Basil of Caesarea even speaks of human beings adorning and completing creation,[29] while his younger brother, Gregory of Nyssa, speaks of elevating and exalting nature.[30]

There is a profound connection between humankind and nature. This is why Basil urges people to discover natural evidence of the divine: "Creation should penetrate you with such great admiration that everywhere, wherever you may be, the smallest plant should bring before you the clear remembrance of the Creator."[31] In the

---

[28]Origen of Alexandria, *Contra Celsum* IV, 76.

[29]Basil the Great, *Hexaemeron*, Book II, 6.

[30]Gregory of Nyssa, *On the Creation of Man*, ch. 2.

[31]Basil the Great, *Hexaemeron*, Book III, 2. See also his *Hexaemeron*, Book V, 7 and Ambrose, *Hexaemeron*, Book III, 13. Glacken writes of the Cappadocian bishop, "Basil's physico-theology is the best of its kind until the works of John Ray, the father of natural history in the late seventeenth century, and William Derham, the father of natural theology in the early eighteenth century; these men had, however, the benefits of the heady discoveries which Galileo, Descartes, Newton, and others had heaped upon the student of nature and the servants of God alike." Glacken contrasts Basil's view with Augustine's in the latter's equivalent to Basil's *Hexaemeron*, namely the

classics of patristic thought, there is not really any concept of an isolated nature (physis), which appears mostly among the Greek philosophers. By the same token, there is no sense of *natura naturans*, which seems to emerge predominantly in the Middle Ages. Adam and Eve are like everyday, ordinary people, living in a garden.

Of course, this association or analogy between Creator and creation, whereby traces of the Creator are divined in the wonder of creation, does not imply any identification or leveling of the two. The distinction between God and the world, encapsulated in the doctrine of creation *ex nihilo*, remains unequivocal and lies at the very heart of a Christian attitude toward nature and creation. Even any comparison or parallel of the earthly world to "mother nature" is simply regarded as a means of alerting us to as indeed averting us from any muscular (or masculine) violation of nature. The earth is created; it is a work of God that is filled with divine grace and transforming energy. Creation is never confused with or even compared to the Creator. Instead, the Creator is ever contemplated in and through creation. It is the obligation of religious thinkers and communities to define this relationship correctly, but deniers and disdainers present an imbalanced view of sin and free will, of greed and asceticism, that distorts this relationship altogether.

Denial or Confession?

Critics have denounced Ecumenical Patriarch Bartholomew for consistently castigating the deliberate or indifferent degradation of the environment as sinful. The patriarch's encyclical of 1994 was the first time that any religious leader had identified harming the environment with committing sin. And in a public address in 1997, the patriarch stated unequivocally,

> To commit a crime against the natural world is a sin. For humans to cause species to become extinct and to destroy the biological diversity of God's creation ... for humans to degrade the integrity of Earth by causing changes in its climate, by stripping it of its forests, or by destroying its wetlands ... for humans to injure

---

De Genesi ad literram libri duodecim, where the Bishop of Hippo observes that "the earth and earthly things are to be spurned when we compare them with the greater glories of the City of God." See Glacken, *Traces on the Rhodian Shore,* 194 and 196.

other humans with disease and contaminate Earth's waters, land and air with poisonous substances … these are sins.[32]

The patriarch's audience included then US Secretary of the Interior, Bruce Babbitt, representing President Bill Clinton, as well as oceanographic explorer Jean-Michel Cousteau and the Sierra Club's executive director Carl Pope. The last of these still acknowledges that this event was his first striking encounter with the intersection of faith and the environment.

The patriarch's undiluted words represented a radical, indeed revolutionary shift in emphasis on a subject so fundamental to theology and at the same time so objectionable to the layperson. The national environmental news journal, *Greenwire*,[33] highlighted the patriarch's words as the "quote of the day." But of course, it was much more than this. Bruce Babbitt declared that the pronouncement would be seen in the future as one of the seminal religious statements of our time. Larry Stammer, religion writer for the *Los Angeles Times*, called it "an unprecedented religious defense of the environment … the first time that a major international religious leader has explicitly linked environmental problems with sinful behavior."[34]

Such a radical statement of faith and revolutionary concept of sin are far removed from any enterprise of ecological terrorizing or political fear-mongering, of which the ecumenical patriarch is often accused by his detractors.[35] This incorrect thinking about sin—arguably a denial of sin—is a form of pride and prejudice, a uniquely human attribute. It belongs to Adam; it is part and parcel

---

[32]Bartholomew address in Santa Barbara, California, 1997, in John Chryssavgis, ed., *On Earth as in Heaven: Ecological Vision and Initiatives of Ecumenical Patriarch Bartholomew* (New York: Fordham University Press, 2011), 99. Also see "Exclusive: Patriarch Bartholomew on Pope Francis' Climate Encyclical," http://time.com/3926076/pope-francis-encyclical-patriarch-bartholomew/ (accessed September 1, 2018).

[33]*Greenwire*, November 10, 1997.

[34]*Los Angeles Times*, Sunday, November 9, 1997.

[35]See Butler and Morriss, *Creation and the Heart of Man*, 7 and 63, where the authors instruct the worldwide leader of the Orthodox Church on the biblical and patristic roots of their approach, while advising Orthodox readers to "reject the tendency toward apocalyptic rhetoric among many environmentalists." See also the editor of their book, Dylan Pahman—in his "Climate Change, the Green Patriarch, and the Disposition of Fear," *First Things*, December 3, 2013—who accuses the patriarch for "using the tragedy [of ecological disaster] to advocate for a political cause through a disposition of fear."

of "original sin"—what Orthodox Christian theology prefers to call "ancestral sin," which never introduces a sense of false delusion or defensive sensitivity but always implies a constant struggle to avoid brokenness and mortality.

Over the centuries, but especially during the Middle Ages, sin has undoubtedly been perceived and promoted through the very narrow lens of transgression, which added an exclusively legalistic and moralistic dimension to the notion of wrongdoing and culpability. Instead of defining sin as a breakdown in relationships—whether among people, between people and the planet, or with God—it was reduced to a list of transgressions or misdemeanors before a sadistic, stringent father figure somewhere in the distant heavens.

Of course, nowadays, it is scarcely acceptable to speak of sin. Sin fatigue has led to a dilution and demolition of the notion of sin. In the words of Richard Dawkins, "The Christian focus is overwhelmingly on sin sin sin sin sin sin sin. What a nasty little preoccupation to have dominating your life."[36] Ironically, Dawkins repeats the word seven times, wittingly or unwittingly perhaps echoing the medieval concept of seven deadly vices. It is true that theologians have for far too long focused on the individual implications of sin. However, the environmental crisis reminds us of its cosmic consequences and global connotations, which are more than merely social, spiritual, or psychological. Every act of exploitation, pollution, or destruction of the natural environment is an offense against God. In *A History of Sin*,[37] John Portmann of the University of Virginia includes "harming the environment" as one of the "modern sins," even quoting Ecumenical Patriarch Bartholomew. And, in *Laudato Si'*, Pope Francis twice acknowledges this unprecedented and unusual notion of ecological sin advanced by the patriarch.[38]

Distortion or Connection?

In addition to a distorted theology of stewardship and sin, climate deniers and disdainers are characterized by a skewed concept of free

---

[36]Richard Dawkins, *The God Delusion* (Boston, MA: Houghton Mifflin, 2006).
[37]John Portman, *A History of Sin: Its Evolution to Today and Beyond* (Lanham, MD: Rowman and Littlefield, 2007).
[38]Pope Francis, *Laudato Si'*, paragraphs 8 and 9.

will and greed, as well as asceticism and compassion, all of which will be discussed more extensively in the chapter that follows. At this point, it is sufficient simply to recall that sin involves choice, a gift of free will from God. Are we willing to choose to make sacrifices, or are our choices based on the self-centeredness and individualism? Can Christians in good conscience support a radical approach to private liberty and private property? Is there no authority or morality beyond one's own opinion and desire? In this respect, is it wrong—if not dangerous—to confound libertarian values with religious principles, particularly Christian virtues?

Such libertarian ideology and mercenary selfishness is diametrically opposed to the Christian gospel. Moreover, it is incompatible with religious asceticism, which aims at restraining the crude and irrational passions of greed or avarice, along with envy or lust that are the drivers behind the market economy and free trade. The jungle ethic of survival of the fittest is fundamentally irreconcilable with the Eucharistic ethos; the former suggests a "dog eats dog society,"[39] while the latter resonates the words of Christ at the last supper: "Take, eat ... my body; drink of this my blood" (Mt. 26:26-28). For deniers and disdainers, environmentalism has become a conspiracy against commerce and the freedom to consume whatever we want whenever we want. By contrast, a sacramental worldview emphasizes personal communion, not individual consumption; it embraces human persons, not financial profits. As John Steinbeck wrote in *The Grapes of Wrath*, "A bank or a company ... [are] creatures [that] don't breathe ... They breathe profits ... It is just so."[40]

What we face today is ultimately a choice about what sort of human beings we want to be. To this end, Christian Scripture provides a compelling argument and a clear picture of what humanity should resemble in light of its creation by a loving God and its reconciliation by the divine Word.[41] How could it be otherwise for a religion based on the cosmic reconciliation of two poles: the incarnation of the Word in flesh and the transformation of the entire creation by the Creator?

---

[39]From Mike Wallace's 1959 interview with Ayn Rand, where Wallace observed, "What you are describing becomes a 'dog eats dog' society."
[40]John Steinbeck, *The Grapes of Wrath* (New York: The Viking Press, 1939).
[41]Rowan Williams, *Faith in the Public Square* (London: Bloomsbury, 2012), 206.

9

Asking the Right Questions

The Devil's Advocate, Part 2

Greed or Grace?

The Blinding Dazzle of Markets

God's gift of free will threads the narrative of our relationship with him from the original Garden of Eden to the contemporary issues of climate concern. But free will also has other corollaries—both bad and good—including sin and greed, asceticism and compassion. How will we exercise our free will when it comes to these principles and caring for creation? The answers affect our relationship not only with God but also with creation and other people; at the same time, the answers refute the claims of those who deny that we are abusing creation.

It is clear, then, that misdirected free will results in the sin of greed, of overconsuming and overspending on misguided priorities. Disdainers concerned about the economic impact of environmental solutions contend that Orthodox theologians are unacquainted with the intricacies of economy and the markets. This is as superficial and simplistic a criticism as the stereotypical claim by presidential candidates and conventional politicians that religion should steer away from science, while the church should shy away from politics.[1] Still, theologians cannot take a pass on

---

[1] See J. Couretas, "Patriarch, Pope and a Bishop's 'Radical Ecology,'" Acton Institute Powerblog, June 23, 2015: "Bartholomew and his clergy continue to scold, seemingly unaware that theological platitudes about 'charity over greed and frugality over wastefulness' don't cut it when economic growth and jobs are on the line."

economics, especially since financial issues appear to be a principal priority when it comes to climate action; ironically, by contrast, they rarely seem to be but an incidental concern when discussion revolves around military conflict and national security or military pride and global terrorism.

Only humility and justice can ultimately reconcile an otherwise divided world, while preserving a planet otherwise exploited by greed and overconsumption. Many will recall President George W. Bush seizing an extraordinary opportunity to set things straight in the wake of the terrorist attack in New York City on September 11, 2001. He appeared on television and declared, "Americans are asking, 'What is expected of us?' " As I watched, I waited desperately for the answer; I thought he might perhaps advise—something we were told was equally infused into his blood as any predilection to war—"Read the Bible!" "Attend church!" or simply "Fast!"[2] Instead, he advocated: "Go shopping and spend money, go out and travel ... " Such counsel certainly adheres to and affirms the former president's market creed: "There's only one history, and it's the history of freedom."[3]

We are clearly responsible for understanding how the markets have changed us by changing the way we perceive the world and our place in the world. That, however, requires more than simply fiscal awareness; it involves what the Shepherd of Hermas in the early second century called "a great understanding"[4] and what Austro-Hungarian economic sociologist Karl Polanyi in the early 1940s called "a great transformation."[5] Embracing the privileges of capitalism does not mean excusing its inherent deficiencies

---

[2]After all, other leaders have proposed such measures in the past; see, for example, the Presidential Proclamation by John Adams in 1798, in R. D. Chatham, *Fasting: A Biblical-Historical Study* (South Plainfield, NJ: Bridge Publishing, 1987), 163f.

[3]Raj Patel, *Stuffed and Starved*, 140. On the deeper connection between what we consume and what we believe, see Michael Schut, ed., *Food and Faith: Justice, Joy and Daily Bread* (Denver, CO: Living the Good News, 2006). On the ethical dimensions of food and farming, see also Joyce D'Silva and John Webster, eds., *The Meat Crisis: Developing More Sustainable Production and Consumption* (London and Washington, DC: Earthscan, 2010).

[4]Shepherd of Hermas, *Mandate* IV, ii, 2.

[5]Karl Polanyi, *The Great Transformation: The Political and Economic Origins of Our Time*, 2nd paperback ed. (Boston, MA: Beacon Press, 2001).

or dangers; nor again is consumer economy justified by an ethic of convenience. The cross as a symbol of sacrifice and sharing mitigates the glare of the market. People must learn—or relearn—that the benefit of asceticism, just as the opposite of consumption, is neither thrift nor waste; it is fairness and generosity, which result in compassion and communion.

Today's free market mentality—where great predators roam and the law of the jungle reigns—is hardly an expression of fairness or philanthropy. Otherwise, how can coal be considered good simply because "it is widely available, inexpensive, and easy to use."[6] Or why would stealing $500 amount to a felony and larceny, punishable no less than by imprisonment, when the financial speculation in stocks that deprives millions of their homes and savings is rewarded by state support and amnesty?[7] "The dazzle of free markets has blinded [people] to other ways of seeing the world ... This is not only delusional—it also distorts the way we see other people. Seeing fellow human beings as mere co-consumers blinds us to the deeper connections between us, and distorts our political choices."[8] Ultimately, it comes down to free will, the choice between greed and grace. Carbon may not be the devil; and green is not necessarily the messiah. However, greed is undeniably the enemy—a matter of spirituality and not prosperity.

Simply put, creation is—at least from a religious perspective—a divine gift, while the economy and politics of the market is a human fabrication. Libertarians casually adapt the biblical mandate of creation care, frequently adopting the notion of stewardship, while conveniently advancing the politics of land appropriation and exploitation. In actual fact, fundamental biblical and spiritual norms are inverted, while selfishness is exalted as normal conduct and altruism is relegated to noble disposition. In both cases, the false theology and the faithless management forewarned by the prophet Isaiah are brazenly disregarded.

---

[6]Butler and Morriss, *Creation and the Heart*, 77.
[7]See Slavoj Žižek, *Trouble in Paradise: From the End of History to the End of Capitalism* (Brooklyn, NY: Melville House, 2015), which illustrates in a provocative, yet constructive way the contradictions of contemporary capitalism.
[8]Raj Patel, *The Value of Nothing: How to Reshape Market Society and Redefine Society* (New York: Picador, 2009), 3 and 22.

Woe to those who decree iniquitous decrees, and the writers who keep writing oppression; to turn aside the needy from justice and to rob the poor of my people of their right. (Isa. 10:1-2)
Everyone who thirsts, come to the waters; and he who has no money, come, buy, and eat! Come, buy wine and milk without money and without price. Why do you spend your money for that which is not bread, and your labor for that which does not satisfy? (Isa. 55:1-2)

For some inexcusable reason and by some indefensible process, disciples of Ayn Rand and other libertarians have managed to reverse biblical norms, blatantly exalting selfishness and brazenly condemning benevolence. Any ethical guidelines that are not compatible with or accommodated by a facile, laissez-faire libertarianism are substituted by a moral consensus that assigns a dominant role to the market. These assumptions and preferences— which harbor a prevailing market that shapes the needs and satisfactions central to personal pleasure and profit—are not even called to question.

The great driver, and at the same time the great donor, behind this market philosophy is of course the multinational or global corporate mentality. This philosophy—for want of a better term, since minimal critical reflection is ever involved—is bipartisan or nonpartisan. Thus, former US House of Representatives Speaker John Boehner can freely admit, "Businesses need to be set free. [T]hey've been antagonized by a government that favors bureaucrats over market-based solutions."[9] Frequently large corporations and oil magnates—or their financial surrogates and foundations—fund think tanks such as the Acton Institute, which shelters a broad "ecumenical" variety of protestant proponents of the uncontested market economy, who in turn influence public policy makers.

Correcting the Glare

With regard to environmental change, the emphasis should be on its religious synonyms: conversion or transformation. Otherwise,

---

[9]See http://www.nytimes.com/2011/09/16/us/politics/jobs-speech-by-house-speaker-john-boehner.html?r=0 (accessed September 1, 2018).

we are not really facing reality; we are actually in denial. In the aftermath of a worldwide financial breakdown and meltdown in 2008, how can we justify uncritically following the same patterns and practices? To quote Larry Lohmann, a prominent climate change thinker in the UK, "[The] climate problem isn't a new problem; it's a continuation of old problems."[10] For instance, when it comes to solutions like cap-and-trade, are we neglecting that it is not so much the "cap" as it is the "trade" itself that ultimately matters?

Enough is enough. Thomas Hobbes' Leviathan defines human nature as competitive, even bellicose; Jean-Jacques Rousseau' *Discourse on Inequality* turned this on its head, claiming that it was still possible for people to check their instincts and learn to be "satisfied." And John Locke's "life, liberty, and property" in *The Two Treatises of Civil Government* differs minimally from the determinative axiom of "Life, Liberty, and the pursuit of Happiness" in the US Declaration of Independence. "What needs to be plucked out of markets is the perpetual and overriding hunger for expansion and profit that has brought us to the brink of ecological catastrophe; what needs to be plucked out of us is the belief that markets are the only way to value our world."[11]

An opinion piece by Paul Farrell on the *Wall Street Journal* webpage on February 16, 2015, was entitled: "Planet Earth is the Titanic, Climate Change Is the Iceberg," which I paraphrase,

> Yes, the world is sinking. And the band keeps playing: On the Titanic, first violinist, Big Oil's Koch Brothers' Empire. For them capitalism is the solution to everything; everyone has a price, especially politicians. Second chair, the world's moral authority, Patriarch Bartholomew and Pope Francis warning that capitalism is the "root cause of the world's problems." No harmony. And playing a mean solo flute, Mother Nature, who doesn't care what the Kochs do, nor what religious leaders say.

The problem is not who should speak for science or economy, but rather who should be silent on growth and greed. Activity

---

[10]Patel, *The Value of Nothing*, 162.
[11]Ibid., 188.

in a consumer society is invariably guided by the incentive and imperative to satisfy an insatiable and irrational preference for the lowest cost produced by demand of a given commodity at any expense to the common interest.[12]

Have we honestly become so addicted to fantasies about riches without risk and profit without price? Do we honestly believe that our endless and mindless manipulation of the earth's resources comes without cost or consequence? Our economy and technology are toxic when divorced from our vocation to see the world as God would. And if God saw the world as "very good" on that sixth day of creation, then we too are called to sense in our world the promise of beauty and to perceive the world in its unfathomable interrelatedness.

Fortunately, an emerging global campaign to encourage divestment points out that carbon-intensive projects and investments are not just bad for the environment, but in fact they constitute bad economics, with assets that can never be realized in a carbon constrained world. Fossil fuel companies base their market value on their reserves in coal, gas, and oil. But it is becoming increasingly clear that a significant proportion of these reserves can never be used without causing catastrophic climate change.[13]

Realistically, most people will not voluntarily choose to sacrifice profits or change practices. The primary purpose and main method of capitalism is to get people to make more money and live more luxuriously. Any shift or change could disrupt a market fundamentalism that rests on such pillars as privatization and deregulation—with all the corollary consequences for lowering corporate taxation and reducing public spending. However, there ultimately needs to be a choice between profit and principle; that choice, I would argue, is the challenge of the cross as laying down one's life for another. As 2016 Nobel Laureate Bob Dylan put it,

---

[12]See, for example, the formative works by J. O'Neill, *Ecology, Policy and Politics: Human Well-Being and the Natural World* (London: Routledge, 1994), and *The Market: Ethics, Knowledge and Politics* (London: Routledge, 1998).

[13]On October 8, 2013, Paul Thornton, letter editor for the *Los Angeles Times*, wrote: "Letters to the editor that say 'there's no sign humans have caused climate change' do not get printed … Simply put, I do my best to keep errors of fact off the letters page; when one does run, a correction is published. Saying 'there's no sign humans have caused climate change' is not stating an opinion; it's asserting a factual inaccuracy."

You may be a preacher with your spiritual pride
But you're gonna have to serve somebody . . .
[I]t may be the devil or it may be the Lord
But you're gonna have to serve somebody.

Christian Scripture adopts a starker, stricter articulation: "You cannot serve God and mammon" (Lk. 16:13). To claim otherwise would be tantamount to either holy ignorance—no longer easy to explain or excuse[14]—or, in the case of most well-intentioned people, unholy resistance. Since the mid-twentieth century, science has generally ceased to be regarded as doctrine and is now embraced as method; it no longer exists in an ivory tower but—in its interface and intercourse with society—has today become intertwined with technology, economy, and politics. Still, unholy resistance is in fact a much more subtle temptation, much more toxic a contamination.

So there are many forms of denial. Some may denounce the science; but most deny the consequences of the science. When it comes to meeting the greatest challenge of our times in addressing the environmental crisis, we are either too skeptical or too sluggish to respond. We are either too critical of ecological issues, which we dismiss as merely political or fashionable, or else too cautious of scientific data, about which we are often uninformed or even in denial. There is undoubtedly good reason for our skepticism and suspicion. Simply put, we have too much at stake! If we take seriously into consideration the issues before us, then our lifestyles would, to a greater or lesser degree, be immediately impacted and disturbed. It is far more convenient to presume guiltlessness and preserve the status quo.

Tampering with the markets might involve laws to protect the environment and spending to enforce them. Yet, while it may be possible to convince individuals and perhaps institutions to embrace "green" priorities or even to endure financial loss, overcoming arrogance and ignorance is neither simple nor straightforward. It comes as no surprise, then, that conservatives like to ridicule the

---

[14]As Garry Wills put it in the *New York Review of Books* (June 18, 2015): French anthropologist Olivier Roy defines "holy ignorance" not as the failure of intelligence, but rather as the proud refusal to know things tainted by the arrogance of inevitability. Professor Roy writes, "There is a close link between secularization and religious revivalism, which is not a reaction against secularization, but the product of it. Secularism engenders religion."

use of Styrofoam cups or solar power in communities. Of course, abandoning Styrofoam at the very least reveals an awareness of issues that is far less discernible in drilling for or living with oil. Nevertheless, climate solutions also call for far more radical changes in spiritual healing and social justice. Again, this has less to do with customs than choices; "[I]t has less to do with the mechanics of solar power than the politics of human power."[15] Which may well explain why climate change has conservatives feeling very threatened and judgmental. It is simply much easier to deny it—a criticism and reservation to which we now turn our attention.

Conservation or Conversion?

In Orthodox tradition and theology, grace is a gift of the Spirit and compassion a fruit of asceticism—at least of asceticism understood correctly and practiced authentically. Deniers and disdainers misunderstand the notion of ascesis, perceiving it as one in a long list of religious principles or disciplinary practices. Furthermore, many of them regard any concern for environmentalism as "inversely proportional to our effectiveness in transfiguring the environment."[16] Any appreciation for the ascetic principles in Christianity is incorrectly considered as being "in line with free market principles of voluntary activity and lifestyle choices."[17] The conviction is that asceticism is not imposed; nor can it deny others the benefits of creation.[18] And while such critics would espouse the Gospel commandment to "seek first the kingdom of heaven," they would interpret it narrowly in light of the subsequent clause of that commission, namely that "all these things on earth will be yours as well" (Mt. 6:33). Any other interpretation is renounced and rejected as yielding to "the temptation of putting the ascetical tradition in the service of another agenda."[19]

Of course, adopting theological and spiritual terminology in order to imbue this with political and economic ideology is the sin

---

[15]Naomi Klein, *This Changes Everything: Capitalism vs. the Climate* (New York: Simon & Schuster, 2014), 25.
[16]Butler and Morriss, *Creation and the Heart*, 58.
[17]Ibid., 57.
[18]Ibid., 59.
[19]Ibid., 53.

of religious mercenaries, sometimes disguised as staunch champions of the patristic tradition. Climate deniers may themselves be critical of "impractical or facile policy recommendations" as well as of "naïve or even willful ignorance of contemporary economics."[20] Nonetheless, their attitudes, arguments, and actions seem to echo John Adams rather than John Chrysostom; and their actions reflect the way of the market but not the mystic.

This may be why, despite the alarming statistics and abundant information at our disposal, we appear to be all the more distant from any solution? From an Orthodox spiritual viewpoint, I know that my church tells me to stop and reflect. That, I feel, is what I am also called to do as a theologian and clergyman.

Allow me, then, to respond by doing what I am ordained to do: namely, not by advancing political or liberal priorities or addressing conservative or consumerist predilections, but rather by preaching the Crucifixion and Resurrection of Jesus Christ, proclaiming the power of silence and tears, and communicating a sacramental worldview. I believe it is as critical to speak honestly from one's own perspective as it is to learn humbly from one another's. And my personal perspective revolves around and centers on liturgy. That is where my mind drifts when I hear the notions of "con-serving" or "pre-serving," and sacrament or sacredness. I immediately contemplate serving at the altar of the world, con-celebrating what Maximus the Confessor in the seventh-century called "a cosmic liturgy." In such a worldview, everything bears a sacramental seal and everything enjoys a sacred significance.

There is a moment in the Divine Liturgy of the Orthodox Church, when the deacon—as I have now repeatedly and respectfully done for over three decades—stands in the middle of the temple and, in apostolic conviction and fervor, chants aloud: "Let us stand well; let us stand in awe." As a venerable mentor once told me, the deacon is not merely reminding people to be upstanding; in fact, the deacon is saying, "Don't just do something; stand there!"

It is true that, before we can act—and we should be humble enough to recall, from time to time, that it is our "acting" that got us into this mess in the first place—we should first refrain from

---

[20]Ibid., 10–11. See also the mistrust of government on p. 73: "Man's fallen nature should make us wary of centralizing power in the hands of government officials who are not exempt from that fallen nature."

acting! We should ruminate and meditate on the way we are living, on what we are doing. If we are going to effect a shift in our attitude and change our lifestyle in order to regulate or reverse the environmental crisis, we must first of all transform the way we perceive our world and ourselves; we must change our worldview, our image or "icon" of the world. This calls for a change of mindset, a conversion of heart that is the essence of repentance and its Greek concomitant *metanoia*.

Contemplative silence or stillness for the purpose of change or conversion creates the time and space for what Olivier Clément calls a "wondering and respectful distance" between the world and us.[21] Human beings can keep nature "at a distance, at arms length, so to speak; and so they can reflect on and transform it."[22] This is not a distance in the sense of separation between humankind and other creatures, but rather a capacity that allows every created being to exist in itself and for its Creator, beyond and before any services it provides to the rest of the ecosystem. Such is the essence of at-one-ment or reconciliation with the world; it implies sharing the same space with all of God's creation—the literal meaning of the Greek word for "forgiveness" (synchoresis).

Perhaps this is what we are called to proclaim and provide for our world; perhaps what we are called to do is not so much acquire or produce something for the planet, but rather to relinquish and surrender something to our planet. We need to offer nature and creation more space for healing and restoration. It is a process analogous to reparations that human communities, too, require for reconciliation and rehabilitation. In this light, land rights and water rights are the other side of the same coin we might label as fundamental human rights. In this context, our discourse should be less about rights or privileges and more about responsibilities or obligations. Preserving God's creation is about protecting all people. Indeed, indigenous peoples of the world are especially

---

[21]Olivier Clément, *The Roots of Christian Mysticism: Texts from the Patristic Era with Commentary* (London: New City, 1993), 141.

[22]From an address by literary critic and philosopher Terry Eagleton, entitled "Nature, Marx, and Badgers," delivered on June 9, 2015, at Halki Summit II, a conference organized by the Ecumenical Patriarchate. Eagleton went on to say that human peculiarism does not have to betray exceptionalism or hubris; it may simply define the peculiar relationship of human beings to the rest of nature.

conscious of and sensitive to the fact that all people are called to care for all creatures.

Regrettably, however, while we should be preserving larger parts of the planet—scientists recommend conserving at least half of the planet—in reality we are only protecting 15 percent of our earth from exploitation and 2 percent of our oceans from overfishing. Creation is more or less being treated like a Ponzi scheme where individuals or corporations withdraw resources but never deposit replacements, always with the false assurance and immediate gratification of new investment. Surely it does not take the training of an economist to recognize that this is the securest and swiftest way to failure and devastation.

The liturgy proposes a broader and farther-reaching perspective. Cosmic liturgy includes humankind as it is: a curious, inventive, adventurous creature. It also has room for a proper use of the world through creativity and technology, including a diverse range of solutions to environmental problems. Moreover, this vision of the cosmos is predisposed to solutions that work with nature, recognizing the embedded wisdom that also forms part of the cosmic "praise." In this panorama, it would not be unreasonable to conceive that those mosquito-infested salt marshes and sand dunes that block our view of the sea may actually serve an invaluable purpose when menacing storms arise. There is an asceticism involved in suspending our own preconceived ideas of how the world should be and instead acknowledging that nature sometimes know best, so that we might actually try to work with natural systems rather than conquer them.

These broad perspectives inform the discipline in our day-to-day lives related to greed, consumption, and compassion. In practical terms the ascetic approach is not merely a matter of consuming less, although this too is an important part of creation care. Asceticism has more to do with making the right choices, in our personal lives as in our everyday interactions.

Numerous practical ideas are available and readily accessible for those interested in their ecological footprint on the planet and their environmental impact on its population. Many congregations and communities have made considerable progress in this regard. Seeking their counsel or offering advice is undoubtedly a fundamental form of sharing and communion, especially in supporting parishes still making or considering initial steps. Individuals and groups may consult professional environmental auditors, often freely at the disposal of local communities.[23]

Individuals can also make a difference by becoming sensitive to what they use (energy-efficient light bulbs and heating/cooling systems) and what they can reuse (recycled paper, bags, ink cartridges, glassware, and cutlery), what they waste (electricity, water, heat, energy, even cups and plates) and what they can do (carpooling or support of local products). These efforts can entail absorbing expenses and changing longstanding practices in the early stages—beyond ideological opposition in the pews—so it is hardly surprising that such practical ideas often encounter some resistance.

Letting go of old consumption habits and destructive lifestyle choices involves the ascetic principle of detachment. When we learn to let go of something, we also learn what is truly worth holding on to. Detachment becomes a surrender of greed and a school of grace. This means that detachment teaches us how to shed excess luggage in order to travel and tread more lightly—and the truth is that we can always do with far less than we imagine or manage. The context here is a struggle to be less centered on ourselves and the world in order to concentrate more on others and God.

Attachment or Detachment?

As we move away from hardened habits and espouse a spirituality of detachment, we literally go through the stages of withdrawal. After all, our culture conditions us to believe that the more we have, the better off we are. By contrast, the context of the desert fathers and mothers taught them that the less they had, the more they could be. It is simply impossible to be whole or be caring—literally to pray or to share something precious, even to hold a lover's hand— when our fists are tightly clenched.

Essentially, this means that love is the only and ultimate purpose of detachment. We are, as Abba Isaiah of Scetis put it, called "to

---

[23]For practical details on how to achieve greater awareness and environmental action in your community, see Frederick Krueger, ed., *Greening the Orthodox Parish: A Handbook for Christian Ecological Practice* (Santa Rosa, CA: The Orthodox Fellowship of the Transfiguration, 2012).

love to love."[24] Nothing is more despicable in light of biblical commandments and evangelical precepts than insensitivity and indifference to others, which, as the same Abba Isaiah assures us, is tantamount to an absence of sensitivity to and awareness of God.[25] In brief: love is life; and God is love (1 Jn 4:8).

In this sense, detachment means becoming transparent, both in relationships with other people as in attitudes toward material things and creation:

> Abba Agathon was walking with his disciples. One of them, on finding a small green pea on the road, said to the old man: "Father, may I take it?" The old man, looking at him with astonishment, replied: "Was it you that put it there?" "No," said the brother. "How then," continued the old man, "can you take up something, which you did not put down?"[26]

The aim of such absolute detachment is the practice of letting go, the starting point and ending point of authentic living and authentic action, a state where we are no longer conditioned by the burden of necessity but prepared for the novelty and surprise of grace.

Arguably the clearest evidence that we are laboring for such compassionate sensitivity and caring responsibility lies in the fulfillment of the apostolic mandate to "bear one another's burdens" (Gal. 6:2). Not wounding one's neighbor, while bearing one another's burdens—sometimes slightly, at other times fully, but at the very least partially—is the clearest and most concise definition of the Christian life in the *Letters* of the mid-sixth century elders, Barsanuphius and John.[27]

Such is the alternative worldview of asceticism, where what we learn first and foremost is to see that we are all mutually interdependent—to perceive the world as intimately interconnected, even beyond our wildest imagination—and where we discover that nothing living is self-contained but rather reflects the fragility of the

---

[24]Isaiah, *Ascetic Discourse* XVI. For the discourses, see *Abba Isaiah of Scetis: Ascetic Discourses*, trans. John Chryssavgis and Robert Penkett (Kalamazoo, MI: Cistercian Publications, 2002), 119–30.

[25]*Ascetic Discourses* V (69–76), XVI (119–30), XVIII (139–42), and XXVI (211–18).

[26]Agathon 11, *Sayings*, Ward, 19.

[27]See their *Letters* 70–3, in *Barsanuphius and John: Letters*, trans. John Chryssavgis, 2 vols. (Washington, DC: The Catholic University of America Press, 2006), 93–9.

whole world: "If one member suffers, all suffer together with it" (1 Cor. 12:26). There is no autonomy, only a distinction between a sense of responsibility and a lack thereof. To speak of such awareness and perception is to adopt an alternative way. Ultimately, it is to identify the tension within our soul and the conflict within our world between two wills or two laws, as Paul describes this in Romans, Chapter 7: "I delight in the law of God, in my inmost self, but I see in my members another law at war with the law of my mind and making me captive to the law of sin that dwells in my members" (vv. 22–23).

This struggle is the very essence of asceticism, and it is an icon of the cross that promises neither comfort nor complacency.

The "ascetic imperative"[28] implies more than simply living or living simply. It issues into compassion and concern for all people, to the least of our brothers and sisters, as well as to all creation, to the last speck of dust. Compassion is what Christians are called to be and supposed to be about—a compassion extended to every living being and every natural landscape. Beyond the scriptural "water to drink" (Mt. 25:42) or the proverbial "cup of cold water" extended to every stranger,[29] Christian compassion should be expanded to the reverence for and sustenance of every living creature.

What is ultimately called for is radical repentance, nothing less than a transformation of accustomed ways. The question is, [A]re we willing to change or will resistance continue? Are we willing to take the steps necessary for personal transformation? Are we willing to take the steps necessary for societal transformation? A stellar example of how to raise such awareness in hearts and in communities can be seen in the extensive environmental ministry of Ecumenical Patriarchate Bartholomew, whose focus is on creation as the body of Christ. The patriarch considers both the planet and all people as the incarnate body of the Creator, an inseparable and interconnected part of the living God. He is a contemporary witness to the sacramental worldview.

---

[28]From an address by Elizabeth Theokritoff at a conference on creation care sponsored by The Orthodox Fellowship of Transfiguration and held at the Greek Orthodox Cathedral in Washington, DC (November 11, 2013). The theme of the conference was "On Earth as it is in Heaven: Putting Orthodox Theology and Ecology into Practice."

[29]See Lynn White Jr., "The Future of Compassion," *The Ecumenical Review* XXX, no. 2 (April, 1978): 98–109, cited in Charles Birch, *Regaining Compassion for Humanity and Nature* (Kensington: New South Wales University Press, 1993), 9 and 76.

FIGURE 5 *Mosaic in the apse of the Basilica di Sant'Apollinare in Classe, Ravenna © Gordon Sinclair/Alamy Stock Photo.* ***See p. 192***

10

The Green Patriarch

A Contemporary Worldview and Witness

In 2006, renowned Harvard professor and winner of a Pulitzer Prize, E. O. Wilson, addressed a "letter to a southern Baptist pastor," the religious affiliation of his own childhood in Alabama, on the moral precept that he was convinced should be shared by people of all beliefs:

> I am puzzled that so many religious leaders, who spiritually represent a large majority of people around the world, have hesitated to make protection of the Creation an important part of their magisterium. Do they believe that human-centered ethics and preparation for the afterlife are the only things that matter?
> ... I am heartened by the movement growing within Christian denominations to support global conservation. The stream of thought has arisen from many sources, from evangelical to unitarian. Today it is but a rivulet. Tomorrow it will be a flood.[1]

Over the last three decades, one religious leader has discerned the signs of the times and called people's attention to the ecological

---

[1] E. O. Wilson, *The Creation: An Appeal to Save Life on Earth* (New York and London: W.W. Norton, 2006), 5–6 and 8.

and social situation relating to creation care.[2] The worldwide leader of the Orthodox churches, Ecumenical Patriarch Bartholomew has persistently proclaimed the primacy of spiritual values in determining environmental ethics and action.

No other church leader has been recognized throughout the world for so many years for his persistent leadership and dynamic initiatives in addressing the theological, ethical, and practical imperative in relation to the critical environmental issues of our time as Ecumenical Patriarch Bartholomew, who has long placed the protection of the natural environment at the head of his church's agenda, developing ecological programs, as well as chairing international gatherings and interfaith symposia.

The Making of a Patriarch

When Pope Francis released his environmental encyclical, *Laudato Si'*, on June 18, 2015, it was not surprising that he singled out and highlighted the example of Ecumenical Patriarch Bartholomew, dubbed as "the green patriarch"—a phrase publicized by the media in 1996 and formalized in the White House in 1997 by Al Gore, then vice president of the United States.

Bartholomew was born Demetrios Archondonis on February 29, 1940, on the island of Imvros, modern day Turkey.[3] The residents of this island, like the inhabitants of so many other regions of Asia Minor, have been known through the centuries for their profound tradition and pious devotion, and in general for their cultivation of spiritual values. As the young Demetrios, Patriarch Bartholomew was raised to work the earth of the heart, leading to the personal

---

[2]The ecological crisis calls for the wisdom and faith of the world's religions to raise awareness to the wonder and beauty of creation. For a general response by and challenge to the global faith community, see Mary Evelyn Tucker, *Worldly Wonder: Religions Enter Their Ecological Phase* (Chicago, IL and La Salle, IL: Open Court, 2003). See also John Grim and Mary Evelyn Tucker, *Ecology and Religion* (Washington, DC: Island Press, 2014). For a broad survey and brief introduction to diverse religious worldviews, see Richard Foltz, ed., *Worldviews, Religion, and the Environment: A Global Anthology* (Belmont, CA: Thomson Wadsworth, 2003).

[3]For a complete biography of the Ecumenical Patriarch, see John Chryssavgis, *Bartholomew: Apostle and Visionary* (Nashville, TN: HarperCollins, 2016).

transformation necessary to preserve the green of the environment as ecumenical patriarch.

His theological training also attracted the young Demetrios to move beyond the library and to breathe the air of the *oikoumene*, the breadth of the universe of theological communication and ecclesiastical reconciliation. In later years, he would see a similar connection between church and environment:

> For us at the Ecumenical Patriarchate, the term ecumenical is more than a name: it is a worldview, and a way of life. The Lord intervenes and fills His creation with His divine presence in a continuous bond. Let us work together so that we may renew the harmony between heaven and earth, so that we may transform every detail and every element of life. Let us love one another. With love, let us share with others everything we know and especially that which is useful in order to educate godly persons so that they may sanctify God's creation for the glory of His holy name.[4]

In 1961, the young Demetrios graduated from the Patriarchal School of Halki, which for 127 years trained numerous clergymen and theologians of the Ecumenical Patriarchate for ministry in many Orthodox churches throughout the world until it was forced to close its doors officially in 1971. This school was to be—and still remains—the venue for numerous meetings and seminars on environmental issues during his tenure as patriarch. In 1961, Demetrios was ordained to deacon, receiving the monastic name "Bartholomew."

From 1963 to 1968, Bartholomew attended several prestigious centers of scholarship and ecumenical dialogue, including the University of Munich (Germany), the Ecumenical Institute in Bossey (Switzerland), and the Institute of Oriental Studies of the Gregorian University in Rome (Italy), where he received his doctorate in Canon Law. Upon completion of his studies, Bartholomew returned to Constantinople where, in 1969, he was ordained to the priesthood.

---

[4]See Ecumenical Patriarch Bartholomew address to the Scenic Hudson, November 13, 2000, in *On Earth as in Heaven: Ecological Vision and Initiatives of Ecumenical Patriarch Bartholomew*, ed. John Chryssavgis (New York: Fordham University Press, 2012), 116.

From 1972, he served as director of the newly established special Personal Office of the late Patriarch Demetrios, and in 1973 was elected Metropolitan of Philadelphia.

He attended General Assemblies of the World Council of Churches—even serving as vice-chairman of the Faith and Order Commission as well as member of its Central and Executive Committees—from 1968 to 1991. These were critical and formative years for the development of the ecological sensitivity of this influential international organization.

In 1990, Bartholomew was elected Metropolitan of Chalcedon, the most senior rank among the bishops in Constantinople at the time. And in October 1991, he was elected ecumenical patriarch, "first among equals" among all Orthodox patriarchs and prelates. From the moment, and indeed from the very address, of his enthronement, Bartholomew outlined the dimensions of his leadership and vision within the Orthodox Church: the vigilant education in matters of theology, liturgy, and spirituality; the strengthening of Orthodox unity and cooperation; the continuation of ecumenical engagements with other Christian churches and confessions; the intensification of interreligious dialogue for peaceful coexistence; *and the initiation of discussion and action for the protection of the environment against ecological pollution and destruction.*

The Making of a Movement

The environmental vision and initiatives of the Ecumenical Patriarchate date back to the mid-1980s, when it organized and chaired the third session of the Pre-Synodal Pan-Orthodox Conference in Chambésy (October 28–November 6, 1986). While the decisions of this meeting were not binding, serving only as recommendations, nevertheless the representatives attending the meeting expressed and emphasized their concern for the abuse of the natural environment by human beings, especially in affluent societies of the Western world. The meeting also underlined the importance of respecting the sacredness and freedom of the human person created in the image and likeness of God, the missionary imperative and witness of the Orthodox Church in the contemporary world, as well as the harm wrought by war, racism, and inequality on human societies and the natural environment.

Thereafter, and especially as a result of the General Assembly of the World Council of Churches held in Vancouver (1983), several Inter-Orthodox meetings were organized on the subject of "Justice, Peace, and the Integrity of Creation" and attended by Orthodox representatives.

Three significant consultations followed: the first in Sofia, Bulgaria (1987). The second consultation, in Patmos, Greece (1988), marked the nine-hundredth anniversary since the foundation of the historic Monastery of St. John the Theologian on the island of Patmos. This historic island in the Mediterranean will later become the focus of a new initiative of the current ecumenical patriarch. However, in September 23–25, 1988, Ecumenical Patriarch Demetrios, under whose spiritual jurisdiction the monastery lies, assigned Metropolitan John of Pergamon as his representative to a conference organized by the Ecumenical Patriarchate, with the support of the Hellenic Ministry of Cultural Affairs, on the theme "Revelation and the Future of Humanity." One of the primary recommendations of this conference was that the Ecumenical Patriarchate should assume the responsibility of appointing a particular day of the year designated and dedicated for the protection of the natural environment.

This conference proved to be a catalyst for the direction of many subsequent patriarchal initiatives on the environment. The Christmas encyclical letter, signed by Patriarch Demetrios, looked forward to the Patmos celebrations and symposium of 1995. A third Inter-Orthodox consultation was held in Minsk, Russia (1989), while an environmental program was also piloted in Ormylia, Greece (1990).

In 1989, the same Patriarch Demetrios, immediate predecessor of Patriarch Bartholomew, who was his closest theological and administrative advisor in these and other matters, published the first official decree, an encyclical letter sent out "to the whole Church." Demetrios was widely known for his softness and meekness. Therefore, it always seemed so fitting that it was during his tenure that the Orthodox Church invited people to dedicate a day of prayer for protection of the environment, which human beings have treated so harshly; Demetrios encouraged his faithful to walk gently on the earth, just as he had in his life and ministry.

This encyclical, proclaimed on the occasion of the first day of the new ecclesiastical calendar, known as the *indictus*, formally established September 1 as a day for all Orthodox Christians within the jurisdiction of the Ecumenical Patriarchate to offer prayers for the protection and preservation of the natural creation of God. Since that time, a similar statement and spiritual reminder is issued every year, on the first day of September, to Orthodox faithful in North and South America, Western Europe, and the Great Britain, as well as in Australasia.[5]

The following year (1990), the foremost hymnographer of the monastic republic on Mount Athos, Monk Gerasimos Mikrayiannanites (d. 1991), was commissioned by the Ecumenical Patriarchate to compose a service of supplication, with prayers for the protection of the environment.[6] The Orthodox Church has always and traditionally prayed for the environment. However, whereas formerly Orthodox faithful prayed to be delivered from natural calamities, from June 6, 1989, the ecumenical patriarch called Orthodox Christians to pray for the environment to be delivered from the abusive acts of humans. Thus, most of the prayers

---

[5]Echoing and citing this appeal by the Ecumenical Patriarchate, and in response to the World Summit on Sustainable Development scheduled for Johannesburg, the central committee of the World Council of Churches passed a resolution (Document GEN 17, 6.2) in its meeting of August 26–September 3, 2002, urging member churches to mark September 1 each year as a day of prayer for the environment and its sustainability. This recommendation was based on a note from its program committee observing: "Some churches have acted with courage and vision in advocating for a sustainable earth. The call of His All-Holiness Bartholomew I, the Ecumenical Patriarch of Constantinople, to Christians around the world to celebrate September 1st as Creation Day so as to pray for the World Summit on Sustainable Development, stands testimony to the commitment of the churches to the earth." The European Conference of Churches (CEC) followed suit. Thus, the Second European Ecumenical Assembly (Graz Austria, 1997) recommended following the initiative of the ecumenical patriarch and promoted September 1 as the Day for Creation and September 1 to October 4 as a Time for Creation. The Third European Ecumenical Assembly (Sibiu, Romania, 2007) formally adopted the two recommendations. In 2015, Pope Francis inaugurated September 1 as a day of prayer for the natural environment for the Roman Catholic Church throughout the world. The Anglican Communion followed suit the next year. Indeed, in 2017, for the first time ever, Pope Francis and Patriarch Bartholomew issued a joint statement on the occasion of September 1.

[6]This service was published in 1991 and translated into English by Fr. Ephrem Lash in England. It was among the last services to be composed by Fr. Gerasimos. The translation appeared as *Office of Vespers for the Preservation of Creation* in *Orthodoxy and Ecology: Resource Book* (Bialystok: Syndesmos, 1996). A second English translation appeared in the United States entitled *Vespers for the Protection of the Environment* (Northridge, CA: Narthex Press, 2001).

composed by Fr. Gerasimos are supplications for repentance, invitations for conversion, and cries of nostalgia for a lost paradise, from which we have been alienated by destroying the world.

Seminars, Symposia, and Summits

A month after his election to the throne of Constantinople, in November 1991, Ecumenical Patriarch Bartholomew initiated and convened an ecological meeting on the island of Crete. The title of the gathering was: "Living in the Creation of the Lord." That convention was attended and officially opened by Prince Philip, the Duke of Edinburgh and International Chairman of the World Wildlife Foundation.

Four months later, Bartholomew called a meeting of all Orthodox patriarchs and primates, who gathered at the Phanar (the offices of the Ecumenical Patriarchate in Istanbul) in March 1992 for an historical expression of unity in theological vision and pastoral concern. Here, the ecumenical patriarch again introduced the topic of the protection of the natural environment and asked from all the leaders of the Orthodox churches to inform their communities about the critical significance of this issue for our times. The official message of the Orthodox primates to their churches throughout the world officially approved and endorsed the patriarchal initiative to establish September 1 as a day of Pan-Orthodox prayer for the environment.

In the summer of the same year, the Duke of Edinburgh accepted an invitation to visit the Phanar and address an environmental seminar at the Theological School of Halki. The ecumenical patriarch returned the visit to the duke, meeting with him in November 1993, at Buckingham Palace where they sealed a friendship of common purpose and active cooperation for the preservation of the environment.

Another ecological seminar was convened two months later at the historical Theological School of Halki, the first of five successive annual summer seminars held there on diverse and focused aspects of the environment. Topics ranged from "Environment and Religious Education" (1994), "Environment and Ethics" (1995), "Environment and Communications" (1996), "Environment and Justice" (1997), and "Environment and Poverty" (1998).

These unprecedented seminars were designed to promote environmental awareness and action inspired by the initiatives of the Ecumenical Patriarchate, seeking to engage leading theologians, environmentalists, scientists, civil servants, and other experts. Speakers included religious leaders, governmental authorities, scientists and ethicists, academicians and intellectuals, as well as artists and journalists. Participants represented all major Christian denominations and faith communities.

In 1994, the University of the Aegean conferred an honorary doctoral degree on Patriarch Bartholomew, the first of a long series of awards and honorary degrees presented to the patriarch in recognition of his efforts and initiatives for the environment, which included the first international Visionary Award for Environmental Achievement from the New York-based organization Scenic Hudson in 2000 and the Sophie Prize of Norway in 2002. Later, for "defining environmentalism as a spiritual responsibility" Ecumenical Patriarch Bartholomew was named to *Time* 100, the magazine's list of the one hundred most influential people in the world for 2008.

Convinced that any appreciation of the environmental concerns of our times must occur in dialogue with other Christian confessions, other religious faiths, as well as other scientific disciplines, Patriarch Bartholomew established in 1995 the interfaith and interdisciplinary Religious and Scientific Committee co-chaired by the Most Reverend Metropolitan John (Zizioulas) of Pergamon, professor of theology at King's College (London) and the University of Thessalonika (Greece), together with Dr. Jane Lubchenco, distinguished professor of marine biology at Oregon State University and subsequent administrator of National Oceanic and Atmospheric Administration.

The Religious and Scientific Committee—coordinated from 1995 to 2012 by Maria Becket, a Greek activist for social justice and creation care—convened eight international, interdisciplinary, and interreligious symposia in order to study and reflect on the fate of the world's rivers, seas, and oceans that cover two-thirds of the planet's surface.[7] These symposia gathered scientists, environmentalists,

---

[7]For more details on Symposia I–VIII, convened between 1995 and 2009, see http://www.rsesymposia.org/. For a broad interfaith approach to creation care, see the publications from a series of twelve conferences entitled "Religions of the World and Ecology," organized by Mary Evelyn Tucker and John Grim at Harvard's Center

journalists, policy-makers, and representatives of the world's major religions in an effort to draw global attention to the plight of waters from the Aegean and Black Seas to the Danube and Amazon Rivers.

Symposium I: Revelation and the Environment convened in 1995, under the joint auspices of Patriarch Bartholomew and Prince Philip for the nineteen-hundredth anniversary of St. John's book of Revelation. Traveling on ship through the Aegean and the Eastern Mediterranean and concluding on the island of Patmos, the two hundred participants of this symposium identified the pollution of the world's waters as a threat to the survival of the planet and recommended the creation of a common language for scientific and theological thought to overcome centuries of estrangement and misunderstanding between reason and faith.

It is critical to the entire vision of the patriarch that the first symposium began with an emphasis on and an interpretation of the book of Revelation, the closing book of the New Testament. Although, in many people's minds, "apocalypse" would seem to imply destruction and holocaust, nevertheless only a literalist and fundamentalist would accept this as an accurate interpretation of the term. Such a view would espouse the notion that the world— whether wealth and power or oppression and poverty—is irrelevant or inconsequential for salvation since everything would (sooner or later; but preferably sooner) be caught up in the rapture of a final conclusion and revelation. In fact, Revelation signifies a vision that evil can be conquered by good, that ugliness can be overcome by beauty. Revelation is a book of imagination and poetry. The Greek word (apocalypsis) implies unveiling; it is a disclosure of possibilities, and specifically a manifestation of the infinite possibilities of working together for a new heaven and a new earth, for a better environment and world to leave behind for future generations.

Symposium II: The Black Sea in Crisis was held in 1997 under the joint auspices of the ecumenical patriarch and Jacques Santer, president of the European Commission. This time, the symposium

---

for the Study of World Religions from 1996 to 1998. http://fore.yale.edu/religions-of-the-world-and-ecology-archive-of-conference-materials/. See Roger Gottlieb, ed., *The Oxford Handbook of Religion and Ecology* (New York: Oxford University Press, 2006), 407–9. Ten publications resulted from these conferences, with Tucker and Grim as the series editors. See also John Grim and Mary Evelyn Tucker, *Ecology and Religion* (Washington, DC: Island Press, 2014), esp. 96–108. URLs in this chapter were accessed and verified on September 1, 2018.

undertook a concrete case study, visiting the countries that surround the Black Sea and assembled local religious leaders and environmental activists, as well as regional scientists and politicians for a case study of the relationship between faith and science. A direct result of this second symposium, the Halki Ecological Institute was held in 1999 to promote and provide wider regional collaboration among theologians and educators, as well as scientists and journalists.

During the second symposium, it became evident that no solution to the ecological collapse of the Black Sea could be determined without addressing the degradation of the rivers that flow into that sea. Therefore, *Symposium III: River of Life—Down the Danube to the Black Sea* took place in 1999 under the joint auspices of Patriarch Bartholomew and Romano Prodi, president of the European Commission. Symposium III focused on the ecological impact of war, urban development, industrialization, shipping and agriculture, and war, especially in the aftermath of the military and ethnic conflict in the Former Republic of Yugoslavia.

Symposium IV: The Adriatic Sea—a Sea at Risk, a Unity of Purpose addressed the ethical aspects of the environmental crisis. Held in 2002, again under the joint auspices of the Ecumenical Patriarch and Romano Prodi, the symposium opened in Durres, Albania, and concluded in Venice, Italy. Two unique events during this symposium turned more than a new page in the book of Nature, sealing them as memorable occasions in the book of History. On June 9, 2002, the ecumenical patriarch celebrated the Divine Liturgy of St. John Chrysostom in the Church of Sant' Apollinare in Classe near Ravenna, Italy, for the first time in twelve centuries. The next day, June 10, 2002, during the closing ceremony, another historical moment of ecumenical and environmental significance unfolded as Bartholomew jointly published a document of environmental ethics with Pope John Paul II via satellite link-up from Rome. The Venice Declaration was the first text ever cosigned by the two religious leaders on ecological issues and emphasizes that the protection of the environment is the moral and spiritual duty of all.[8]

Symposium V: The Baltic Sea—A Common Heritage, A Shared Responsibility was organized in 2003, moving from Gdansk,

---

[8]Joint Declaration with Pope John Paul II, Venice-Vatican, June 2002 in Chryssavgis, *On Earth as in Heaven*, 335.

through Kaliningrad, Tallinn, and Helsinki, and concluding in Stockholm. The Baltic Sea is surrounded and polluted by nine countries with widely dissimilar economies and communities, as well as social structures and religious cultures. The end of the Cold War had permitted the renewal of political, economic, social, cultural, and religious ties between this region and countries comprising the European Union, and the wider world. Organized under the patronage of the ecumenical patriarch and Romano Prodi, the symposium sought to draw lessons from the Baltic—its diversity, problems, and history—in order to illustrate the challenges faced by humanity in that region. The direct result of this symposium was the North Sea Conference, cosponsored by the Ecumenical Patriarchate and the Church of Norway.

Symposium VI: The Amazon—Source of Life was held in 2006 on the Amazon River under the joint patronage of the ecumenical patriarch and Kofi Annan, secretary-general of the United Nations. Participants journeyed from Manaus, through Santarem and Jau, meeting at the crossing of the Rio Negro and the Rio Solimoes for a special ceremony of the blessing of waters by the ecumenical patriarch and local indigenous leaders.

Symposium VII: The Arctic–Mirror of Life was held in 2007, raising global awareness about the melting ice caps of Greenland. The symposium was cosponsored by the ecumenical patriarch, José Manuel Barroso (president of the European Commission) and Kofi Annan (then former secretary-general of the United Nations). The symposium examined the plight of indigenous populations, the fragility of the sea ice, and the encroachment of oil exploration in a region generally considered to be one of the first victims of human-induced climate change. On September 7, 2007, the patriarch led a moment of silent prayer before the melting icebergs—a symbol of profound repentance for humanity's responsibility in exacerbating global climate change.

The next symposium, *Symposium VIII: Restoring Balance—the Great Mississippi River*, was held in 2009 along the banks of the Mississippi in New Orleans. As one of the world's greatest rivers, with the third largest drainage basin on the planet, the Mississippi has been acutely devastated by human domination in a chain of cities along its length, discharging domestic and industrial waste into the river for nearly two centuries. As he declared the symposium open, Bartholomew perceived and underscored the fate of the Mississippi waters primarily as an ethical crisis.

The successful series of waterborne symposia ultimately turned the patriarch's attention to a new method in greening people's hearts and minds. Thus, from large-scale conferences, the Ecumenical Patriarchate today prefers to concentrate on smaller-scale conversations in an effort to address specific subjects and reach out to particular segments of society. In this endeavor, it has worked in partnership with Southern New Hampshire University, the first carbon-neutral campus in its home state of New Hampshire. As a result, a series of consultations known as Halki Summits (originating on the island of Halki in Turkey) now assemble smaller, focused groups in a specific discipline. At the heart of the discussion is the belief that no effort can be successful without a fundamental change in values as manifested in ethics, spirituality, and religion.

The inaugural Halki Summit in 2012 explored the impact of "global responsibility and environmental sustainability" on organizations and corporations, while in 2015, the second Halki Summit focused on the influence of literature and the arts. The third Halki Summit, organized in 2019, focused on educational institutions and theological seminaries in an effort to raise ecological awareness and create environmental programs among future teachers and clergy.

In 2018, the Ecumenical Patriarchate organized a ninth international symposium, entitled "Toward a Greener Attica— Preserving the Planet and Protecting Its People." This symposium opened at the Acropolis Museum in Athens and sailed along the picturesque islands of Spetses and Hydra in the Saronic Gulf, assembling prominent religious and civil leaders, scientists and journalists, as well as political legislators and social representatives, who deliberated on the impact of climate change but also on the pressing challenge of the refugee crisis in Greece, the Mediterranean and Middle East as a result of regional war, poverty, and persecution. Speakers included Christians, Jews, Muslims, and Hindus, while participants traveled from all over the world, including Greece and Turkey, Britain and Europe, the United States and Canada, as well as India and Africa. The symposium underlined and demonstrated how all religions and races, just as all disciplines and organizations, must work closely together in order to address climate change. To this end, the role and responsibility of the Ecumenical Patriarchate has been on the one hand to mark the spiritual roots of the ecological crisis and on the other hand to mobilize all people of good will to respect God's creation and inspire transformation in all communities.

"Greener Attica" brought the pioneering ecological activities of the Green Patriarch full circle—beginning in 1995 in the Mediterranean Sea and returning in 2018 to the Saronic Gulf surrounding the historical city of Athens.

Ancient Teachings for Modern Times

Bartholomew's writings and vision faithfully reflect the ecology and traditions of the Orthodox Church: its views on humility, asceticism, and sin; its praxis derived from the liturgy, communion, pastoral care and icons, even eco-justice. Perhaps the most prominent feature of Bartholomew's ecological writings, however, is the mark of humility. Bartholomew always defers: to God, to the saints, to his predecessors, to his contemporaries, even to scientific knowledge. The overwhelming sense of humility is extended not only upward (before the grace of God) and backward in time (before the face of tradition), but also sideward (before every human face) and downward (before the beauty of the natural world). In other texts, Patriarch Bartholomew speaks of humility before the earth and even of dialogue with nature.[9] This is the way of the sacraments.

This arguably also constitutes the fundamental ground for the patriarch's authority. He is always striving to discern the larger picture. He recognizes that he is standing before something greater than himself; he belongs to an "unbroken" succession that long predates him and will long outlast him. He is a part of this tradition, and cannot conceive himself apart from it. Therefore, he speaks of self-emptying (kenosis), of ministry (diakonia), of witness (martyria, a Greek term that conveys martyrdom and suffering), and of thanksgiving (eucharistia, a Greek term that also implies liturgy).

The same signature of humility is evident on other levels as well. In his enthronement address, Bartholomew describes the Ecumenical Patriarchate as a spiritual institution; it is not, he insists, a powerful

---

[9]See Bartholomew's address at the Halki Ecological Institute (1999), 167; in the encyclical for September 1 (2001), 47–9, he underlines the inherent danger of human arrogance over nature, in Chryssavgis, *On Earth as in Heaven*.

establishment in secular terms. The same point is underlined elsewhere, such as in his address in Kathmandu (2000). On other occasions, the emphasis is on simplicity—the technical term is *asceticism* (or the ascetic life).[10] In this respect, specific reference is made to the monastic tradition and particularly to the disciplined existence of monks on Mount Athos for over one thousand years. The emphasis in the enthronement address is also on liturgy as the source and essence of Orthodox theology and spirituality.[11]

The notion of liturgy leads to what is arguably the most distinctive characteristic of Bartholomew's vision, again foreshadowed from the day of his enthronement, namely the central and crucial concept of communion. In everything that Bartholomew says and does in light of the environmental crisis, he is aware that all Orthodox must be included.[12] Indeed, not only should all Orthodox Christians be in communion, but also all Christians in general should be in communication. In addition, all religions should be in cooperation;[13] all sciences and disciplines should be committed;[14] all cultures and ages should concur; and even atheists should be seen to contribute, as people of good will, in the movement toward transforming creation.

---

[10]This emphasis is found in several texts, such as the opening address at the Black Sea Symposium II, Trabzon, Turkey (1997), 81–2; the keynote address in Santa Barbara, CA (1997), 97–8; the meditation before the cross, Danube Symposium III, Germany (1999), 220–1; the closing address at the Adriatic Symposium IV, Venice (2002), 222–3; the address at the Baltic Symposium V at Utstein Monastery, Germany (2003), 199–204. Also see the patriarch's article in the *International Journal of Heritage Studies* (2006), 125–6; as well as the patriarchal encyclical for September 1 (1994), in Chryssavgis, *On Earth as in Heaven*, 34.

[11]The emphasis on liturgy is found in the closing ceremony of the Revelation Symposium I, Patmos (1995), 174; the opening address of the Amazon Symposium VI, Amazon River (2006), 150–1; as well as the encyclical for September 1 (1994), 34–5. Above, ibid.

[12]See "Address of Ecumenical Patriarch Bartholomew at the Opening Session of the Meeting of the Orthodox Primates at the Phanar," 5/31/92, at Orthodoxy & the Environment—Patriarchal Addresses, http://www.patriarchate.org/.

[13]See his opening address for the Revelation Symposium I, Istanbul (1995), 215; as well as his message for World Oceans Day at the Baltic Sea Symposium V, Stockholm (2003), 340–1, in Chryssavgis, *On Earth as in Heaven*.

[14]See especially the opening of the Revelation Symposium I, Istanbul (1995), 216–9; the opening address of the Black Sea Symposium II, Trabzon, Turkey (1997), 82–3; and the closing address for the Amazon Symposium VI, Manaus, Brazil (2006), 191. Above, ibid.

It is for this reason that Patriarch Bartholomew considers his efforts for the protection of the environment as an obligation, not as a way of submitting to contemporary fashions or political statements. His commitment to and involvement in environmental issues is not a matter of public relations but of theological conviction. This is apparent in his repeated phrase: "We cannot remain idle!"[15] He makes it clear that he will not cease proclaiming the importance of the environment.[16] It is, he believes, an almost "apostolic commission."[17]

Never Conforming, but Ever Transforming

For Ecumenical Patriarch Bartholomew, his ecological vision is a matter of truthfulness to God, humanity, and the created order. In fact, it is not too far-fetched to speak of environmental damage as being a contemporary heresy or natural terrorism; he condemns it as nothing less than sin![18] The environment is not a political or a technological issue; it is, as Bartholomew reiterates in so many interviews, primarily a religious and spiritual issue. Religion, then, has a key role to play; and a spirituality that is not involved with outward creation is not involved with the inward mystery either.[19]

The patriarch offers no apology for his traditional Orthodox theological background and approach.[20] Moreover, he offers no apology for his criticism of a-religious responses to the environment,

---

[15]Encyclical (signed by Patriarch Demetrios) for September 1 (1989), 24; and closing address for the Revelation Symposium I, Patmos (1995), 175. See also his homily during the Baltic Symposium V, Helsinki (2003). Above, ibid., 190.

[16]See his closing address at the Danube Symposium III, Romania (1999). Above, ibid., 277.

[17]See his opening address at the Black Sea Symposium II, Trabzon, Turkey (1997). Above, ibid., 84.

[18]See his encyclical for September 1 (1994), 33; opening ceremony first summer seminar, Halki (1994), 238; keynote address at Santa Barbara, CA (1997), 99; and his article in *Seminarium*, Vatican (2010), 137–9. On the notion of "spiritual pollution," see his address to the Bankers Association, Athens (1999). Above, ibid., 263.

[19]On the role of religion, see his address at the Danube Symposium III, Bulgaria (1999), 274–5; on spirituality, see his encyclical for September 1 (1994). Above, ibid., 34–5.

[20]See "Address to the Orthodox Primates," 5/31/92, http://www.patriarchate.org.

whether these derive from scientific or moral sources.[21] Finally, he offers no apology for his harsh criticism of false technological promises about "progress" and "development."[22] He is candid about the thirst of Western civilization for another worldview and an alternate spirituality.[23]

Indeed, he is not afraid to adopt "politically incorrect" language concerning the centrality of the human person within creation.[24] It is not anthropocentrism that is the problem, he would argue; it is *anthropomonism*[25]—namely, the exclusive emphasis on and isolation of humanity at the expense and detriment of the natural environment. Nature is related to people and people to nature.[26] If Bartholomew is radical[27] in the theological articulation of his vision, it is because his worldview is rooted (the literal sense of the word "radical") in his church tradition.

All of this leads to another dimension of the patriarch's environmental initiatives, namely the deeply pastoral attitude toward those whom he addresses. Whether speaking to colleagues among the worldwide Orthodox primates (as in his address in 1992), or to individual leaders and churches (as in Galati in 1999), or else to Orthodox faithful throughout the world (as in all of the encyclicals for September 1), Ecumenical Patriarch Bartholomew is sensitively, thoughtfully, and gradually educating and molding with "paternal admonition."[28]

---

[21]Encyclical for September 1 (1996), 37–8; his words at the University of the Aegean (1994), 66–8; and his address in Japan (1995), 251–2, in Chryssavgis, *On Earth as in Heaven.*
[22]Encyclical for September 1 (1994). Above, ibid., 33.
[23]See the opening ceremony of the summer seminar, Halki (1995). Above, ibid., 162.
[24]See his encyclicals for September 1 (1993, 32; 1995, 36; 1997, 39–41; 1998, 41–3; 2001, 47–9); as well as his addresses at opening of the Black Sea Symposium II (1997), Turkey, 79; in Japan (1995), 253–7; at the Halki summer seminar (1998), 244–9; and at the opening of the Danube Symposium III, Germany (1999). Above, ibid., 85–90.
[25]See especially his address at the presentation ceremony of the Sophie Prize (2002), 73. In the Christmas encyclical of 1994, Bartholomew underlines the importance of Christocentrism. Above, ibid., 227.
[26]See especially, his address to the Bankers Association, Athens (1999), 261; and the encyclical for September 1 (2001). Above, ibid., 47–9.
[27]See "Address to the Orthodox Primates," 5/31/92, http://www.patriarchate.org.
[28]Encyclical for September 1 (1996), in Chryssavgis, *On Earth as in Heaven,* 37.

Bartholomew will frequently relate the environment to a familiar aspect of Orthodox spirituality, such as to the icons that decorate Orthodox churches. Symbols are important in Orthodox thought, worship, and life.[29] Creation itself is likened to an icon,[30] in the same way as the human person too is created "in the image [or, icon] and likeness of God" (Gen. 1:26).[31] So the patriarch will invite the Orthodox to contemplate the Creator through the icon of creation. Creation is a visible and tangible revelation (apocalypse) of the presence (parousia) of the Word of God.[32] Humanity is called to wonder at creation, but not to worship creation. Otherwise, the natural world is reduced from the level of icon to the level of idol.[33] It is in the same vein that Patriarch Bartholomew will refer to human beings as created and intended by God to serve as "priests" in the created world.[34]

Bartholomew believes that a particular ethos is called for in our response to the environmental crisis. This ethos is divinely inspired, even imposed, by God.[35] And it is an ethos incarnated and communicated by the saints![36] The saints inform and re-form the world with their presence and their prayer. They remind us, says Bartholomew, that the personal responsibility and the slightest action of even the feeblest among us can change the world for the better.[37]

The ecumenical patriarch is well aware that environmental issues are intimately connected to and dependent on numerous social

---

[29]See his Christmas encyclical (1994), 227; the opening address during the Revelation Symposium I, Istanbul (1995), 216; and his address at the Institute of Marine Research during the Baltic Sea Symposium V, Norway (2003). Above, ibid., 204–8.

[30]See his homily in Santa Barbara (1997), ibid., 152–3.

[31]See address at the Black Sea Symposium II, Turkey (1997), ibid., 79.

[32]Apocalypse is perceived both as the end (as in the encyclical for September 1 [1989], 24) and the epiphany of God (as in the opening address of the Revelation Symposium I, Istanbul, 1995). Above, ibid., 215.

[33]See the opening address at the Black Sea Symposium II, Turkey (1997), 82; the encyclical for September 1(1999), 45; and the address to the Bankers Association, Athens (1999). Above, ibid., 261.

[34]See, for instance, his address at the Halki summer seminar (1992), 195; and the keynote to the Baltic Sea Symposium V, Germany (2003). Above, ibid., 202.

[35]See his address at the University of the Aegean (1994), 66–8; at the Halki summer seminar (1995), 160–2; and his keynote address in Santa Barbara (1997), 100; but especially the encyclical for September 1(1997). Above, ibid., 40–1.

[36]Encyclical for September 1 (1998), 43. Above, ibid., 45.

[37]See especially the encyclical for September 1(1998), ibid., 43.

issues[38] of our times and our ways. These include war and peace,[39] justice and human rights,[40] as well as poverty[41] and unemployment.[42] Even when the environment does not appear to be the central issue of his address, nevertheless the interconnectedness of the above-mentioned problems with the destruction of our planet is profoundly apparent. It is not by chance that the term "eco-justice" has been coined in ecumenical church circles to describe the cosmic interconnection between creation and creatures, between the world and its inhabitants. We have, in recent years, become abundantly aware of the effects of environmental degradation on people, and especially the poor.

For Bartholomew, then, "eco-justice" is not an exercise in public relations; nor is it merely a fashionable advocacy. It is, rather, a deep theological, liturgical, and spiritual conviction. It is the understanding that Christianity is essentially and profoundly maximalist, materialist, and environmentalist. For the patriarch, the environment is not only a political or a technological issue; it is, as his sacramental vision implies, primarily a religious and spiritual issue. The profound disfiguration and degradation of creation, the disharmony and environmental destruction that are now "everywhere present" become a form of sacrilegious "graffiti" on the holy temple of the earth that can only be erased by cleansing our personal temples and by eliminating the sinful causes of ecological destruction in our minds and souls. This is why religion has a key role to play.

---

[38]See his address at City University, London (1994), ibid., 146–8.
[39]See his addresses at the opening of the Revelation Symposium I, Istanbul (1995), 216, 220; at the opening of the Danube Symposium III, Germany (1999), 85–6; the encyclical for September 1 (1998), 42–3; the address to the Bankers Association, Athens (1999), 261–4; and his message in Thebes, Greece (2005). Above, ibid., 266–8. See also "Address during the Prayer for Peace in Novi Sad, Serbia" 10/22/99, http://www.patriarchate.org.
[40]See the foreword for the Halki summer seminar (1997), in Chryssavgis, On Earth as in Heaven, 163–5.
[41]See the encyclical for September 1 (1994), 34; the foreword for the Halki summer seminar (1998), 244–50; his address to the European Parliament, France (1994), 288–91; and the statement to the World Council of Churches (2004). Above, ibid., 338–9.
[42]See his "Keynote Address at the Millennial Youth Congress," Istanbul, 6/18/00 at http://www.patriarchate.org.

"Our mission," declares Bartholomew, "is to make it well known throughout the world that we are all the caretakers and not the owners of our common *oikos* [earthly home] ... Churches have, through sermons, catechism, and continuous education, a serious responsibility to inform our faithful about these matters" (September 16, 2015). And as the patriarch introduces the task of caring for creation, he points to the added dimensions of our mission as caretakers of creation. We are to commit ourselves to protecting and advocating the rights of the most vulnerable:

Scientists calculate that those most harmed by global warming will be the most vulnerable and marginalized ... And there is a bitter injustice about the fact that those suffering its worst ravages have done least to contribute to it. The ecological crisis is directly related to the ethical challenge of eliminating poverty and advocating human rights. This means that global warming is a moral crisis and a moral challenge. The dignity and rights of human beings are intimately and integrally related to the poetry and—we would dare to say—the rights of the earth itself. (Philippines, February 26, 2015)

Conclusion

The Way Forward

From even before his election in 1991, I have worked with Ecumenical Patriarch Bartholomew on the issue of creation care, witnessing not only the time and effort he has devoted, but experiencing my own transformation through his vision and inspiration. Whether at a large environmental conference or in a quiet forest alone, I am grateful for this journey with His All-Holiness and for the opportunities it has afforded. One extraordinary privilege was attending the formal publication of the green encyclical letter issued by Pope Francis on June 18, 2015.

Laudato Si': On Care for Our Common Home was jointly released in the new synod hall of the Vatican by His Eminence Peter Cardinal Turkson of the Pontifical Council for Justice and Peace and His Eminence Metropolitan John of Pergamon, senior bishop and theological spokesman of the Ecumenical Patriarchate. Needless to say, theologians and environmentalists, politicians and pundits have already interpreted the encyclical in numerous and diverse ways, often—as Cardinal Turkson likes to remark—reading into the text far more than the drafters themselves probably envisaged.

However, I would like to offer some personal insights into the ecumenical and ecological contexts of this important papal statement, which is not only intended for Roman Catholics but for all Christians. Indeed, Cardinal Turkson observed that his office recognized from the outset that this encyclical was not merely destined for Christian believers, but for all people of goodwill concerned about the welfare and sustainability of the planet.

Communion: An Act of Openness

Let me, then, offer some glimpses into less apparent dimensions of this extraordinary document in order to provide some background and insight into a very crucial dimension and connection: namely, the relationship between a pope and a patriarch in our times.

Almost exactly one year before the publication of *Laudato Si'*, Pope Francis and Ecumenical Patriarch Bartholomew traveled together to Jerusalem in order to celebrate the fiftieth anniversary of the historical visit there in 1964 by their predecessors, Paul VI and Athenagoras. Later that year, December 2015 marked another milestone, namely the fiftieth anniversary of what is known as "the lifting of the anathemas"—namely, the eradication by the two same visionary prelates (Pope Paul VI and Ecumenical Patriarch Athenagoras) from the memory of the church of the tragic excommunications that led to the unfortunate estrangement between the Roman Catholic and Orthodox Churches, the division almost one thousand years ago in 1054 between the Western and Eastern churches known as the "great schism."

Through their pioneering and daring initiatives, Pope Paul VI and Ecumenical Patriarch Athenagoras broke a long and painful silence of ten centuries in their vision and dedication to fulfill Christ's final commandment and fervent prayer that his disciples "may be one" (Jn 17:21). Moreover, for over five hundred years, the leaders of the two ancient and most senior Christian communions had neither spoken to nor communicated with one another. So when Pope Paul and Patriarch Athenagoras met in Jerusalem, it was the first time that a Roman pontiff and an Eastern patriarch were meeting face-to-face since the Council of Florence in 1438.

More recently, when in March of 2013 Ecumenical Patriarch Bartholomew decided personally to attend the inaugural mass of Pope Francis in St. Peter's Square, his spontaneous gesture signaled another first: it was the first time that the leader of either church had ever participated in such an event.

Moreover, each year, June 29 and November 30 mark the patronal feasts of the Church of Rome and the Church of Constantinople respectively, where once again Ecumenical Patriarch Bartholomew is officially represented at the Vatican for the solemn celebration of the Feast of Ss. Peter and Paul, while Pope Francis is formally represented at the Phanar for the thronal Feast of St. Andrew. On occasion, the leaders themselves have attended these seminal events. Above and beyond the theological dialogue that commenced in 1980 on the island of Revelation, Patmos, this powerful tradition of formal exchanges between the two churches, which began in 1969, would constitute a significant step on the way toward reconciliation.

What I would submit, therefore, by way of providing some personal and ecumenical background for the papal encyclical letter on creation care is that it had long been anticipated not only from an ecological perspective, but also in the context of inter-Christian openness between two contemporary religious leaders, who are profoundly and steadfastly committed to restoring communion between their two churches, which Constantinople likes to characterize as "sister churches" while Rome is fond of describing as "two lungs breathing together."

Compassion: An Act of Responsibility

If commitment to communion is what attracts Pope Francis and Ecumenical Patriarch Bartholomew to a joint ecumenical witness in a world otherwise divided by political and economic tension, as well as by religious and racial conflict, responsibility for compassion is undoubtedly what impels them to a shared concern for the exploitation of people and of the planet.

For almost thirty years, Ecumenical Patriarch Bartholomew has emphasized the spiritual dimension of the ecological crisis and even introduced the revolutionary concept of ecological sin in order to expand our understanding of repentance from what we have hitherto considered purely as an individual wrongdoing or social transgression to a much broader, communal, generational, and environmental abuse of God's creation.

And since his election, the pope assumed the name of St. Francis of Assisi as an unmistakable indication of his priority for and sensitivity to the marginalized, the vulnerable, and the oppressed in our global community. This is why, in his environmental encyclical, Pope Francis encourages us to pray: "O God, bring healing to our lives, that we may protect the world and not prey on it ... Touch the hearts of those who look only for gain at the expense of the poor of the earth."

Cooperation: An Act of Caring

What the papal encyclical has reminded us so powerfully and permanently is that preserving nature and serving neighbor are inseparable; they resemble two sides of the same coin. In fact, Pope Francis and Ecumenical Patriarch Bartholomew have repeatedly underlined the profound connection between environmental justice and social justice, declaring solidarity with people suffering from war and persecution, as well as poverty and hunger. The two religious leaders have, from the very outset of their institutional and personal relations, demonstrated that they understand the vocation and vision of the church. They know what matters, or at least what *should* matter, in the church; and they understand what the responsibility and priority of the church should be in the contemporary world.

Theological dialogues and ecumenical relations are of paramount importance, but they are often carried out in order to *gain* something, whether to achieve greater clarity or advance toward fuller unity. Nevertheless, on April 16, 2016, the visit to the island of Lesbos in Greece by Pope Francis and Ecumenical Patriarch Bartholomew, along with the local Archbishop Ieronymos of Athens and All Greece, in fact aimed at *giving* something: namely, hope to hundreds of detainees and desperate refugees from the Middle East and Northern Africa. In this regard, the event in Lesbos, which received international attention, indicated a practical and pastoral response by the churches of the East and West to a tragic crisis in our world. At the same time, it marked a powerful reassessment of how ecumenical relations can advance human rights at a time when the world is either turning its face away from the victims of religious extremism and persecution or else deciding their fate on exclusively financial terms and national interests. The power of ecumenism lies in beginning to open up beyond ourselves and our own, our communities and our churches. It is about learning to speak the language of care and compassion. It is giving priority to solidarity and service.

Inspiration: An Act of Example

I believe that it is indeed providential that these two bishops are leading their respective churches at this critical moment in time. Just as previously with Popes John Paul II and Benedict XVI, Patriarch Bartholomew and Pope Francis have issued joint statements—in Jerusalem (June 2014) and Istanbul (November 2014)—drawing attention to the plight of Christians in the Middle East, as well as an exceptional statement in September 2017 highlighting the importance and impact of climate change. Their "Joint Message on the World Day of Prayer for Creation" was an "urgent appeal to those in positions of social and economic, as well as political and cultural responsibility to hear the cry of the earth and to attend to the needs of the marginalized, but above all to respond to the plea of millions and to support the consensus of the world for the healing of our wounded creation."

There is no doubt in my mind that the favorable reception—but at the same time I would venture to add: the adverse reaction to and harsh criticism—of these two leaders advancing and advocating for the care of God's creation is arguably the greatest testimony and evidence that they are most definitely on the right track. For this reason alone, they deserve our prayer and praise, while their enlightened example and instruction merit our attention and imitation.

Perhaps everyone can gradually embrace their vision of creation as sacrament, learning to respect and care for the cosmos that God fashioned, reconciled and transfigured with love.

ORIGINAL SOURCES

Introduction

Portions of this chapter first appeared in John Chryssavgis, *Beyond the Shattered Image: Insights into an Orthodox Christian Ecological Worldview* (Minneapolis, MN: Light & Life, 1999 [out of print]), 1–15; and in *The Wiley Blackwell Companion to Religion and Ecology*, ed. John Hart (Oxford: Wiley Blackwell, 2017), 273–85.

Chapter 1: The Lens of Grace

An early version of this chapter appeared in Chryssavgis, *Beyond the Shattered Image*, 16–27.

Chapter 2: Transcendence and Immanence

An early version of this chapter appeared in Chryssavgis, *Beyond the Shattered Image*, 71–89.

Chapter 3: The Desert Is Alive

This chapter is based on material in Graeme Ferguson and John Chryssavgis, eds., *The Desert Is Alive: Dimensions of Australian Spirituality* (Melbourne: Joint Board of Christian Education, 1990 [out of print]); and in Chryssavgis, *Beyond the Shattered Image*, 90–117. Some research was conducted in preparation for the International Conference on Patristic Studies held in Oxford (1991) and appeared in *Studia Patristica* XXV (Leuven, 1993).

Chapter 4: Divine Sophia

This chapter is based on material that originally appeared in the journal *Phronema* 8 (1993): 19–32; and in Chryssavgis, *Beyond the Shattered Image*, 141–64.

Chapter 5: Ecology and Mystery

An early version of this chapter first appeared in Chryssavgis, *Beyond the Shattered Image*, 28–65; and as "The Earth as Sacrament," in *The Oxford Handbook of Religion and Ecology*, ed. Roger S. Gottlieb (Oxford, UK: Oxford University Press, 2006), 92–114.

Chapter 6: On Earth as in Heaven

Parts of this chapter originally appeared in Chryssavgis, *Beyond the Shattered Image*, 120–39; and as "A New Heaven and a New Earth," in *Toward an Ecology of Transfiguration: Orthodox Christian Perspectives on Environment, Nature, and Creation*, ed. John Chryssavgis and Bruce V. Foltz (New York: Fordham University Press, 2013), 15.

Chapter 7: Living Cosmology

An early version of this chapter appeared in Mary Evelyn Tucker and John Grim, eds., *Living Cosmology: Christian Responses to Journey of the Universe* (Maryknoll, NY: Orbis Books, 2016), 99–106.

Chapter 10: The Green Patriarch

Parts of this chapter first appeared as an introduction in *Cosmic Grace, Humble Prayer: The Ecological Vision of the Green*

Patriarch, ed. John Chryssavgis (Grand Rapids, MI: Eerdmans, 2003 [out of print]); and in *On Earth as in Heaven: Ecological Vision and Initiatives of Ecumenical Patriarch Bartholomew*, ed. John Chryssavgis (New York: Fordham University Press, 2012), 1–22. Also see John Chryssavgis, *Bartholomew: Apostle and Visionary* (Nashville, TN: HarperCollins, 2016).

Conclusion

Originally delivered on the floor of the UN Economic and Social Council chamber, this chapter appeared with the title "Pope Francis' *Laudato Si'*: A Personal Response, an Ecumenical Reflection," *Phronema* 32, no. 2 (2016): 17–21; and with the title "An Eastern Orthodox Perspective on *Laudato Si'*," *First Things* (July 6, 2015).

FURTHER READING

Books

Bartholomew, Ecumenical Patriarch. *Encountering the Mystery: Understanding Orthodox Christianity Today*. New York: Doubleday, 2008.

Chryssavgis, John. *Light through Darkness: The Orthodox Tradition*. Maryknoll, NY: Orbis, 2004.

Chryssavgis, John. *On Earth as in Heaven: Ecological Vision and Initiatives of Ecumenical Patriarch Bartholomew*. New York: Fordham University Press, 2012.[1]

Chryssavgis, John and Bruce V. Foltz, *Toward an Ecology of Transfiguration: Orthodox Perspectives on Environment, Nature, and Creation*. New York: Fordham University Press, 2013.

Foltz, Bruce V. *The Noetics of Nature: Environmental Philosophy and the Holy Beauty of the Visible*. New York: Fordham University Press, 2013.

Gregorios, Metropolitan Paulos (Verghese). *Cosmic Man: The Divine Presence*. New Delhi: Sophia, 1980. [This book also appeared as *The Human Presence: An Orthodox View of Nature*. Geneva: WCC, 1978.]

Guroian, Vigen. *Inheriting Paradise: Meditations on Gardening*. Grand Rapids, MI: Eerdmans, 1999.

Hart, David Bentley. *The Beauty of the Infinite: The Aesthetics of Christian Truth*. Grand Rapids, MI: Eerdmans, 2004.

Keselopoulos, Anestis G. *Man and the Environment: A Study of St. Symeon the New Theologian*. Crestwood, NY: St. Vladimir's Seminary Press, 2001.

Limouris, Metropolitan Gennadios, ed. *Justice, Peace, and the Integrity of Creation: Insights from Orthodoxy*. Geneva: WCC, 1990.

Nellas, Panayiotis. *Deification in Christ: Orthodox Perspectives on the Nature of the Human Person*. Crestwood, NY: St. Vladimir's Seminary Press, 1987.

---

[1] I am indebted to Fredric Nachbaur, Director of Fordham University Press, for his generous permission to use material from my introduction and the texts of this book.

Schmemann, Alexander. *For the Life of the World: Sacraments and Orthodoxy*. New York: St. Vladimir's Seminary Press, 1973.

Sherrard, Philip. *The Eclipse of Man and Nature*. Northumberland, UK: Lindisfarne Press, 1987.

Sherrard, Philip. *Human Image, World Image: The Death and Resurrection of Sacred Cosmology*. Ipswich, UK: Golgonooza Press, 1992.

Stăniloae, Dumitru. *The Experience of God: The World, Creation and Deification*. Brookline, MA: Holy Cross Orthodox Press, 2005.

Stefanatos, Joanne. *Animals Sanctified: A Spiritual Journey*. Minneapolis, MN: Light & Life, 2001.

Theokritoff, Elizabeth. *Living in God's Creation: Orthodox Perspectives on Ecology*. Crestwood, NY: St. Vladimir's Seminary Press, 2009.

Ware, Metropolitan Kallistos (of Diokleia). *Ecological Crisis, Ecological Hope: Our Orthodox Vision of Creation*. New York: Fordham University Office of Public Affairs, 2006.

Ware, Metropolitan Kallistos (of Diokleia). *Through the Creation to the Creator*. London, UK: Friends of the Centre Papers, 1997.

Woloschak, Gayle E. *Beauty and Unity in Creation: The Evolution of Life*. Minneapolis, MN: Light & Life, 1996.

Articles

Bordeianu, Radu. "Maximus and Ecology: The Relevance of Maximus the Confessor's Theology of Creation for the Present Ecological Crisis." *Downside Review* 127 (2009): 103–26.

Brock, Sebastian. "Humanity and the Natural World in the Syriac Tradition." *Sobornost/ECR* 12, no. 2 (1990): 131–42.

Guroian, Vigen. "Ecological Ethics: An Ecclesial Event." In *Ethics after Christendom: Toward an Ecclesial Christian Ethic*, edited by Vigen Guroian. Grand Rapids, MI: Eerdmans, 1994.

Ignatius IV, Patriarch of Antioch. "Three Sermons on the Environment: A Theology of Creation; A Spirituality of the Creation; The Responsibility of Christians." *Sourozh* 38 (1989): 1–14.

Louth, Andrew. "Between Creation and Transfiguration: The Environment in the Eastern Orthodox Tradition." In *Ecological Hermeneutics: Biblical, Historical and Theological Perspectives*, edited by D. G. Horrell et al. Edinburgh: T&T Clark, 2012.

Stăniloae, Dumitru. "The World as Gift and Sacrament of God's Love." *Sobornost* 5, no. 9 (1969): 662–72.

Zizioulas, Metropolitan John (of Pergamon). "Preserving God's Creation: Three Lectures on Theology and Ecology." *King's Theological Review* 12 (1989): 1–5, 41–5; 13 (1990): 1–5.

INDEX

Printed in the USA
CPSIA information can be obtained
at www.ICGtesting.com
LVHW012156261123
764988LV00039B/1116

9 780567 680709